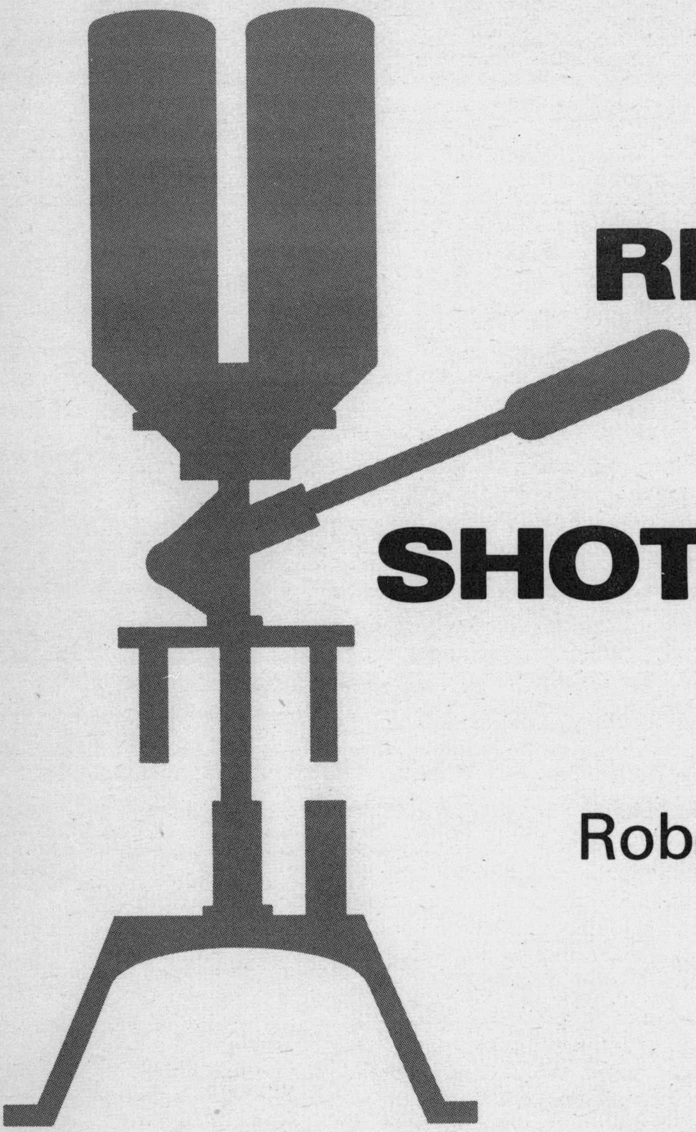

RELOADING FOR SHOTGUNNERS

Edited by
Robert S.L. Anderson

DBI BOOKS, INC., NORTHFIELD, ILL.

STAFF

EDITOR
Robert S. L. Anderson

ASSISTANT TO THE EDITOR
Lilo Anderson

ASSOCIATE EDITOR
Harold A. Murtz

COVER PHOTOGRAPHY
John Hanusin

PRODUCTION MANAGER
Pamela J. Johnson

PUBLISHER
Sheldon L. Factor

CONTENTS

Why Reload?

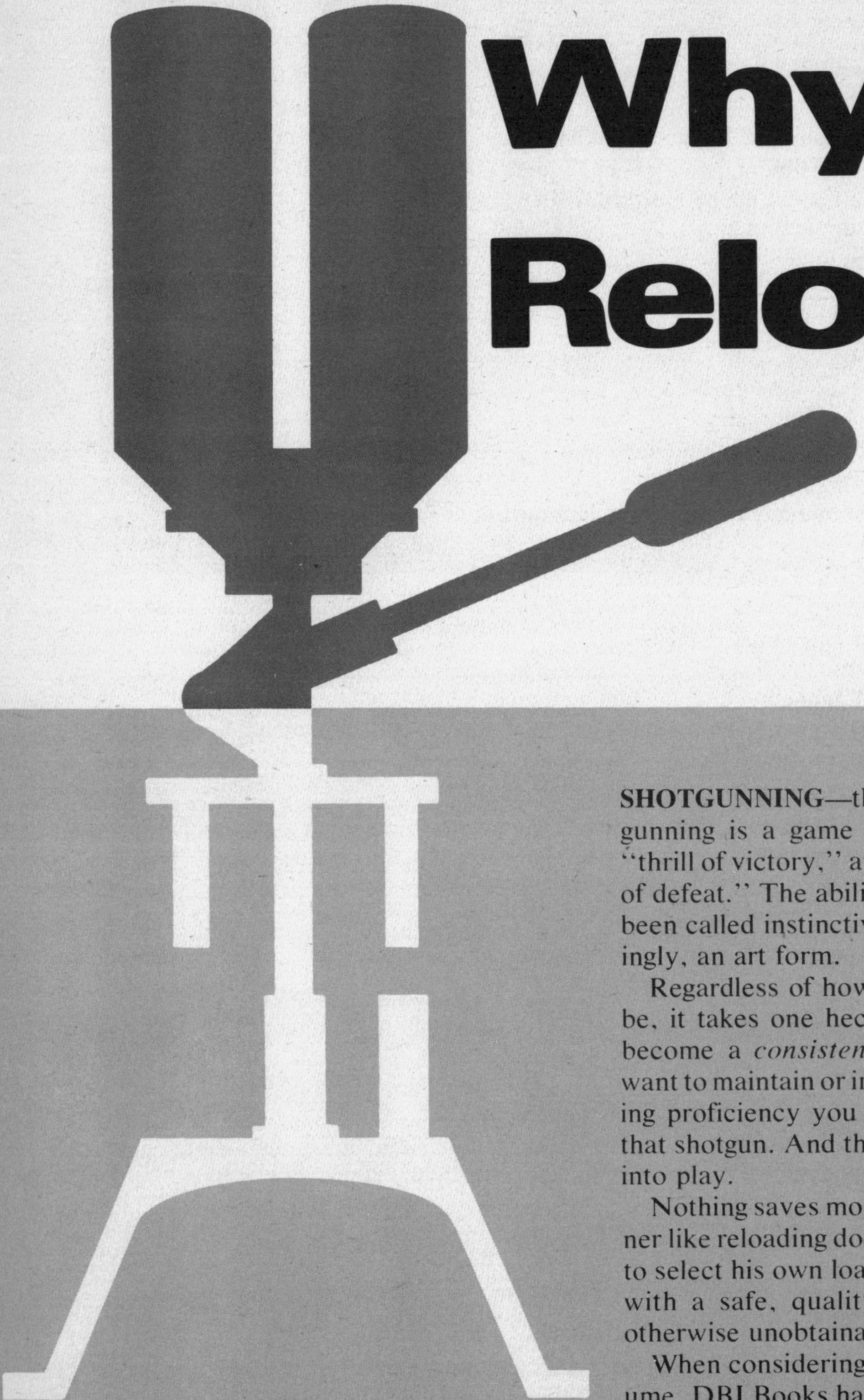

SHOTGUNNING—there is nothing like it. Shotgunning is a game where a hit becomes the, "thrill of victory," and a miss means the "agony of defeat." The ability to hit with a shotgun has been called instinctive, natural and, not surprisingly, an art form.

Regardless of how natural it may or may not be, it takes one heck of a pile of shotshells to become a *consistently good* wingshot. If you want to maintain or improve a level of wingshooting proficiency you are going to have to shoot that shotgun. And this is where reloading comes into play.

Nothing saves money for the average shotgunner like reloading does. It also allows the shooter to select his own load, oftentimes providing him with a safe, quality shotshell that would be otherwise unobtainable in the marketplace.

When considering the undertaking of this volume, DBI Books had to answer the old question faced with every new effort—is there a need?

REALIZED SAVINGS THROUGH RELOADING

Gauge	Shot Charge/oz.	Powder Charge	Savings
10 gauge 3½"	2	4¼ dram	77 percent
12 gauge 3"	1⅝	4 dram	70 percent
12 gauge 2¾"	1½	Magnum	65 percent
12 gauge 2¾"	1¼	3¾ dram	62 percent
12 gauge 2¾"	1⅛	3 dram	59 percent
16 gauge 2¾"	1	2½ dram	61 percent
20 gauge 3"	1¼	Magnum	67 percent
20 gauge 2¾"	⅞	2½ dram	56 percent

Quite frankly we decided rather quickly that a need did, in fact, exist. There have been comparatively few efforts devoted to shotshell handloading. While no one book on such a topic could be complete, we felt that we could provide the shotshell reloader with not only updated information, but new material as well. An example of new material would be the superb job Ed Matunas did in compiling some 70 pages of load data. Every load listed comes complete with Ed's specific recommendations for load application, be it Skeet, trap, upland game, etc.

The subjects covered by our carefully selected experts will help make your shotshell reloading a pleasant chore-free procedure which will produce the results you have the right to expect.

If you haven't already started to reload shotshells then consider the fact that the *average* shotshell reloader saves from 56 to 77 percent off the cost of a box of factory shells.

No one can afford to ignore such savings.

When armed with enough knowledge to produce good, safe ammunition, reloading becomes not only a way to save money but also an enjoyable hobby. It's a hobby that will also allow you to produce shotshell loads not duplicated by factory ammunition. To find out more about this aspect, see Ed Matunas' article on "Wildcatting the 12-Gauge."

As time goes on we will keep abreast of your reactions to our newest effort. We hope you will agree that this volume has helped make shotshell reloading an easy and enjoyable pastime that will result in superb field performance. And, if you are like most reloaders, the money you save will probably be spent in giving you the opportunity to shoot, shoot and shoot some more. With this increase in your shooting activity you can expect to be well on your way to becoming a fantastic wingshot. Or, if you already so qualify, reloading will enable you to maintain that high level of proficiency.

THE PURPOSE of handloading, whether it be for metallic rifle and pistol ammo or shotshells, is to save money. For the rifleman, handloading offers some additional advantages in producing ammo better suited to his particular rifle. In many cases, the result is a cartridge exhibiting better accuracy than the factory round. But, alas, the shotgunner doesn't reap this benefit from his hull-stuffing. Factory shotshells are so good the handloader has to work hard and intelligently just to equal them. Beat them? Never. Equal them? Yes!

There's a certain amount of economy inherent in the reloading process resulting from the reuse of the shell or casing, one of the more expensive parts of the finished cartridge. The other components must be purchased and used for each loading.

Using the Omark Savings Computer for Handloaded Shotshell ammunition, I computed a savings of $18 per 100 12 gauge, 1⅛-ounce reloads. This is, of course, based on today's component prices in my geographic (Southwest) location: shot ($17.50 per 25 pounds), powder ($5 per pound can and 17.5 grains of powder per reload), primers ($1.75 per 100) and wads ($3.75 per 250) against factory loads at $28 per 100. Certainly, your own savings could be greater or less than this depending upon whether you pay retail or discount prices. But it's safe to say that you can save anywhere from $10 to $20 per 100 pounds, or a minimum of $2.50 per box of 25.

You can save more dramatically on a per-

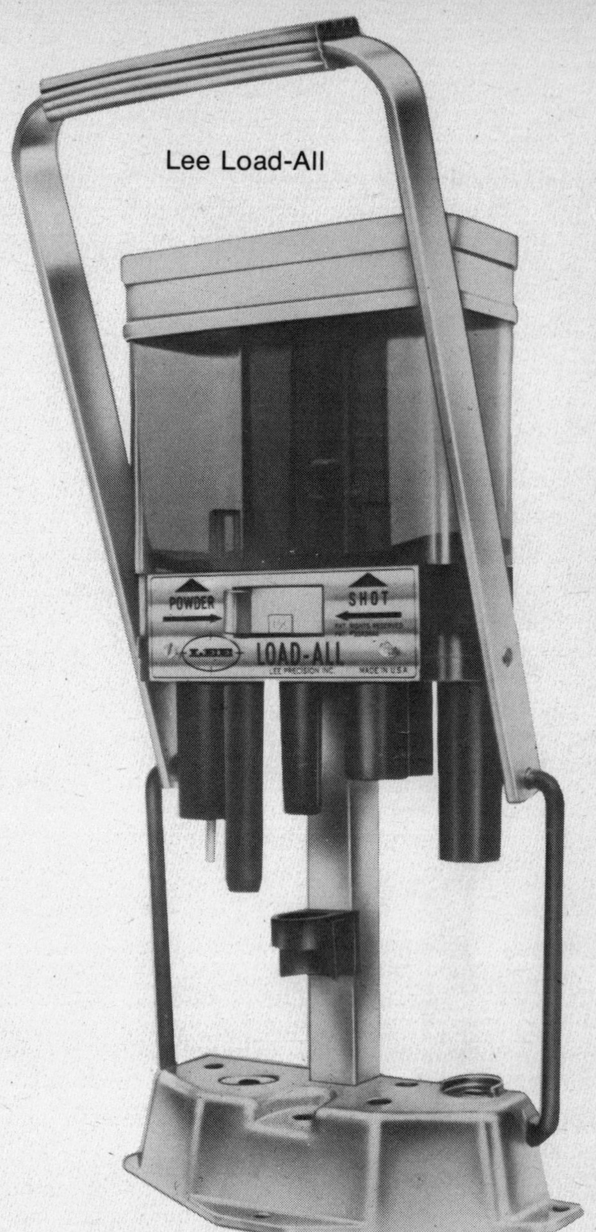

Budget $hotshells–

reload basis if you shop wisely for components. They can usually be obtained more cheaply if purchased in large quantities; that is, powder by the 4-pound caddy or keg, primers by the thousand(s), and so on.

I'm told that in some areas you can purchase reclaimed or salvaged shot at a *big* savings. I've never used this type of shot and can't vouch for its shootability but with shot being one of the most expensive components, anything that'll cut costs can have a profound affect on your overall savings.

The area where most beginning shotshell reloaders go astray (from an economic standpoint), is in the choice of reloading equipment. With the range of available tools running from the hand-operated variety all the way up to the progressive machines that can supply most shooting clubs, the handloader has to first decide what category he fits into with respect to the volume of shells he will need over a given period of time.

It could be your own choice of reloading tools that might ruin the economical equation relative to your reloading needs. For example, if you buy

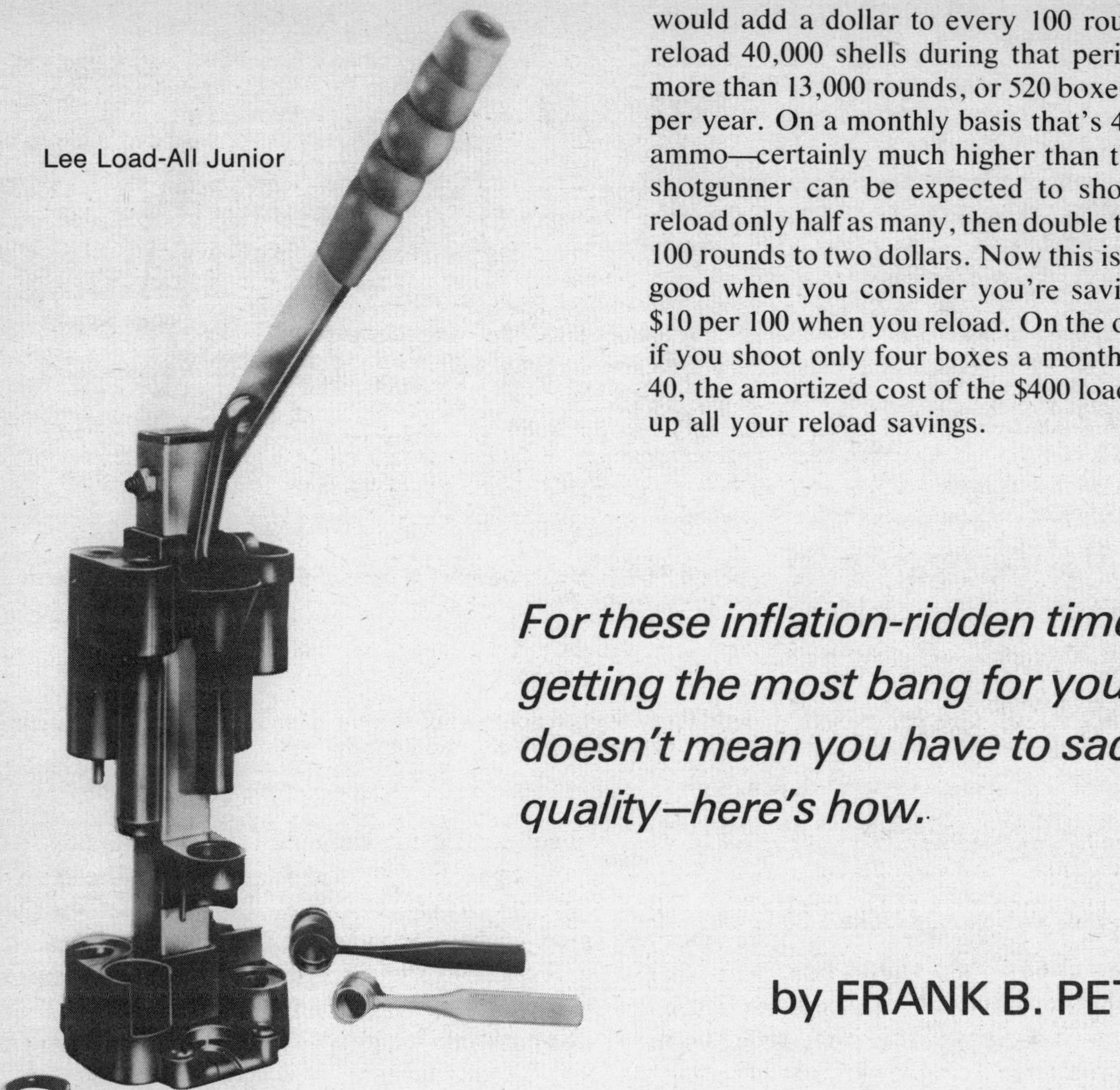

Lee Load-All Junior

would add a dollar to every 100 rounds if you reload 40,000 shells during that period. That's more than 13,000 rounds, or 520 boxes of ammo, per year. On a monthly basis that's 43 boxes of ammo—certainly much higher than the average shotgunner can be expected to shoot. If you reload only half as many, then double the cost per 100 rounds to two dollars. Now this is still pretty good when you consider you're saving at least $10 per 100 when you reload. On the other hand, if you shoot only four boxes a month instead of 40, the amortized cost of the $400 loader will eat up all your reload savings.

by FRANK B. PETRINI

the Load-All Way

a $400 progressive loader to knock out a couple of boxes of shells every month, it'll take a long, *long* time to recover that big initial cost. To be fair about it you should amortize its cost over the cost of all your reloads.

I usually consider a 3-year period reasonable to pay off a piece of new equipment. I take the cost of the item and spread it across the number of reloads I expect to produce over that length of time. If the cost per reload is prohibitive I avoid the purchase.

Using the 3-year rule, a $400 shotshell press

Certainly, you can work with any payback period that you like, but I've found that the 3-year rule is a reasonable one and, over the years, it has saved me money on what later have turned out to be unnecessary and costly purchases.

It's when a shooter gets up to 100 to 200 rounds a month that handloading becomes feasible; but, it's this shooter who must be careful in his choice of reloading tools.

After pondering this subject for a number of weeks and discussing it with fellow shooters, I concluded that a complete loading setup in the

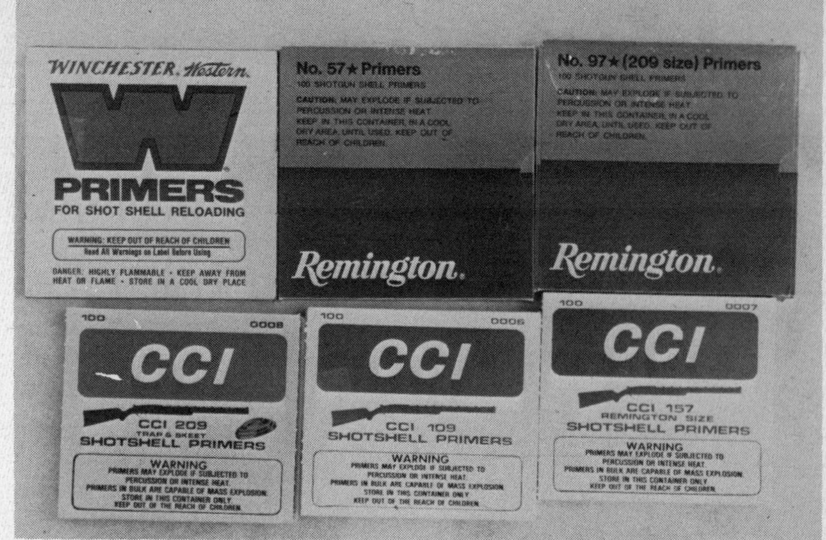

(Above) All brands of popular shotshell primers can be used with the Load-All charge tables.

(Left) If you plan on doing a fair amount of shooting, you can economize further by buying powder in bulk form.

$35 to $40 range would be just the ticket for most shotgunners that I know. These guys shoot maybe a maximum of 50 boxes a year (that's 1250 shells) or 150 in 3 years. That $40 investment spread over about 4000 shells comes to just about a dollar per hundred, a reasonable figure.

In addition, if a press in this price range were capable of producing a couple of boxes of reloads per hour then there would be little chance of it becoming tedious and the savings in ammunition costs would be pretty good.

I've been doing most of my shotshell reloading for some years with an old Pacific loader of considerably higher price than the $40 limit, so I ordered out one of the new Lee Load-Alls from Lee Precision, Inc., Hartford, WI 53027. This one seems to meet all the requirements at a fantastic retail price of only $36.98.

When the Lee Load-All was first introduced a few years back, it created quite a stir, not only because of its low price but also because of its ingenious design. Except for its base, supporting column and handle, it's entirely made of plastic —the dies are made of hard nylon.

The press comes complete with shot and powder bushings for throwing just about all popular powder charges and shot weights. The press I received is in 12 gauge and comes with eight shot bushings for throwing shot weights ranging from 1 ounce to 1⅞ ounces. Incidentally, these bushings are preset for No. 6 shot. Smaller shot will give slightly heavier charges while larger shot will come in slightly lighter. The only exception is the 1⅛-ounce bushing which was designed to dispense this weight of 7½ and 8 size shot for trap and Skeet shooters.

In addition, 16 powder charge bushings are included that throw charges running from 10.6 grains of Hercules Green Dot to 47.9 grains of Hodgdon's HS5. As the powder charge weight goes up from bushing to bushing, the increase in bushing powder capacity is only 5 percent. This means you'll never be more than 2½ percent from any desired load.

Actually, in examining these bushings and the Bushing Capacity Chart included with the Load-All, I found it inconceivable that the bushings supplied could not meet 100 percent of the average shotgunner's needs, for either clay or live birds.

The Load-All is a multiple station press with an overhead arm which, when pulled down, drives the press head with the powder and shot reservoirs and nylon dies downward to the casing being reloaded. To complete the circuit the arm must be pulled down below the front edge of the

(Above) The 16 powder bushings provided with the Load-All allow the handloader a large selection of usable loads both for target and hunting. (Below) The Lee Load-All has eight shot bushings that provide the handloader with a wide range of shot weights.

 # LOAD-ALL BUSHING CAPACITY CHART

This is a reference charge only to determine the charge of each type of powder each bushing will dispense.

These are not recommended charges as not every bushing is usable with each type of powder.

	BUSHING	.095	.100	.105	.110	.116	.122	.128	.134	.141.	.148	.155	.163	.171	.180	.189	.198
HERCULES	Green Dot	10.6	11.2	11.8	12.3	13.0	13.7	14.3	15.0	15.8	16.6	17.4	18.3	19.2	20.2	21.2	22.2
	Red Dot	10.7	11.3	11.9	12.4	13.1	13.8	14.5	15.1	15.9	16.7	17.5	18.4	19.3	20.3	21.4	22.4
	Herco	13.9	14.6	15.3	16.1	16.9	17.8	18.7	19.6	20.6	21.6	22.6	23.8	25.0	26.3	27.6	28.9
	Unique	14.7	15.6	16.3	17.1	18.0	18.9	19.8	20.8	21.9	22.9	24.0	25.3	26.5	27.9	29.3	30.7
	Blue Dot	18.1	19.1	20.1	21.0	22.2	23.3	24.5	25.6	26.9	28.3	29.6	31.1	32.7	34.4	36.1	37.8
	2400	21.0	22.1	23.2	24.3	25.6	27.0	28.3	29.6	31.2	32.7	34.3	36.0	37.8	39.8	41.8	43.8
HODGDON	X58	10.7	11.3	11.9	12.4	13.1	13.8	14.5	15.1	15.9	16.7	17.5	18.4	19.3	20.3	21.4	22.4
	Trap 100	13.3	14.0	14.7	15.4	16.2	17.1	17.9	18.8	19.7	20.7	21.7	22.8	23.9	25.2	26.5	27.7
	H4227	20.2	21.3	22.4	23.4	24.7	26.0	27.3	28.5	30.0	31.5	33.0	34.7	36.4	38.3	40.3	42.2
	HS6	21.9	23.0	24.2	25.3	26.7	28.1	29.4	30.8	32.4	34.0	35.7	37.5	39.3	41.4	43.5	45.5
	H110	22.5	23.7	24.9	26.1	27.5	28.9	30.3	31.8	33.4	35.1	36.7	38.6	40.5	42.7	44.8	46.9
	HS7	22.9	24.1	25.3	26.5	28.0	29.4	30.8	32.3	34.0	35.7	37.4	39.3	41.2	43.4	45.6	47.7
	HS5	23.0	24.2	25.4	26.6	28.1	29.5	31.0	32.0	34.1	35.8	37.5	39.5	41.4	43.6	45.7	47.9
DU PONT	Hi Skor 700X	12.2	12.8	13.4	14.1	14.9	15.6	16.4	17.2	18.1	18.9	19.8	20.9	21.9	23.0	24.2	25.3
	PB	12.9	13.6	14.3	15.0	15.8	16.6	17.4	18.2	19.2	20.1	21.1	22.2	23.3	24.5	25.7	26.9
	SR 4756	14.2	14.9	15.7	16.4	17.3	18.2	19.1	20.0	21.0	22.1	23.1	24.3	25.5	26.8	28.2	29.5
	SR 7625	14.9	15.7	16.5	17.3	18.2	19.2	20.1	21.0	22.1	23.2	24.3	25.6	26.9	28.3	29.7	31.1
	IMR 4227	20.2	21.3	22.4	23.4	24.7	26.0	27.3	28.5	30.0	31.5	33.0	34.7	36.4	38.3	40.3	42.2
WIN.	452 AA	13.3	14.0	14.7	15.4	16.2	17.1	17.9	18.8	19.7	20.7	21.7	22.8	23.9	25.2	26.5	27.7
	473 AA	16.0	16.8	17.6	18.5	19.5	20.5	21.5	22.5	23.7	24.9	26.0	27.3	28.7	30.2	31.8	33.3
	540	22.8	24.0	25.2	26.4	27.8	29.3	30.7	32.2	33.8	35.5	37.2	39.1	41.0	43.2	45.4	47.5
	571	22.9	24.1	25.3	26.5	28.0	29.4	30.8	32.3	34.0	35.7	37.4	39.3	41.2	43.4	45.6	47.7
NOBEL	Nobel 60	11.4	12.0	12.6	13.2	13.9	14.6	15.4	16.1	16.9	17.8	18.6	20.0	20.5	21.6	22.7	23.8
	Nobel 62	12.5	13.2	13.9	14.5	15.3	16.1	16.9	17.7	18.6	19.5	20.5	21.5	22.6	23.8	25.0	26.2
	Nobel 64	13.1	13.8	14.5	15.2	16.0	16.8	17.7	18.5	19.5	20.4	21.4	22.5	23.6	24.8	26.1	27.3
	Nobel 78	9.8	10.3	10.8	11.3	12.0	12.6	13.2	13.8	14.5	15.2	16.0	16.8	17.6	18.5	19.5	20.4
	Nobel 80	10.0	10.5	11.0	11.6	12.2	12.8	13.4	14.1	14.8	15.5	16.3	17.1	18.0	18.9	19.9	20.8
	Nobel 82	10.9	11.5	12.1	12.7	13.3	14.0	14.7	15.4	16.2	17.0	17.8	18.8	19.7	20.7	21.7	22.8
ALCAN	Al-120	11.8	12.4	13.2	13.6	14.4	15.1	15.9	16.6	17.5	18.3	19.2	20.2	21.2	22.3	23.4	24.6
	AL-5 AL-7	17.1	18.0	18.9	19.8	20.9	22.0	23.0	24.1	25.4	26.6	27.9	29.3	30.8	32.4	34.0	35.6
	AL-8	15.2	16.0	16.8	17.6	18.6	19.5	20.5	21.4	22.6	23.7	24.8	26.1	27.4	28.8	30.2	31.7

metal base. Because of this the press has to be mounted within an inch of the edge of the table or bench.

To produce a setup as portable as possible, I mounted the 12-gauge Load-All on a sheet of ¾-inch particle board which was then clamped onto one of my reloading benches. This same arrangement can be used on a kitchen table but, here, Lee recommends that felt be glued to the bottom of the board to avoid table damage.

A handy charge table is included with the press giving popular loads with all common 12-gauge shot weights. This table, in essence, is a guide to choosing the correct powder bushing for use with a specific powder to produce the desired velocity. The dram equivalent is also specified to provide comparison to the factory product. For your convenience, complete Lee charge tables are presented here for 12, 16 and 20 gauge Load-All presses. You will also find a Load-All bushing-capacity chart as well as Load-All Junior charge tables.

Two bushings are specified for each load, one for plastic shells with a plastic base wad or no base wad at all (examples are Winchester AA, Remington RXP, and Federal Champion II shells), the other for paper shells or plastic shells with paper base wads.

As an example, I wanted to produce some target loads shortly after my Load-All arrived. I wanted to load specifically for trap and Skeet in an effort to use up a good supply of once-fired 2¾-inch Winchester AA 12-gauge casings. The answer was a relatively light 1⅛-ounce load of 7½ shot. An equivalent 2¾ dram load that would produce 1145 fps was available in the load chart which also gave me my choice of any one of eight popular powders. I chose Dupont Hi Skor 700X. The table listed Lee bushing number 134 for use with the all plastic Winchester casings. From the capacity chart I found that this bushing should throw a charge of 17.2 grains of Dupont powder.

As a check, I referred to the current Dupont *Handloader's Guide* and found their recommended load of 17.5 grains of 700X with 1⅛ ounces of shot would produce 1135 fps with 7900 pounds of chamber pressure. The Lee data relates very closely.

The Dupont info was based on the Winchester 209 primers and WAA12 wads I planned to use. So everything was consistent.

Now for a word of warning. While rifle and pistol ammo handloaders freely substitute brands of brass, primers and bullets when using published load data, doing so with shotshell reloading is inviting disaster.

For example, with a change of primer in the above load—from Winchester 209s to Federal 209s—the Dupont Guide shows a 17-grain charge of 700X (½-grain less) will give 1145 fps, or 10 fps more. More importantly, it'll produce 9500 pounds of chamber pressure, an increase of *20 percent* over the same load with the Winchester primers. While this may not be a big deal in a light target load it can have serious implications in heavier ones.

A change of shell has even more significance. Paper casings or plastic ones with paper base wads require more powder to produce the same velocity than the all-plastic shells. To use a heavy charge recommended for the former in the latter can have serious repercussions, one of which may be damage to the shotgun and shotgunner.

The Lee charge tables make no specific reference to brands of primers but a comparison of the data relative to information published by the powder manufacturers leads me to conclude that Lee recommended loads are slightly low, enough to mask the effects of changes in this one component.

The recommended loads are well thought out and provide for just about all 12-gauge uses. But for increased flexibility for the budget minded, free literature is available from the major powder manufacturers. For yours, send to Dupont (Dupont Sales Division, Wilmington, DE 19898); Winchester (Winchester-Western, New Haven, CT 06504); Hercules (Hercules, Inc., 910 Market St., Wilmington, DE 19899) and Hodgdon (Hodgdon Powder Co., 7710 W. 50 HiWay, Shawnee-Mission, KS 66202).

To install the proper bushings in the Load-All you must first remove the thin metal nameplate providing access to the charge bar. Do this with the powder and shot reservoirs empty or you'll have a mess on your hands. The shot bushing is inserted into the right bushing slot, the powder charge bushing in the left. Then replace the nameplate.

To fill the powder and shot hoppers, first slide the charge bar to the left, placing it in the proper position for the first shell to be loaded. Next, the hoppers can be filled with the proper powder and shot. To insure uniform charges it's best to keep

LEE LOAD-ALL CHARGE TABLES

HOW TO USE A CHARGE TABLE:

1) Select correct gauge and shell length.
2) Select shot charge and install correct bushing.
3) Select the correct bushing according to powder type and shell type.

IMPORTANT NOTICE: Most loads recommend a different bushing for one piece plastic cases as compared to cases with a paper or composition base wad. Be sure you're in the correct column.

4) Check Nos. 1, 2 and 3 again to make certain you have not made a mistake. The wrong bushing could be extremely dangerous.

12 GAUGE — 2¾" Shells

Plastic shells with paper base wad and paper shells.
Plastic shells with a plastic base wad or no base wad such as Win. AA, Rem. RXP & Federal Champion II.

SHOT	DRAMS EQUIV.	POWDER TYPE	BUSH. NO.	BUSH. NO.
1 OZ.	2¾ 1150 F.P.S.	GREEN DOT	.171	.171
		RED DOT	.155	.163
		X58	.155	.163
		700X	.134	.148
		PB	.155	.163
		SR 7625	.141	.155
		452 AA	.141	.155
		TRAP 100	.141	.155
	3 1220 F.P.S.	GREEN DOT	.180	.180
		RED DOT	.163	.171
		X58	.163	.171
		700 X	.141	.155
		PB	.163	.171
		SR 7625	.148	.163
		452 AA	.148	.163
		TRAP 100	.148	.163
	3¼ 1290 F.P.S.	GREEN DOT	.189	.189
		RED DOT	.171	.180
		X58	.171	.180
		700 X	.148	.163
		PB	.171	.180
		SR 7625	.155	.171
		452 AA	.155	.171
		TRAP 100	.155	.171
1 1/8 OZ.	2¾ 1145 F.P.S.	GREEN DOT	.155	.171
		RED DOT	.155	.163
		700 X	.134	.141
		PB	.155	.163
		SR 7625	.141	.163
		X58	.155	.163
		TRAP 100	.141	.148
		452AA	.141	.148
	3 1200 F.P.S.	GREEN DOT	.163	.180
		RED DOT	.163	.171
		700X	.141	.148
		PB	.163	.171
		SR7625	.148	.171
		UNIQUE	.128	.141
		X58	.163	.171
		TRAP 100	.148	.155
		452AA	.148	.155
		473AA	.141	.148
	3¼ 1255 F.P.S.	GREEN DOT	.171	.189
		PB	.171	.180
		SR7625	.155	.171
		UNIQUE	.141	.148
		TRAP 100	N.R.	.163
		452AA	N.R.	.163
		473AA	.148	.155

N.R. No recommendation.

12 GAUGE — 2¾" Shells

Plastic shells with paper base wad and paper shells.
Plastic shells with a plastic base wad or no base wad such as Win. AA, Rem. RXP & Federal Champion II.

SHOT	DRAMS EQUIV.	POWDER TYPE	BUSH. NO.	BUSH. NO.
1 1/4 OZ.	3¼ 1220 F.P.S.	PB	.171	.180
		540	.128	.134
		473AA	.148	.155
		UNIQUE	N.R.	.141
		HERCO	.163	.180
		SR7625	.155	.171
		SR4756	.189	.198
		HS-5	.110	.116
		HS-6	.128	.134
	3½ 1275 F.P.S.	540	.134	.141
		HERCO	N.R.	.189
		SR4756	.198	N.R.
		HS-5	.116	N.R.
		SR7625	.171	.180
		HS-6	.134	.141
	3¾ 1330 F.P.S.	540	.141	.148
		BLUE DOT	.171	N.R.
		HERCO	N.R.	.198
		SR7625	.171	.189
1 1/2 OZ.	Magnum 1260 F.P.S.	540	N.R.	.141
		571	.148	.155
		HS-7	.148	.155
		HS-6	N.R.	.134
		BLUE DOT	.171	.180

12 GAUGE — 3" Magnum

Paper and plastic shell with a paper base wad.
Plastic shells with a plastic base wad or no base wad such as Winchester compression formed cases.

SHOT	DRAMS EQUIV.	POWDER TYPE	BUSH. NO.	BUSH. NO.
1 5/8 OZ.	Magnum 1280 F.P.S.	571	.148	.163
		540	N.R.	.155
		HS-7	.148	.163
		BLUE DOT	.198	N.R.
		SR4756	.198	N.R.
1 7/8 OZ.	Magnum 1210 F.P.S.	571	.134	.148
		HS-7	.134	.148
		SR4756	.198	.198
		BLUE DOT	.198	.198

The loads on this charge table are extracted from load data published by powder manufacturers. We have no control over the manufacture, storage or use of the components you use, so we cannot accept responsibility for ammunition loaded with this data. The listed loads are the only loads we were able to select that appeared to give uniform and safe results with a variety of components. For additional loads it's necessary to secure that data from a reliable source such as that published by the manufacturer of the powder or a reloading manual published by a competent and responsible company.

LEE LOAD-ALL CHARGE TABLES

HOW TO USE A CHARGE TABLE:

1) Select correct gauge and shell length.

2) Select shot charge and install correct bushing.

3) Select the correct bushing according to powder type and shell type.

IMPORTANT NOTICE: Most loads recommend a different bushing for one piece plastic cases as compared to cases with a paper or composition base wad. Be sure you're in the correct column.

4) Check Nos. 1, 2 and 3 again to make certain you have not made a mistake. The wrong bushing could be extremely dangerous.

20 GAUGE — 2¾" Shells

Paper and plastic shell with a paper base wad.

Plastic shells with a plastic base wad or no base wad such as Winchester compression formed and Remington RXP.

SHOT	DRAMS EQUIV.	POWDER TYPE	BUSH. NO.	BUSH. NO.
7/8 OZ.	2¼	GREEN DOT	.122	.128
		UNIQUE	.095	.095
	1160 F.P.S.	SR7625	.100	.105
		PB	.110	.122
		SR4756	.128	.134
		700X	N.R.	.110
		473AA	.100	.105
		HERCO	.105	.110
	2½	GREEN DOT	.128	.134
		UNIQUE	.100	.100
	1210 F.P.S.	SR7625	.105	.110
		PB	.116	.128
		SR4756	.134	.141
		HERCO	.110	N.R.
1 OZ.	2½	UNIQUE	N.R.	.100
		SR4756	.128	.134
	1165 F.P.S.	SR7625	N.R.	.116
		HERCO	.110	.116
		HS-7	.095	.100
	2¾	SR4756	.134	.141
		SR7625	N.R.	.122
	1220 F.P.S.	540	N.R.	.095
		HERCO	N.R.	.122
		HS-7	.100	.105
		571	.100	.105
		HS-6	N.R.	.095
1 1/8 OZ.	2¾ Magnum 1175 F.P.S.	571	.095	.100
		BLUE DOT	.110	.116
		HS-7	.095	.100

N.R. Indicates Not Recommended.

20 GAUGE — 3" Magnum

Paper and plastic shell with a paper base wad.

Plastic shells with a plastic base wad or no base wad such as Winchester compression formed cases.

SHOT	DRAMS EQUIV.	POWDER TYPE	BUSH. NO.	BUSH. NO.
1 1/8 OZ.	Magnum 1220 F.P.S.	SR4756	.155	.155
		HS-7	.105	.110
		571	.105	.110
		BLUE DOT	.134	.141
1 1/4 OZ.	Magnum	571	.100	.105
		HS-7	.100	.105
	1135 F.P.S.	BLUE DOT	.128	.128
		IMR4227	.180	.189

16 GAUGE — 2¾" Shells

Paper and plastic shell with a paper base wad.

Plastic shells with a plastic base wad or no base wad such as Winchester compression formed cases.

SHOT	DRAMS EQUIV.	POWDER TYPE	BUSH. NO.	BUSH. NO.
7/8 OZ.	2½	700X	.122	.122
		PB	.134	.141
	1190 F.P.S.	SR7625	.128	.134
		SR4756	.155	.163
		RED DOT	.134	.141
		GREEN DOT	.141	.148
		452AA	.116	.122
		473AA	.116	.122
		TRAP 100	.116	.122
		UNIQUE	.110	.110
		X58	.134	.141
	2¾	SR7625	.134	.141
		SR4756	.163	.171
	1230 F.P.S.	473AA	.122	.128
		UNIQUE	.116	.122
		HERCO	.134	.141
1 OZ.	2½	700X	.122	.122
		PB	.134	.141
	1165 F.P.S.	SR7625	.128	.134
		SR4756	.155	.163
		GREEN DOT	.141	.148
		452AA	.116	.122
		473AA	.116	.122
		TRAP 100	.116	.122
		UNIQUE	.110	.116
	2¾	473AA	.122	.128
	1220 F.P.S.	UNIQUE	.116	.116
		HERCO	.134	.141
1 1/8 OZ.	2¾	540	.110	N.R.
		UNIQUE	.110	.116
	1185 F.P.S.	HERCO	.141	.148
		PB	.141	.148
		SR7625	.128	.134
		SR4756	.155	.163
	3¼	540	.116	.122
	1295 F.P.S.	SR4756	.163	.171
1 1/4 OZ.	Magnum 1260 F.P.S.	571	.122	.128
		HS-7	.122	.128

The loads on this charge table are extracted from load data published by powder manufacturers. We have no control over the manufacture, storage or use of the components you use, so we cannot accept responsibility for ammunition loaded with this data. The listed loads are the only loads we were able to select that appeared to give uniform and safe results with a variety of components. For additional loads it's necessary to secure that data from a reliable source such as that published by the manufacturer of the powder or a reloading manual published by a competent and responsible company.

the level of powder and shot above the built-in baffles in each hopper.

At this point loading can begin. Each shell must be taken through eight steps and each station on the base. These are sizing/decapping; priming; insertion of powder, wad, and shot; crimp starting and final crimping. With one hand working the handle, the other is free to move the shell between stations during the following operations: placing the resizing ring over the shell in station one; placing a primer in the well at station 2; taking the resizing ring off at station 2; throwing the powder charge at station 3; positioning the plastic wad and finally throwing the shot charge and crimping.

It's easier to do than to describe; and, while this is no progressive machine by any stretch of the imagination, it takes little practice before you can knock out at least 100 shells an hour. Dick Lee claims 200 and I don't doubt Dick's word. However, the reloader must be organized and dexterous to achieve such production.

As already mentioned, few shotgunners use more than a few hundred rounds a month. This

STEP-BY-STEP WITH THE LOAD-ALL

1. In station 1, the shotshell is resized and decapped.

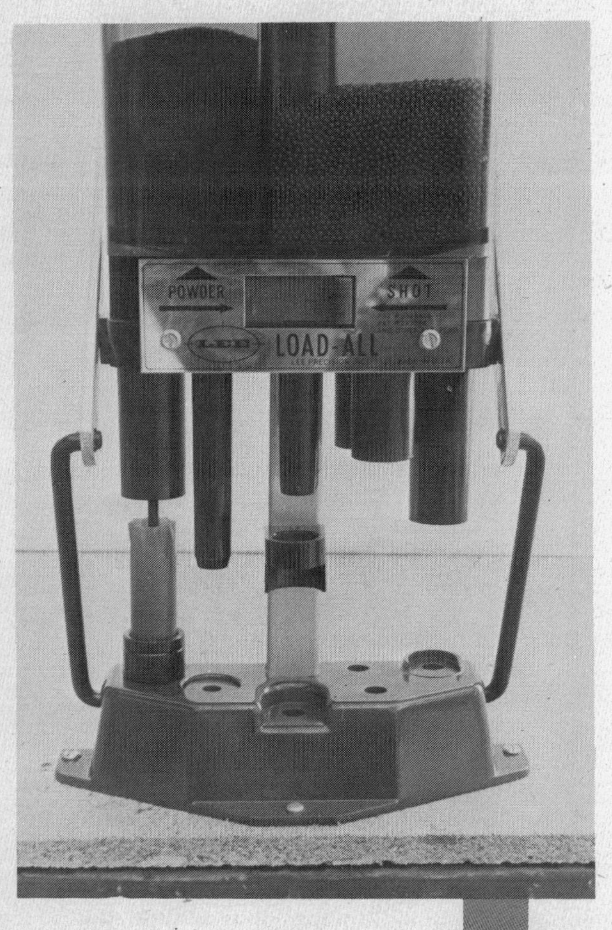

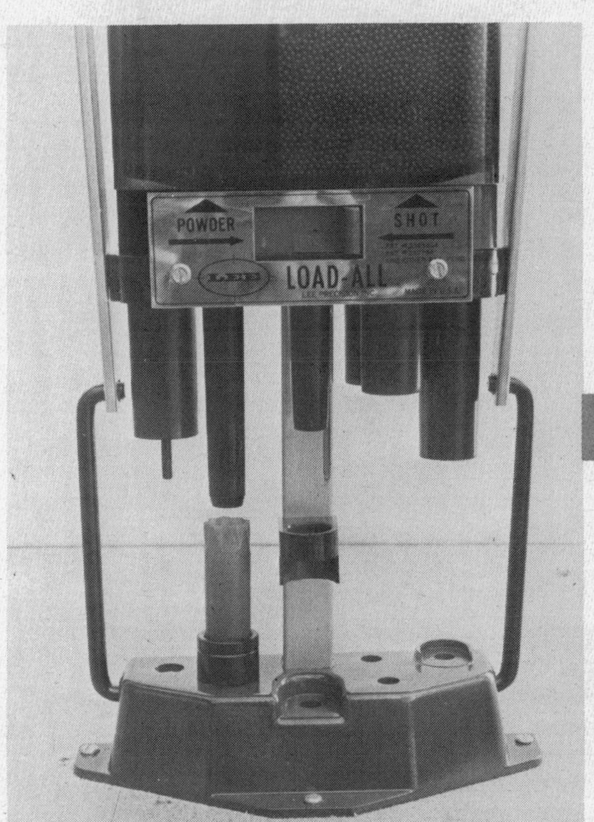

2. In station 2, a primer is first inserted in the well and the shell is placed above in preparation for priming.

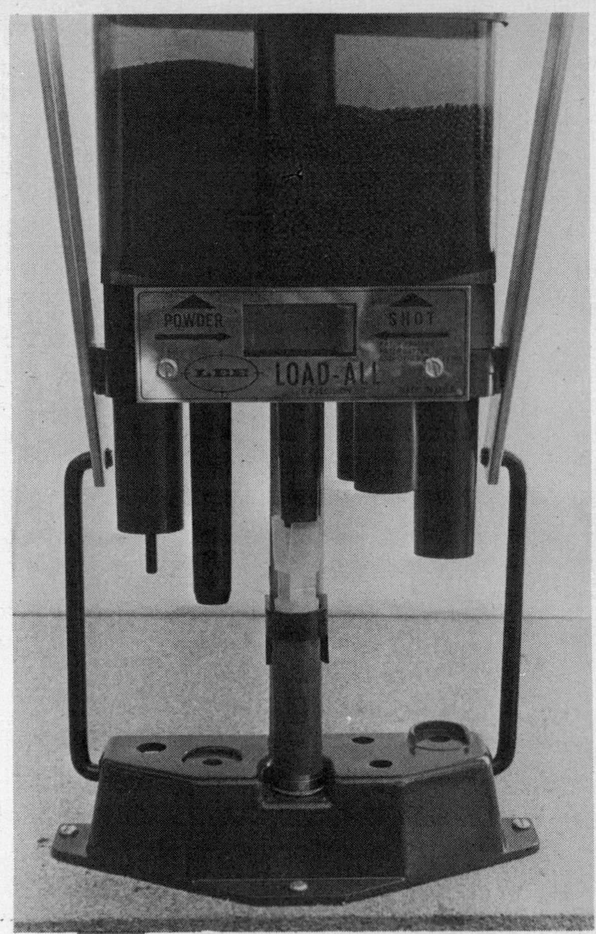

4. In station 3, the shell is first charged with powder.

3. In station 2, while priming, the resizing ring is pushed off the base of the shell freeing its grip on the case.

5. Next, the plastic wad is positioned above the wad guide.

6. After the wad is seated, the shot is dropped into the case.

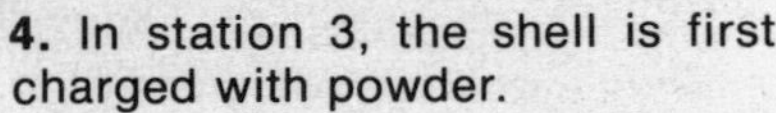

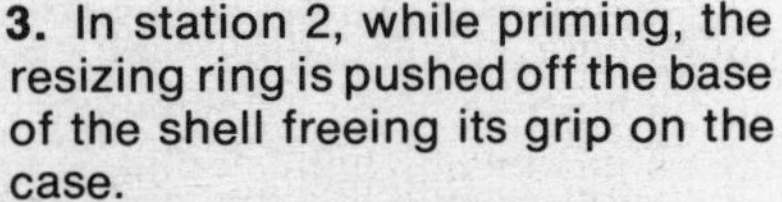

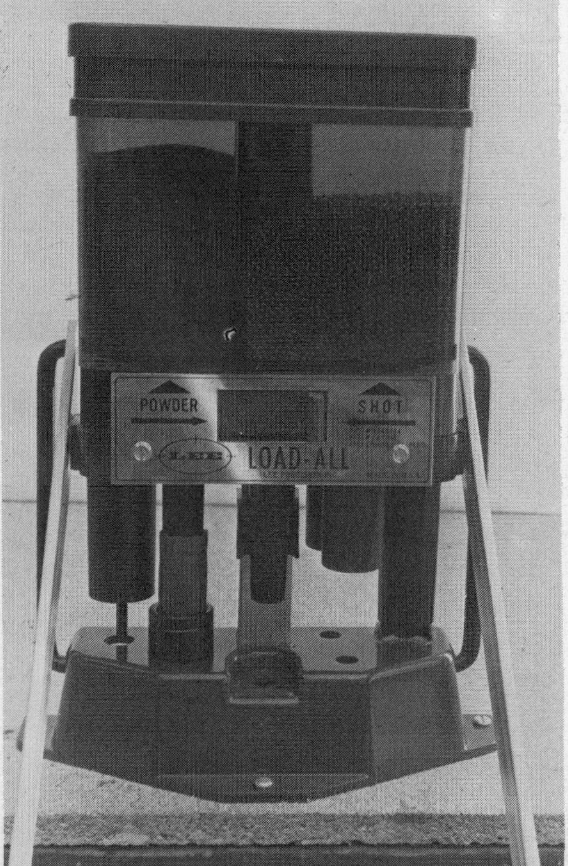

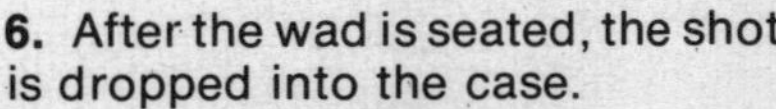

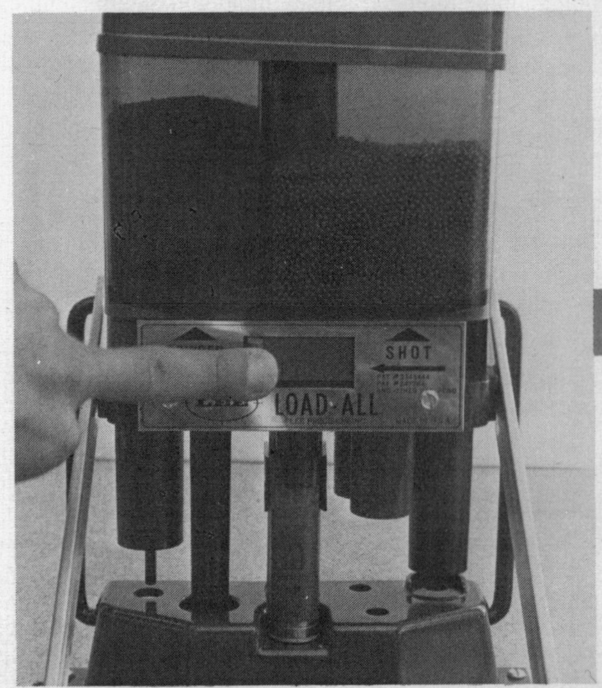

lightweight press can easily meet this quota with just an hour or two reloading time.

The Load-All can also handle 3-inch magnum shells with some modification to the press and procedures. First the wad guide must be moved ¼-inch higher on the column to allow room for the longer casing. Secondly, during the crimp starting and final crimping (stations 4 and 5) you can't pull the handle down to a complete stop. Here you must develop a "feel" for when to stop forming the crimp on the longer shell. Nine recommended "magnum" loads using the Lee bushings are provided in the charge tables.

The Lee Load-All is also available in 16- and 20-gauge versions, with operations exactly the same as those described with the 12.

For the shotshell stuffer interested in economy, the Lee Load-All is the perfect answer to reasonable production at a low base cost. This means cheaper reloads with no appreciable quality loss.

If you're willing to sacrifice a little bit of automation, and a tiny amount of speed, the Lee Load-All Junior press should be investigated. It,

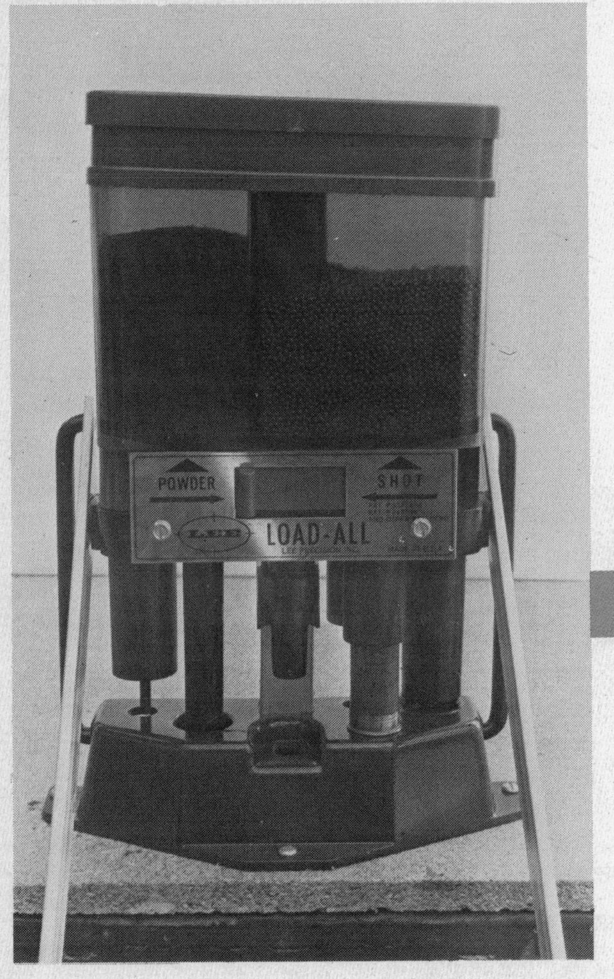

7. In station 4, the crimp is started.

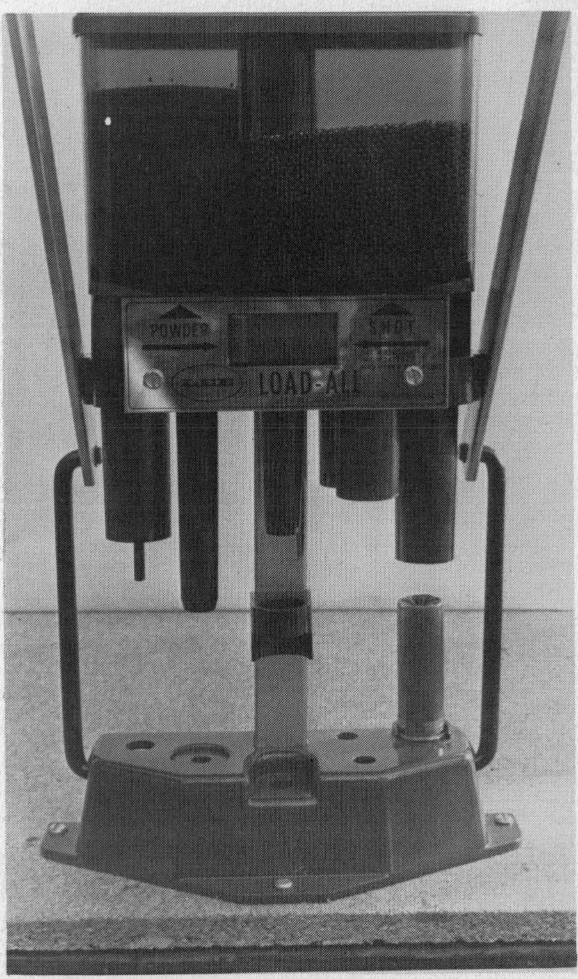

8. In station 5, the final crimp is applied and the reload is finished.

too, is made of plastic and nylon with essentially the same procedures followed as with its big brother. But, appearance-wise, there's little family resemblance since the Junior lacks the large powder and shot hoppers of the other press.

Powder and shot are measured and dispensed with dippers that come with the press. The one used for powder measuring has a volume of 2.5 *cc*s (cubic centimeters). The Junior charge tables show two dozen 2¾-inch, 12-gauge loads for use with this one powder measure. The shot scoop has an adjustable base that can be set to throw from 1 to 1⅝ ounces of shot.

The number of loads listed are just a fraction of those listed in the charts for the bigger press but for most 12-gauge shooters they should meet most uses, with some restriction. For example, I could not use Dupont 700X powder with 1⅛ ounces of shot in my 2¾ inch Winchester AA cases. For a comparable target load I'd have to use Green Dot, Red Dot, or PB, the only propellants listed in the Junior tables. If you can live with the restricted powder set, the Junior can do the job just about as well as the bigger Load-All.

STEP-BY-STEP WITH THE LOAD-ALL JUNIOR

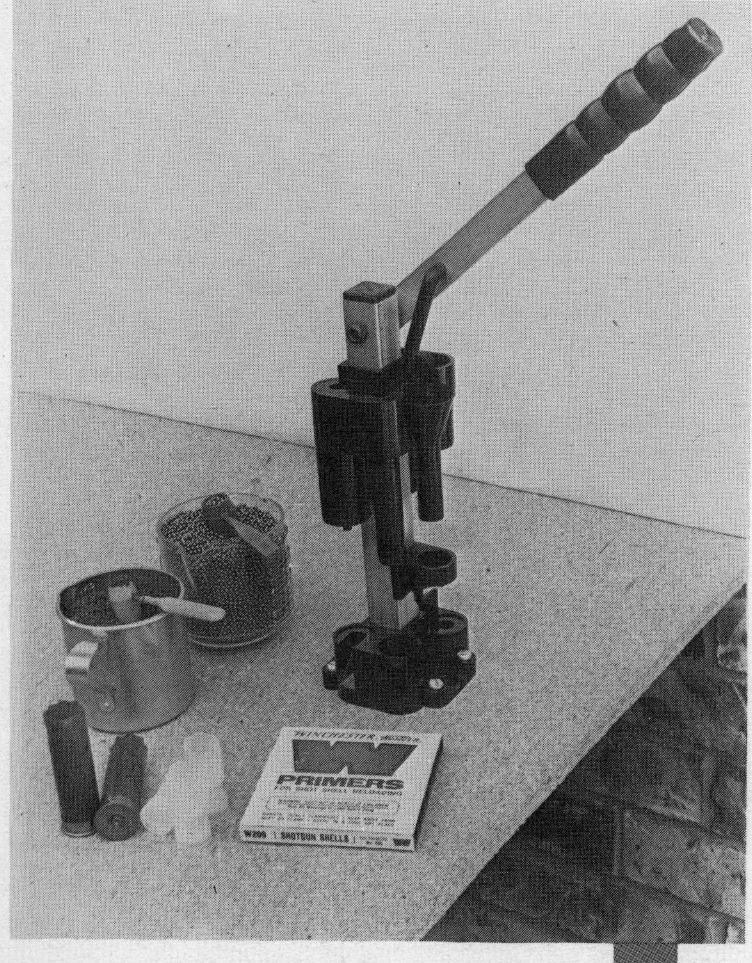

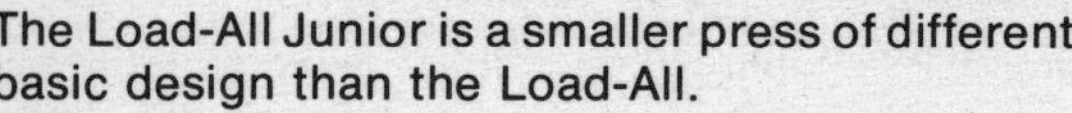

The Load-All Junior is a smaller press of different basic design than the Load-All.

1. In station 1, the case is resized and decapped.

2. In station 2, priming and release of the resizing ring is accomplished.

3. After the shell is charged with the powder dipper, it's placed in station 3, where the wad is positioned and seated.

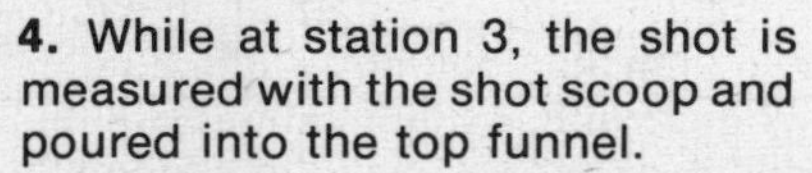

4. While at station 3, the shot is measured with the shot scoop and poured into the top funnel.

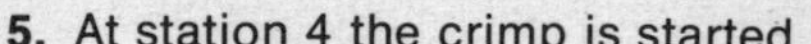

5. At station 4 the crimp is started.

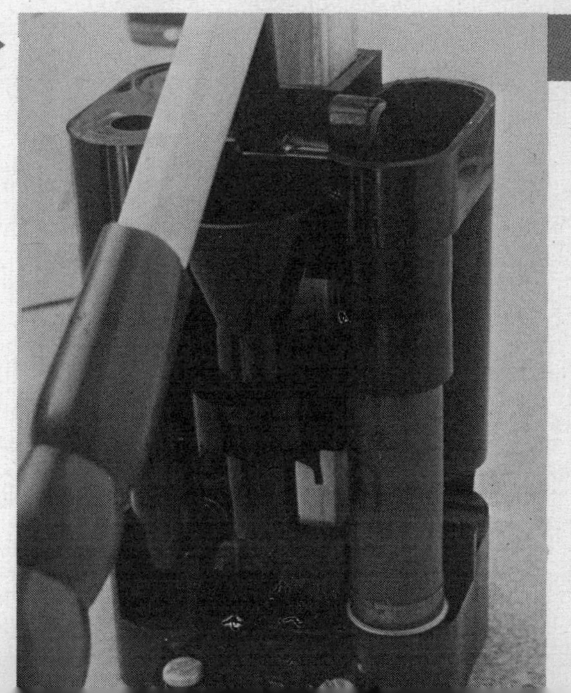

6. Station 5 is for final crimping — the shell is finished.

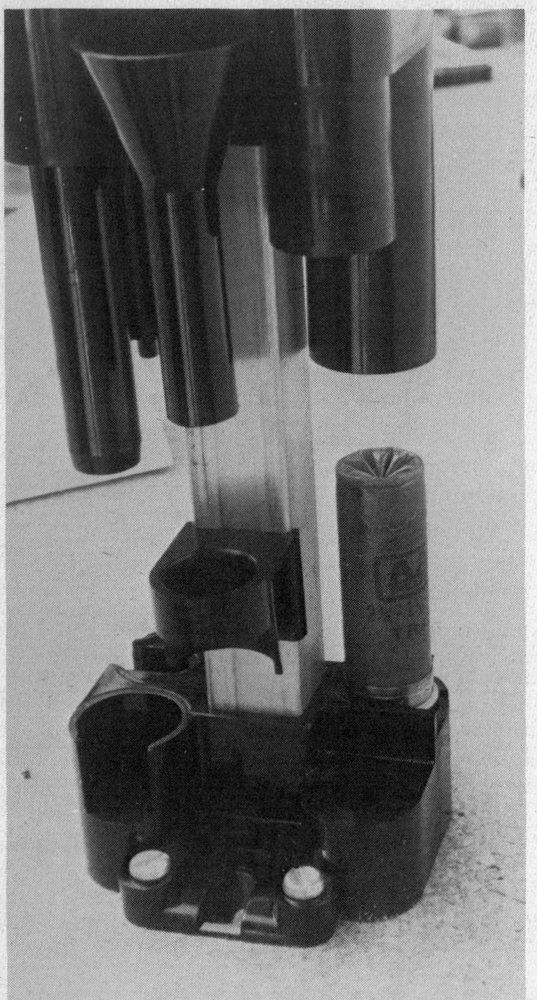

LEE LOAD-ALL JUNIOR 12-GAUGE CHARGE TABLES

PLASTIC CASES

Using 2.5 cc measure
CAUTION: These loads will give the velocity stated only if loaded in all-plastic shells such as Win. AA, Rem. RXP, Fed. Champion II and Win. compression formed cases. They are safe to load in any shell but will give reduced velocity in paper cases or shells with a paper base wad.

SHOT	DRAMS EQUIV.	POWDER TYPE	POWDER GRAINS 2.5 cc measure
1 OZ.	2¾ 1150 FPS	Red Dot P B	17.7 20.7
	3¼ 1290 FPS	SR 7625 • 462 AA Trap 100	23.9 21.4 21.4
1⅛ OZ.	2¾ 1145 FPS	Green Dot P B	17.1 20.7
	3 1200 FPS	Red Dot	17.7
	3¼ 1255	SR 7625	23.9
1¼ OZ.	3¼ 1220 FPS	SR 7625	23.9
1⅜ OZ.	3½ 1275 FPS	571 HS-7	36.8 36.8

PAPER BASEWAD CASES

Using 2.5 cc measure
CAUTION: This data is for paper cases or plastic cases with a paper base wad only. **DO NOT USE** these loads in all plastic shells such as Win. AA, Rem. RXP, Federal Champion II or Win. compression formed cases as dangerous pressure will result.

SHOT	DRAMS EQUIV.	POWDER TYPE	POWDER GRAINS 2.5 cc measure
1 OZ.	2¾ 1150 FPS	SR 7625 452 AA Trap 100	23.9 21.4 21.4
1⅛ OZ.	2¾ 1145 FPS	Red Dot	17.7
	3 1200 FPS	Trap 100 452 AA	21.4 21.4
	3¼ 1255 FPS	473 AA	25.6
1¼ OZ.	3¼ 1220 FPS	473 AA	25.6
	3¾ 1330 FPS	540	36.6
1½ OZ.	Magnum 1260 FPS	571 HS-7	36.8 36.8
3" Shell 1⅝ OZ.	3" Magnum 1280 FPS	540	36.6

Once you get the powder and shot scooping down to a science you should be able to load somewhere around 75 shells per hour. This isn't much slower than the Load-All but is significantly faster than any hand tool. The price is an astonishingly low $14.98.

Incidentally, the Junior is an entirely different design from the Load-All. Its arm doesn't come down lower than the press base during any operation so it's not necessary to mount the press near the edge of the bench as with the "senior" model. The nylon dies of each press are similar and there's no apparent (visual) difference between the reloads from either.

Choosing between the two presses can be reduced to considering a few factors. First is the gauge of shells to be reloaded—the Junior is only available in 12-gauge at this time. Second is price. Third is the convenience of the charge-bar approach to shot and powder measuring versus the scooping technique. Whichever the choice, both presses offer true economy as well as quality. And in shotshell reloading, that's the name of the game. •

STEEL SHOT – the Question of Reloadability

There is indeed a future for those who want to reload steel shot. However, the future will have to be approached by both the reloader and the reloading industry with a great deal of caution.

by CHUCK TURNER

About the Author: Chuck Turner has been in the firearms and ammunition industry for over 28 years, holding executive positions in research, engineering and production. He is currently Technical Advisor to the Sporting Arms and Ammunition Manufacturers' Institute, and to the Association of Firearms and Toolmark Examiners. He is also Chairman of the Shooting Safety Committee of the National Safety Council.

IT WOULD SEEM that the handloading of waterfowl loads with steel shot is fast becoming the holy grail, the promised land of more and more hunters. As federal regulations become more restrictive and the cost of factory loads is pumped up by inflation, the waterfowler feels like he is caught between the shore and the open sea in a leaky boat as an offshore breeze heralds an approaching storm. He is becoming righteously angered and frustrated. In some cases panic has set in leading to attempted remedies far more dangerous than the situation to which he is reacting.

Without getting into the battle of words that has taken place over the last five years, and certainly without wishing to add to the mountains of testimony that have been born over the pros and cons of steel vs. lead shot, let's just discuss the problems of reloading steel shot as they exist now and what the future offers in the way of solutions.

Contrary to some of our experts, the loading of materials other than lead pellets into shotguns was not begun five or six years ago. Early shoulder weapons were really scaled down and very

Ordinary lead shot is cheaply manufactured by running molten lead through a sieve, and through a shot tower, as seen here. The process of making properly hardened steel shot is much more complex and costly. It's still a "manufacturer's only" proposition when it comes to quality steel shot availability.

cumbersome versions of larger, heavier military cannons that fired everything from arrows to stones and yes, even steel balls. The early shoulder weapons, were, in fact, called "hand-cannons" and were smooth bored. They, too, fired arrows, small steel pellets of all shapes and sizes, and just about anything else that would fit down the barrel. It wasn't until the 15th century that lead shot was being made on a large scale in Germany and very soon thereafter in England.

Lead shot had so many advantages both in the manufacture and its ballistics that it was just "no contest." Steel balls as shot for shoulder arms disappeared until the age of the environmentalist dawned in the United States around 1948. Soon after, at least one prominent member of the firearms industry became concerned with the ingestion of lead pellets by feeding waterfowl. Winchester-Western began looking for non-toxic substitutes at that time. The rest of the industry followed very soon. Naturally, the material they were looking for would have to be a metal as heavy, or heavier, than lead that could be formed into spheres at a reasonable cost. They wanted the weight for ballistic reasons, of course. As the industry scientists went down the Specific Gravity tables looking for the higher numbers indicating high weight per unit volume, everything from spent uranium to iron became candidates. There were many of them. The future looked rosy. (Table I gives a few examples.)

The euphoria, often so prevalent in the early stages of a research project, before all of the problems are evaluated, didn't last very long.

Table I

Specific Gravity Comparison

Metal	Specific Gravity
Rhenium	20.5
Tungsten	19.4
Uranium	19.1
Lead	11.3
Copper	8.9
Nickel	8.9
Iron	7.9
Zinc	7.1
Tin	5.7

Reasonable cost eliminated all of the choices except iron.

It didn't take long to find out that if iron was to do the job, then *pure* iron was needed for reasons of its relative softness. Pure iron, in pellet form, and as soft as possible was impossible to obtain. It could be made into wire keeping most impurities (such as carbon) out of it but making pellets was a costly process. Other paths toward a solution were, therefore, tried. Some of these were: coatings for lead, the use of other metals such as copper, zinc and even elaborate processes for combining lead and iron. All of these attempts failed either because they could not stand up to the gastric juices of the waterfowl, or wore away quickly under the abrasive action in the gizzard.

While it takes only a few words to review the research that went on, it took years and many, many thousands of dollars to make very little progress. Just getting ballistic data was difficult and time consuming because pellet forming was something only ball-bearing manufacturers were set up to do and they did not want to make only 10,000 to 15,000 special-diameter balls from metals other than what they were running every day. Putting an even coating of various plastics or metals on the lead pellets was an even more difficult task.

It wasn't until 1965 that Armco Supersoft iron was announced and was quickly tested as material for non-toxic shot. Special pellet making machines were designed and pellets made. It soon became apparent that just forming the almost pure iron wire into spheres would harden it beyond what had been set as the softness goal. Although the shot at that time was called "iron shot," it didn't take long to realize that the name was not quite correct. In order to get the formed pellets down to a reasonable softness they had to be heated to reform the iron microcrystals that had developed during the pellet forming process. During this heat-treat the pellets picked up carbon, even if only a small amount, from the annealing flame. They were no longer iron, they were now steel pellets. Of course, heating the pellets in a special furnace would have eliminated the carbon pick up but the cost would have, once again, become unreasonable.

While all of this history may seem irrelevant to the handloader, it really isn't when you realize that the biggest problem the load-it-yourselfer has is getting steel shot of the proper hardness (or better, softness). More about this later. Let us not, however, give anyone the impression that shot hardness is the only problem with the home-loading of steel shot.

The Case

To the uninitiated the interior shape of the case

Conventional compression-formed hulls have tapered walls that rob the volume needed for steel shot reloading. A new shotshell, the ACTIV, by Rainel de P.R. features straight walls as can be seen here. It may eventually prove to be the ideal steel-shot case for reloaders. The Rainel shell has a steel washer that's an integral part of the head.

would seem to be of little importance. *However,* at least with the powder, wads and primers available to us today, that interior configuration is a *very* important factor.

While the compression formed shells are outstanding hulls for shotshell reloading, the tapered wall robs us of too much needed volume for steel shot reloading. There are also those who warn us they cause high pressure when used with steel shot. I've heard a lot of conjecture about why they produce the high pressures but I've seen no definitive data that really proves it or tells me why. An essentially straight-interior-walled hull, with all other components being correct, may provide the needed volume and produce safe pressures but they just don't seem to have the reloading life most of us want. But, my fellow shotgunners, take heart.

A new shell has recently arrived in the United States from Puerto Rico that should provide us with all of the advantages of both the one piece hull as well as straight wall shells. The new shell is being made by Rainel de Puerto Rico, Inc., and is being marketed in this country under the name ACTIV. I have seen a test report from the H. P. White Laboratory, the well known, respected firearms and ammunition test laboratory, wherein these shells are reported to have equaled the reloadability performance of their prestigious, one piece, U.S. cousins.

The ACTIV shell is indeed a one piece shell that starts out as two pieces, one a biaxially oriented tube, with straight walls, the other an injection molded head with a metal insert for rim strength. These two pieces are then electronically welded together resulting in a one-piece shell with, practically, a straight wall interior configuration that, in addition, needs no brass head whatever! They work. They extract and eject. According to H. P. White they are reloadable many times over. There are also a couple of other shells about to be introduced that are said to be one piece with a straight interior-wall design. I have not had the opportunity to examine these as I have the ACTIV but, in any event, the future is beginning to look up for us.

The Powder

In the very beginning there were conjectures that steel shot would require a hotter primer and faster powder because, "after all, steel is lighter than lead." Hotter primer, yes, faster powder,

no, but not for the reasons given. Anywhere on this earth an ounce and a quarter of shot is an ounce and a quarter whether it is steel or lead. "Ha," you say knowingly. "Then the same powder should work with lead or steel." In fact there have been geniuses among us who have reasoned that you could just open the crimp of a lead-shot load and put in as much steel shot as could be forced in, and away you go. *DON'T DO IT.* First of all, to get almost the same weight of steel shot in there you are going to ruin the wad configuration. It takes a lot more steel shot, by volume, to equal the weight of lead shot. Table II presents some comparisons.

Table II

**Comparative Number of
Lead and Steel Pellets Per Ounce**

Shot		Approx. Number Per Ounce	
Size	Diameter (in.)	Lead	Steel
BB	0.18	50	72
1	0.16	72	103
2	0.15	87	125
4	0.13	135	191
6	0.11	222	316

NOTE: The number per ounce has been calculated assuming 2 percent antimonial lead shot and a steel density of 0.284 pounds per cubic inch.

When you change the wad configuration you are tampering with a very well balanced system and will wind up in trouble, more often than not, by developing high pressures. Let me tell you of a friend of mine who, several years ago, reasoned that he could make that simple substitution. After getting off just one round of his substituted mayhem he found that he had to take his model 12 apart, piece by piece, in order to extract the remains of the shell. He was lucky that it didn't come apart by itself—all at once! Three rounds of those little marvels averaged 29,200 psi each. The nominal average *proof* pressure for that 12 gauge load, according to SAAMI is 18,600 psi. He was over 50 percent overproof! (More about the whys of this later when we discuss the shot itself.)

In general, slower powder speeds must be used with steel shot than with lead. A problem then arises because when slower powder is employed

Pressure testing of steel-loaded shotshells has been an on-going process ever since those shells were introduced. The use of equipment such as this has proven that many home-grown steel-shot loads are exceeding safe limits.

so as to get pressures down to SAAMI recommended levels, dirty burning may set in at colder temperatures. I have seen 28 grains of HERCO loaded into a Federal paper shell (with 1½-oz. of an acceptable steel shot using a Herter wad made for 1½-oz. of lead) produce an average pressure of 14,500 psi for 5 rounds. The load used a W-W 209 primer. The SAAMI Maximum Product Average—which is a statistical technique for estimating the average for a whole lot—for this load is 12,500 psi. Prudent manufacturers load below this for even much greater sample sizes so as to be certain the whole lot will average below 12,500. In addition the handloads chronographed at an average velocity of 1340 fps for those same 5 rounds. SAAMI recommends a velocity Maximum Product Average of 1275 fps. So why not just drop the pressure and velocity? Because as soon as we got the pressure and velocity down to where it should be, dirty burning raised its ugly head.

The Shot

Everything from steel BBs to ball bearings have been experimentally stuffed into shotshells by handloaders since the steel shot regs went into effect. There are plenty of smooth bores that are no longer smooth—they now have "no-twist rifling" all the way to the muzzle.

After a lot of industry research and a lot of wrecked barrels it has been determined that steel shot should have a hardness of no greater than

One of the keys to reloading steel shot is the hardness of the shot. If you must fill those wads up with steel, it is imperative that the shot used has a Diamond Point Hardness no greater than 110. The author is aware of some steel shot (sold to reloaders) with a DPH of 290! It's downright dangerous.

110 DPH (Diamond Point Hardness) maximum with optimum hardness running 90 to 95 DPH or lower. This figure will reasonably protect *most* guns of good quality as long as they have sufficient wall thickness in the barrels. Even with steel shot of 90 to 95 DPH I would suggest that you do not use steel shot loads in expensive side-by-side or over-under double barrels. These guns, even with factory loads, may be damaged. Even with the 90-95 DPH there is no guarantee that heavy-walled, good quality barrels will escape scoring. It does indicate that some of the steel shot I have seen offered for sale to the homeloader is *downright dangerous*. The stuff I am referring to measured a 290 DPH. As far as I know only one company, Superior Steel Ball of Hartford, Connecticut, is the only one making steel shot of acceptable hardness.

One of the problems, I suppose, is that Diamond Point Hardness is not an easy thing to measure. It should be done on a good Rockwell tester, or the equivalent, and must be done very carefully. The variation in shot hardness that is inherent even in the best shot, is quite large. As a result, a large sample must be measured to be assured of reasonably accurate results. For example in order to be 95 percent sure of your results you should measure at least 300 individual pellets that have been picked, at random, from the whole lot. This is a bit more involved than the recommended comparison I have seen of trying to cut both the unknown and a factory-load pellet with a knife. "If they seem the same," one guy proclaimed, "they are close enough . . . " NO WAY.

Steel shot, even at best, is harder than we would like it to be. The hardness, besides causing barrel damage causes pressure problems. Let's now return to that question of why 1¼-oz. of lead shot requires a faster burning powder than 1¼-oz. of steel shot. The harder the shot, the higher the modulus of elasticity. What has elasticity got to do with interior ballistics? Plenty. Let's try, by means of some high-speed imagination "photography" to examine what happens when a primer ignites the powder and the pressure builds in two different shotshells—one containing lead shot, the other steel.

In the lead-shot shell with no buffering material, the shot column gets kicked in the tail with the 11,000 psi or so of pressure. Even with a plastic wad the spheres are rammed into each other and

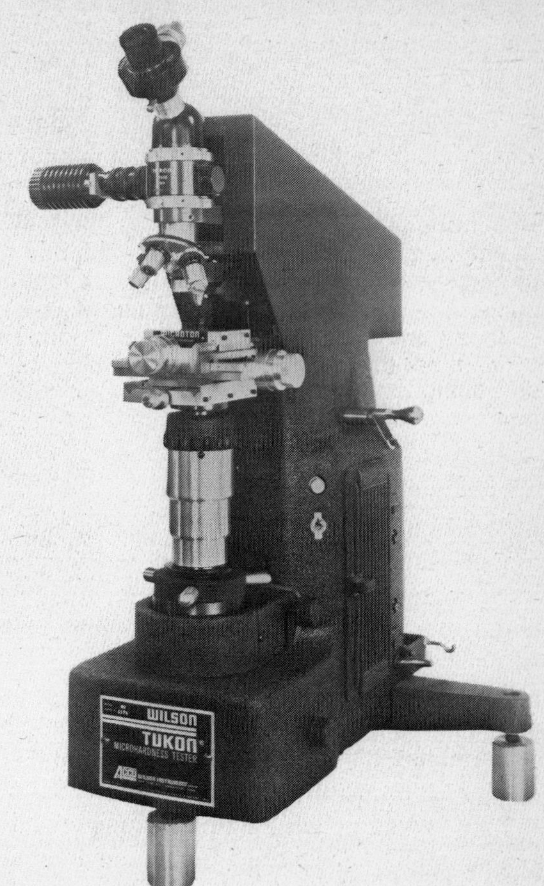

Determining the hardness of steel shot requires the use of sophiciated equipment. Shown here is the "MO Tukon Microhardness Tester." It's doubtful that you'd find this sort of item hanging around the average reloading bench. (Photo courtesy of Measurement Systems Division of Acco Industries, Inc., Bridgeport, CT.)

are deformed. They essentially stay deformed because soft lead shot has a modulus of elasticity of just over 2, and harder antimonial shot a modulus of about 3. This low modulus means very little bounce-back. As the column deforms, it effectively provides a larger burning chamber. If, as it should, the crimp opens at this time and the column begins to move, the "chamber" begins to enlarge rapidly. In order to produce a good velocity/pressure ratio the powder must burn quickly to "fill-in" behind the shot column as it begins to accelerate through the throat and into the barrel.

When steel shot, with a modulus of elasticity of 20 to 30 is used this column reacts very differently. The column is also reduced as the spheres are rammed into each other and deform. But as the steel spheres reach maximum deformation the elasticity characteristic manifests itself and instead of remaining deformed as the lead did, the steel pellets rebound like the steel balls they are and effectively refuse to let the burning chamber expand. They may even begin to reduce it as the powder continues to burn and the pressure continues to rise. In addition, when the wad does move and enters the throat of the barrel, any steel pellets that may have punctured the plastic petals of the wad cause a very high frictional component to develop. This is due, of course, to the point contact of the steel pellets on the steel barrel. Friction is always highest for point contact and when like metals comprise the two rubbing surfaces. Therefore, as the powder continues to produce more and more gas and the chamber does not expand as fast as it must to keep the pressure down, the pressure goes up, but fast!

For this reason, 1) slower burning powders must be used with steel shot, 2) the harder the shot, the higher will be the pressure—all other things being equal and 3) substitution of steel shot, even soft steel, in a load designed for lead shot can be an *extremely dangerous* and ill advised practice.

This modulus of elasticity and frictional component difference between lead and steel shot is also the reason why the balance is so delicate when we start to get pressures down to a reasonable level. Allow for the bounce and you approach the threshold of incomplete burning—resulting in dirt (powder residue). Push the pressures up to ensure complete burning and the bounce and friction could push your pressures into a dangerous region. It takes careful quality control and the pressure measurement of a great many shells to keep the burning clean and the pressure within safe limits.

Ideally we should have a progressive burning powder which would not jolt the column but gently accelerate it most of the way down the barrel. That powder has not yet been developed; however, I'll wager that if that type of powder is ever made, the muzzle pressures it will produce will result in a muzzle blast that will sound like a cannon.

At this point, as far as I can determine, no manufacturer of *properly hardened* steel shot is offering their product for sale to reloaders. Only the future will tell, and it's darned hard to gaze into a crystal ball from even this vantage point.

The Wad

Let no one fool you, this is one of the most *important* components of a shotshell, and because of the hypercritical nature of a steel-shot load the wad becomes a super-sensitive component. In order to ensure the proper rate of pressure build-up, wad collapse must be an engineered feature, properly predetermined and properly controlled. It is not an easy thing to attain. This is especially true in a steel-shot pouch where we must give up the normal cushion space in order to achieve maximum volume for the lighter-than-lead steel pellets. In addition to the cushioning that we look for in a wad, the petals must also protect the barrel wall during barrel travel. To do this under 11,000 psi or so of pressure, while those steel spheres try to penetrate the plastic, takes petals that are tough or thick, or both. If we make them thick enough to withstand the impact and bounce and rebound forces of the steel shot, we lose far too much shot capacity. In short, the petals must be thin and tough.

I have yet to see a wad available to the reloader that will really do the job. It would seem that some sort of thin metal sleeve protected on both sides by high density polyethylene is needed. I'm afraid the cost of such a wad will

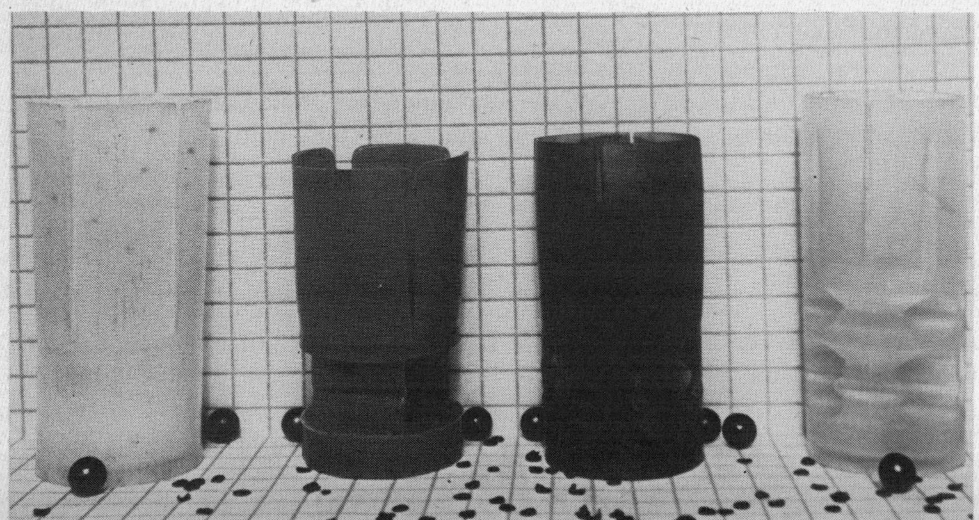

With the standard steel shot wad on the left and plastic lead-type wads to the right the lack of cushioning for steel shot (where the lead-type wads are concerned) is quite obvious.

make it prohibitive unless some smart production man can dream up a way of continuously extruding the cylindrical sandwich and then chopping it to the proper length. Of course, even if someone does this, the very act of adding metal to the collar adds weight to the total column that we must push out of the barrel. Weight that we cannot use to get that bird.

The Primer

Even at best, a good shotshell primer is barely able to do the job that we require for steel shot. Remember, low temperature firings result in too much residue left from partially burned powder. It is not the fault of the primer or the powder. It is the fault of the total system that becomes unbalanced when we add steel shot. Perhaps once the commercial loaders have enough experience with their own steel-load primers, they will put them on the component market. However, until they are positive we cannot get into trouble using them inappropriately or even misusing them, they *won't* take chances putting their components into the hands of reloaders who do *not* have the pressure measuring devices to keep themselves out of trouble.

The Future

While the industry had been working on nontoxic loads when the government regulations hit them, they simply were not ready enough to translate their everyday production components into components for the handloader. *The whole process is still too sensitive to release to the reloader who, for the most part, does not have calibrated pressure measuring equipment.* However, there has been excellent progress in the performance of steel-shot loads over the past few years. The big ammunition manufacturers, nevertheless, feel that a good deal more work remains to be done before steel-shot loading— *outside of a factory*—can approach the reliability of lead-shot loading.

We have seen improved wads and cleaner burning loads but the residue from unburned, or partially burned powder that still results from cold temperature firings is far greater than equal lead loads.

All of the bigger manufacturers, at least, are working on heavier payloads with improved performance. Before they feel sure enough about any development to release it to the handloader, they want hundreds of thousands of factory loads made without any potential safety problems rearing their ugly heads.

I can hear some of you out there saying, "Nuts! The big guys just want to rip us off by forcing us to buy factory loads. We've seen plenty of loads for steel shot recommended for handloaders. They're in just about every magazine you pick up!" Well, my friends, let me point out first of all it wasn't the ammunition manufacturers that pushed steel shot onto us. It was the U.S. government. But of far greater importance is the fact that I'm skeptical of those loads you may find in the magazines, using components made for lead shot.

When those loads show, for example, 11,000 psi (or LUP) with an extreme variation (EV) of 1500 or so for a 3-round sample, I worry. I am familiar enough with statistics to know that an EV of 1500 psi for 3 rounds can mean that an individual round might go as high as 16,500 psi or as low as 5520 psi when we fire enough shots. Furthermore, velocity and pressure measuring systems require constant calibration. In other words, when a writer tells me he has a load that measures an average of 11,000 psi for 3 shots, with an EV of 1500—assuming he really did measure even three rounds—I'm not sure of his 11,000 or his 1500 either, for that matter. Maybe his equipment is only 10 percent off so that the 11,000 is really 12,100. Then those high individual shells might be pushing 17,600 psi! A 16,500 or 17,600 psi shotshell is a proof load and I, for one, am not about to bet my eyes or my hands by shoulder-firing proof loads!

Summary

I, for one, am not going to go out on a limb at this time and recommend the reloading of steel shot. It's that simple. I do, however, recognize that others are advocating—in print—something I don't personally condone. Certainly, this is a free society, and you can choose your own destiny. I do, however, feel that the prudent handloader, will wait a bit longer for the broad range of quality components necessary to *safely* reload steel shot. As mentioned earlier, some of those components may be close at hand. Yes, we are a bit closer to the reality of reloading steel shot than we were 10 years ago. It's only a matter of time. Just how much time is the "future" part of the story that's hard to predict. ●

THERE HAS generally been a tendency to over-simplify the reloading of shotshells. The fact is, however, that there are pitfalls on the way to perfection at the reloading bench, and the best way to avoid those dangers is to acquire a thorough understanding of the theory and practice of this hobby before getting too deeply involved.

The foregoing statement wasn't intended to deter anyone from becoming a handloader. It doesn't mean a beginner will automatically jam his press, concoct dicey loads or blow up his shotgun if he fails to study handloading literature. On the other hand, casual and haphazard approaches to loads and loading can indeed produce faulty performances and gun bursts! Therefore, an intelligent reloader will take a serious look at the basics, the complexities and the potential dangers of his hobby before plunging in.

The best advice that can be given all reloaders venturing into new areas—be they beginners with their first press or old hands trying new equipment or working up specialty loads—is to read instructions and manuals carefully to gain an overall insight. In handloading, there is nothing so dangerous as just a little knowledge that urges hobbyists ahead without them knowing every step and pitfall. This implies the need for patience and forethought, of course. Patience is especially important. Far too many reloaders give no time to setting up and inspecting new equipment; they can't wait to bolt a new press down and to start cranking out loads. A better approach, however, is to spend one evening reading the instructions, securing the press to the bench, and then making a few trial runs to check charge weights and die adjustment. An evening spent in this way will insure safe and smooth operation in the future.

Assuming the press has been secured to a bench that has sufficient work area on both sides, the first step is to weigh powder and shot charges dropped by the bar or bushing. Unfortunately, not many reloaders do this. Gullible chaps that they are, they assume that a powder bushing marked for 22 grains of "Blast-Master" powder is indeed dropping said charge. But the fact is that few charge bars and bushings actually drop their advertised charge weights! Many bars and bushings are ½- to 1½-grains light on powder. Moreover, powders can vary on a lot-to-lot

TROUBLESHOOTING...

. . . or how to stop reloading problems before they start.

by DON ZUTZ

(Left) Here's the end result of a carelessly reloaded shell. That reload blew out the chamber area of a relatively sturdy pumpgun. Those little charges of smokeless powder can develop extremely high pressures.

basis, one lot being fluffier or denser than the other; consequently, a given powder bushing can throw a light charge with one cannister lot of powder while throwing a heavier charge with another lot of the very same propellant.

Checking the powder charge dropped by a bushing/powder combination demands a loading scale. *It is the most important piece of equipment a reloader can have!* There is always an element of danger when one works with gun powder—and how does one know exactly how much powder he is loading if he doesn't weigh it? Take nothing for granted. Bushings can get mixed up; powder lots can vary.

When checking the powder charge of a shotshell press, do *not* just slide the bar back and forth to drop a charge. That gives a misleading result, because the vibrations of normal press operation are missing, and those vibrations have an effect on the way powder settles and packs into the bushing. When a single-stage press handle is worked five or six times between powder chargings, for example, the action will cause powder to settle differently than it does in a progressive-type press which utilizes only one pull of the handle between chargings. The key to accurate and consistent powder charges, then, is scaling a specific amount of propellant that has been taken when the respective press has been run through a normal sequence. This produces the identical vibrations found in actual reloading and gives the best indication of charge weights.

Although shot charges are heavy enough to settle uniformly without worrying about machine vibrations, a serious handloader will also use his scale to determine just how much shot a selected bushing is throwing. Variations can occur here, too. The most important point is that no shot bushing will ever handle all shot sizes equally. Fine pellets (7½s, 8s and 9s) pack more densely than do the bulkier numbers (BBs, 2s and 4s); hence, a given bushing will throw heavier with fine shot than it will with coarse pellets. A 1⅛-ounce charge of shot, for instance, should weigh 492 grains. However, when one given bushing made for 1⅛-ounce loads was checked with different sizes of pellets, it dropped these average amounts:

Shot Size	Actual Weight
No. 2 shot	472.0 grains
No. 4 shot	485.1 grains
No. 6 shot	493.5 grains
No. 7½ shot	504.0 grains
No. 9 shot	505.5 grains

Thus, since the bulkier pellets leave more air space between them, they invariably throw a lighter load of shot through a selected bushing. The difference between 2s and 6s in the above list comes very close to equalling a full 1/16-ounce.

The above table was based on chilled shot, and additional variations can occur when high-antimony or copper-plated shot is used. This is due to the fact that shot possessing both antimony and copper weigh less than ordinary chilled shot which has less than a 2 percent hardener content. There can be another 3-4 percent differential when pellets have a high antimony content or a copper plating. The point is, then, that shot

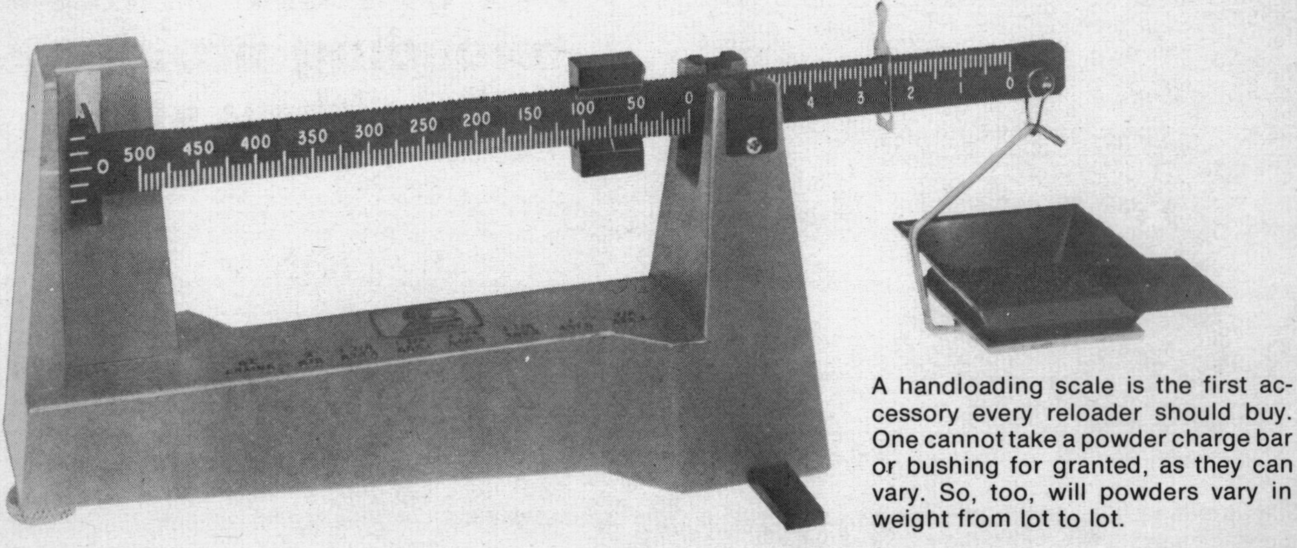

A handloading scale is the first accessory every reloader should buy. One cannot take a powder charge bar or bushing for granted, as they can vary. So, too, will powders vary in weight from lot to lot.

bushings should be checked with the shot to be used for optimum reloading accuracy. Too, shot bushings also become mixed up, and a quick check will determine if the right one is installed.

Most handloader-type scales run no higher than 505 grains. To measure heavier shot charges, the load will have to be split: first weigh 1 ounce (437.5 grains), and then adjust the scale for the remainder.

How do you know if a scale is accurate? There are precise test weights available. A special set of these weights have been made especially for handloaders and is being offered by Paul Yeager through the Dare Gun Room (201-B Paradise Point Road, Grafton, VA 23692). These weights are *precisely* scaled and made in sets to test scales at various levels.

Once the powder and shot bushings have been checked out, attention can be returned to the press itself. The instruction sheet should be read completely, after which a careful trial run can be made to adjust the individual dies and to make certain the linkage is free and moving properly. This shakedown cruise is especially important with progressive presses to establish alignment, indexing and die adjustment for smooth rotation. Many reloaders have spent an entire evening or afternoon tinkering with a new progressive model, and the only advice that can be offered is to have patience and *follow instructions*. There are simply too many different models to allow a step-by-step discussion of them here. In general, however, the basic check points include (A) the setting of the resizing/depriming die to make certain that resizing is indeed full length; (B) an adjustment of the repriming post to affirm proper primer seating; (C) a check of the wad seating ram to insure that the wad is being pressed down to contact the powder and not leave an air space that could produce a ''blooper;'' (D) some trials at the crimp starting station to make certain that the correct style crimp starter (6- or 8-point) is in place and is spinning freely to pick up the grooves; and (E) a careful test of the final crimp die to make those adjustments needed to put a

Most crimp starting die heads are multi-piece units. A spurt of oil from a spray can into the body of the die will prevent rust and keep the spinner head rotating freely to pick up the creases in fired hulls.

nicely rounded shoulder on the finished reloads for positive chambering. Correct all these die settings according to the respective manufacturer's instruction sheet.

Advanced equipment with self-indexing bases, handle-activated charge bar assemblies, and automatic primer feeds must also be adjusted before smooth operation can be expected. Linkage assemblies are almost always at fault when problems arise with the above features; and, corrections must always be made subject to each

Make certain that all nuts and bolts are tightened to insure proper alignment and minimum vibrations. On some models, such as this MEC, the main upright can be raised and lowered to accommodate both magnum- and standard-length cases with the same dies.

individual press. The point is: Don't expect absolute perfection from presses right out of the box! Practically all shotshell presses are mass produced, and the manufacturers assume that buyers will know enough to make final adjustments. If every press were perfectly adjusted at the plant, the prices would be prohibitive.

Once adjusted, shotshell presses are easily maintained. The single most important factor is cleanliness. Gun powder, primers and the dusty residue from both are abrasive and flammable. Frequent dustings with a reasonably stiff nylon brush will eliminate the problem caused by powder residue. Certain popular shotshell propellants, such as Red Dot and Green Dot, can be especially dusty and may require even more frequent dusting. In recent years, it has been found that many ball powders tend to seep between the charge bar and its raceway. As a result, press makers now generally include a brass grommet accessory that seals the space between the charge bar and the hopper—it should be installed immediately.

Occasional lubrication will help keep press movement "slickety-click" while also preventing corrosion. Just don't overdo it, as excess oil

Grease should be used on the stem of the final crimp die of most press-type shotshell reloaders.

or grease will attract all sorts of primer and powder residue. It will only serve to gunk up the machine. Light machine oil will generally suffice on the main upright. The same light oil should occasionally be sprayed into the bore of crimp starting and finishing dies to keep them free of rust and residue; and, a drop of light oil worked into the crimp starting die's rotating head will help keep it spinning freely to pick up the old crimp creases. Finally, use light oil on the contact points of linkage assemblies that activate indexing plates, charging bars and primer feed mechanisms. *Do not* get any oil or silicon spray on the charging bar or into the bar's raceway, as that will contaminate powder and cause a quick build up of residue.

If the charging bar is to be slicked up, it should be done *only* with a dry lubricant, namely, powdered graphite or Motor Mica.

Light oil is a dubious lube for the main scissors-type connections of any press. These require a heavier oil, and some manufacturers recommend EP90. Something like RIG grease is best for the stem and plunger system of crimp finishing dies.

The popular MEC line of reloaders includes some models with collet resizing—this feature requires special attention. Oil and other spray lubricants, such as silicon, are not acceptable. The outer side of the collet segments bear heavily

A graphite-impregnated grease is needed on the outer circumference of collet-type resizing units, such as this MEC "Sizemaster," to insure smooth movement. Without such lubrication, the unit will begin to seize.

against a metal ring known as the "collet closer"—this friction point requires an anti-bind lubricant, such as Antiseize by Locktite or Gunslick by Outers. Failure to apply a graphite-impregnated grease on the outer collet area will result in increased friction, excess wear and potential damage to the collet-resizing unit.

Wet lubricants must be kept off the surface of primer feed trays, but free feeding can be improved by wiping the primer tray with a tissue or a silicon cloth.

Aside from the above lubrication hints, the important step in press maintenance is keeping the nuts and screws suitably tight and the main upright aligned. It is also wise to eyeball the cavity of the repriming station whenever loose shot dribbles on the base plate. If a single piece of shot fell into this void, it could possibly detonate the primer when normal seating pressure is applied.

So much for the press itself. A handloader can also troubleshoot his loading bench and component selection. Cluttered working areas and haphazard component selection are anathema to good reloading. Use a setup that will minimize movement. Set the wad dispenser where it can be easily reached. If you don't have an automatic primer feed, invert the correct number of primers on the bench top for quick pickup and placement. The most efficient way to prepare shells for boxing is to use the MEC E-Z Pak, a holder that receives loaded rounds so they can be packed directly into the box without additional handling. Since much reloading is done in the basement, a

Eyeball the repriming station repeatedly, especially if pellets happen to fall on the base plate. Pellets that trickle into the repriming void, as shown here, can detonate a primer under normal seating pressures.

rubber pad beneath one's feet will make things more comfortable. Indeed, by using some careful judgment in setting up, the reloader will enhance his speed and accuracy. A special reloading bench isn't needed; a workbench will do fine when proper judgment is applied to the organiza-

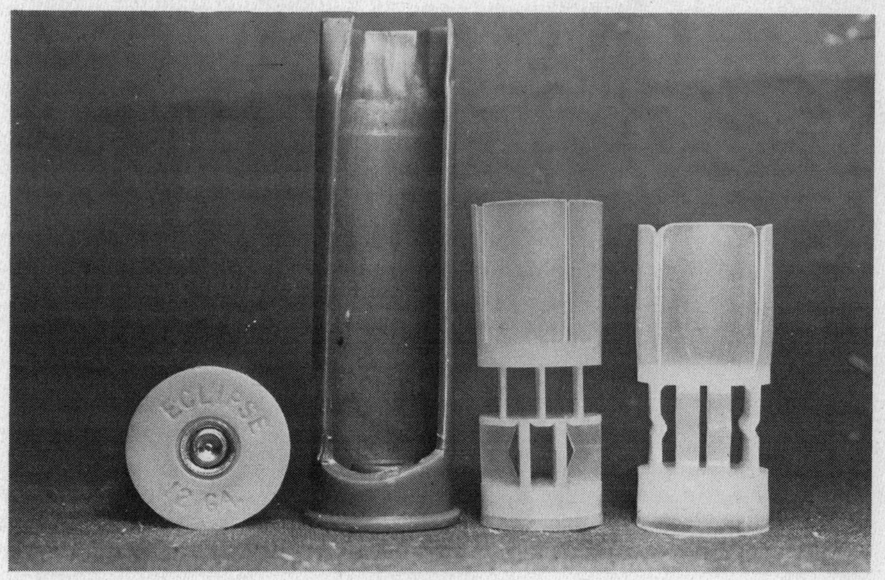

The new all-plastic hull from Eclipse has a gently tapered wall and virtually no base wad; hence, volumteric capacity is extremely high. To handle this abundance of space, Eclipse has provided a special wad which is longer than the conventional WAA12, which is at the extreme right. The Eclipse wad also works well with 1-ounce reloads in conventional cases.

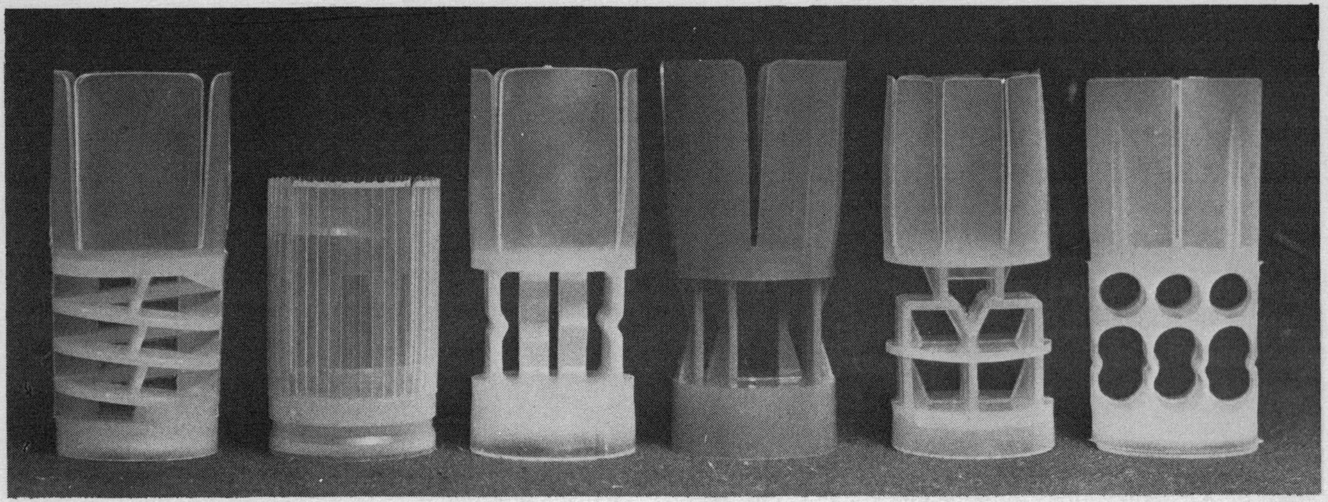

There are wads of different sizes and diameters, some shaped for hulls with an inside taper, others made to fit shells with little or no internal taper. From left, the Federal 12S1 for tapered cases; the Lage Uniwad, which is said to fit both styles; the Winchester AA for taper cases; the Pacific Versalite, also for tapered hulls; the new Windjammer, taper for AAs and Blue Magics; and the Remington RXP-12 for the tapered RXP and AA hulls.

Wad Compatability Table

Tapered Cases	Cylindrical Cases
Windjammer	Federal 12S3 Pushin'-Cushion
Winchester WAA12	Federal 12S4 Pushin'-Cushion
Winchester WAA12R	Lage Uniwad
Winchester WAA12F114	Winchester WAA12R
Remington RXP-12	Ballistic Products BPGS
Lage Uniwad	Ballistic Products Pattern Driver
Pattern Control Post Wad	Remington Power Piston series
Pacific Versalite	Pacific Varilite
Federal Champion II	Federal Champion I

Note: Some of the wads for cylindrical hulls will fit tapered cases with heavy powder charges, as the wad need not be seated so deeply. Tapered cases mentioned above are the Peters Blue Magic, Remington RXP, Winchester compression-formed line, and Federal Champion II. Cylindrical hulls are the Federal paper Champion, Federal Gold Medal, Federal plastic field-style, Remington ShurShot (SP), Winchester (Sears, Browning, etc.) poly-formed.

There are some exceptions where this wad-compatability table is concerned, and you will find those exceptions in the loading tables further on in this book. At this point it should also be said that the depth to which a wad is seated into a taper-walled hull will have a bearing on whether or not a particular shell's taper affects the selection of one wad over another.

tion of the bench and the components on it.

Perhaps the greatest problems arise when reloaders use components indifferently. Reloads assembled with haphazardly selected components can give all sorts of trouble in storage, loading and gun function and ballistic performance. This potential for shotshell faults and failure is generally due to the casual handloader's failure to study the myriad variables found in shotshell construction, hull condition and component compatibility.

For example, not all wads are designed for use in every hull. There are basically two types of shotshell interiors: one has a cylindrical interior as exemplified by the Federal paper Champion, the Federal Gold Medal and the Remington

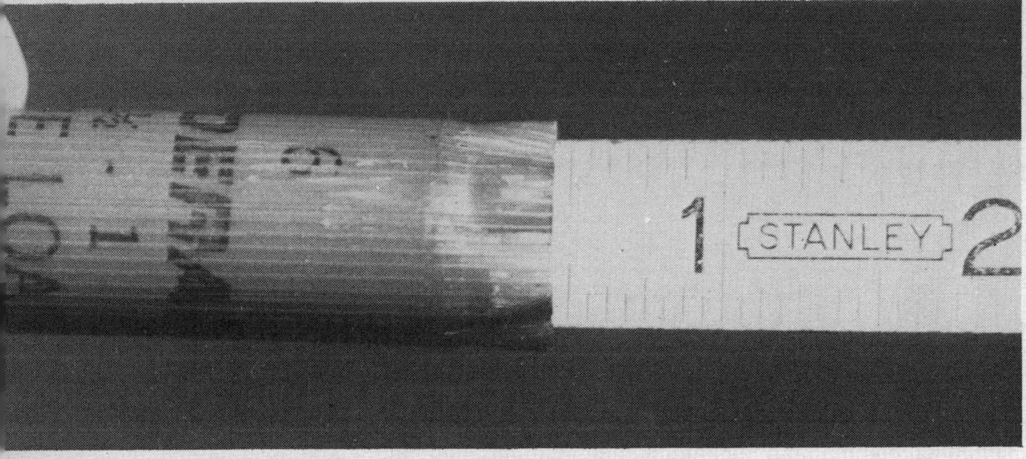

Wads should fit the load properly to leave adequate room for a crimp without bulging and without the need for an over-shot seal. A depth of 7/16-inch will be right for most 12-, 16-, and 20-gauge reloads.

"SP" field-style plastics. The other hull type has a tapered interior, the walls becoming thicker as they near the base. Winchester's compression-formed (AA-type) cases, Remington's RXP, Peters' Blue Magic and Federal's Champion II are examples of such taper-walled hulls. If one wishes the best fit for load balance and gas sealing, he must use wads designed and dimensioned for the specific interior. A tapered wad can be a loose fit in a cylindrical case, and it can permit powder to slip upward betwixt overpowder wad and hull wall when it is jiggled during transit. On the other hand, a thicker wad designed for use in a cylindrical hull may not be able to work down far enough in a tapered hull to reach the powder

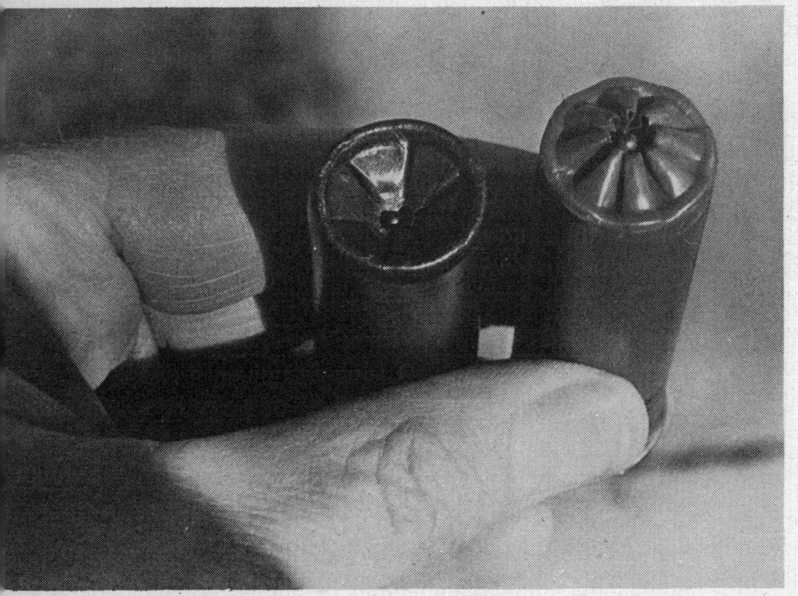

Haphazard wad selection can influence the crimp, leaving it caved in or bulged.

and apply pressure. In this latter case, an air space will be present and result in a "blooper."

Improper wad selection can influence the final crimp. Using a wad that is too long produces a bulged crimp, while a wad that is too short lets the crimp open inwardly in the finishing die. Sometimes, even reloads that come out with a perfect crimp will pop open during storage, thanks to the pressure from a compressed wad returning to its normal length. The most professional answer to these problems is finding the right wad for any given reload. Generally, this will be the wad recommended in published data from reputable labs.

Primer selection also deserves some careful attention. Although they all may make a reload go *Bang!* they aren't all alike. Some have a greater brisance factor than others; however, the actual pressure level depends entirely on the reload's composition. Since primers are different, then, the only way to get the ballistics published with a certain load is to stick with the listed primer. Random primer substitutions negate published data.

There are currently two sizes of battery cup primers: the 209 size and the 57 size. The 209 is now the most popular, and it has a larger diameter than the 57s. The only shotshells still using the 57-size primer are some Remington-Peters field loads.

Primers also have two different types of flash holes: open, or, closed with lacquer or foil. Primers selected for ball-type powders should always have a covered flash hole. If "lumps" of ball powder should trickle into the battery cup itself (which is entirely possible), the condition can (A) stifle the priming thrust to produce a blooper

Primers vary in both diameter and power. Don't assume you can substitute freely and still get the same ballistics and patterns.

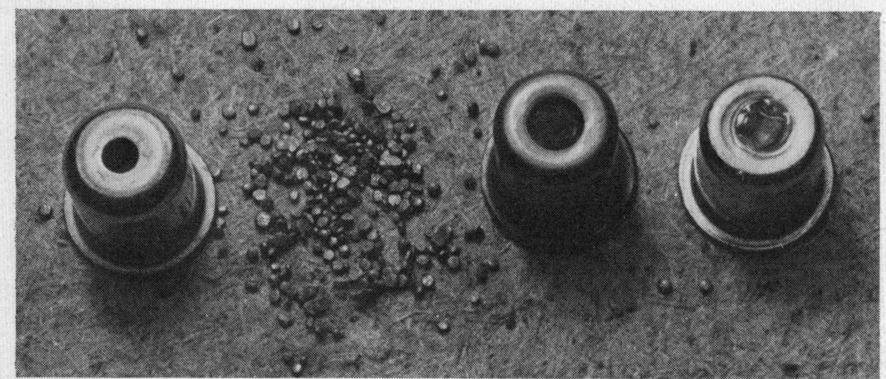

Primers with open flash holes, such as the Remington 97★ on the left, should *not* be used with ball powder. When loading with ball powder, use only those primers with flash holes closed by lacquer or foil, as on the right.

or squib load and/or (B) create excess pressure inside the battery cup unit. This latter situation may not result in a burst gun, but it will loosen the primer sufficiently to enable it to fall out and jam the action of a repeater. Moreover, excess pressure in the battery cup can cause a rearward gas spurt toward the shooter's face and, perhaps, place excess strain on the breech mechanism. At this writing, only Remington's 57★, 97★, and 97-4 have open flash holes, and they should be avoided with the ball powders.

A final step in troubleshooting is avoiding the "blooper," which is normally a result of poor ignition and/or insufficient resistance ahead of the powder gases. Most bloopers come from loads in which the primer thrust doesn't reach the powder full force. This can happen when a hull with a paper or composition base wad, such as the Remington ShurShot (SP), is used. Firing pressures, or the impact from depriming and repriming rams, can loosen base particles which, in turn, fall over the primer's flash hole to stifle the flame. The same blockage can occur when empties are carried in the back of one's hunting coat, because feathers and other debris can work into the hull. Thus, many bloopers can be avoided by eyeballing the interior of each case before starting to reload. And on single-stage

Repriming isn't a foolproof step. Inspect the base of the case and flash hole to make sure that the primer isn't covered with debris that could block the flash and cause a blooper.

presses, it isn't a bad idea to make a second check after the primer has been seated.

Moisture is another cause of bloopers. Carefully inspect all hulls picked up around trap clubs, duck blinds and goose pits. If in doubt, dry them in the hot sun, in an oven at low temperature or atop a space heater.

Weak crimps and improperly selected powder can also produce faulty ignition. Crimps must hold to allow a burning curve to develop. Pairing slow-burning powder with a light shot charge will also give dubious results—the powder will not burn properly if initial pressures can move the payload ahead. Always try to use a fast-burning powder with light shot charges, a medium-speed powder with intermediate-weight payloads, and a slow-burning powder with heavy loads.

Always remember, of course, that the gauge is also important to powder selection. As a rule of thumb, the smaller the gauge, the slower the powder's burning speed will be for a given payload weight. Some publicity has been given in the past to the use of 4227 in 10- and 12-gauge Magnum reloads, but this is to be discouraged; such heavy gobs of ultra-slow-burning powder have not ignited consistently in big-bore shotguns, and they have either "blooped" or left wads dangerously stuck in the bore. Indeed, 4227 has worked horribly in the big bores under cold hunting conditions.

When it comes to storing your powder and primers, select a cool, dry spot. Dampness and heat do nothing for propellant longevity. Also, never store powder in anything other than the containers they came in. Why? If you should, for example, buy an 8-pound caddy of Dupont Hi-Skor, try to use that powder from the can it came in. If you happen to put a quantity of the Hi-Skor into an available (empty) 1-pound can that once held Bullseye, you just might be inviting more danger than you can deal with.

Yes, I know some shooters habitually do this. I don't. Even the best relabeling job in the world might not do the trick. A friend of mine used to habitually repack powder in old, empty, 1-pound cans. Things went famously until his 6-year-old daughter decided to peel all the labels off one afternoon. My friend ended up flushing (wisely) about 8 pounds of various propellants down the drain.

If you haven't figured it out already, here's another warning: Keep your reloading gear and components locked up and away from prying fingers. Kids and gunpowder don't mix.

When it comes to wads, hulls and primers, take the same, organized approach. Separate your

Adjust the final crimp die to insure nicely rounded shoulders on
the finished shells for smooth functioning and easy chambering.

hulls by type and brand—no mixing, please—and
store your wads in the bags they came in. Primers
are like powder—they too belong in the boxes
they came in.

Twenty-five pound bags of lead shot can be as
fluid as blazes, especially when they are partially
full. If you've got a half-full bag of shot, be sure
it's *securely* tied off when put away for storage;
and, try to store that bag on its base not on its
side. If the bag is stored flat, and the tieing-off job
isn't perfect, the shot may, eventually, force the
bag open spilling shot everywhere. If you've ever
tried to recover about 10 pounds of shot from a
shag rug you know what I'm talking about. (At
$15 to $20 a bag, I try to treat my shot like gold.)

It is possible that each handloader should
troubleshoot his own mentality and tempera-
ment. Don't take silly chances by assembling
random batches of components. Don't take
anything for granted; research a load thoroughly
before trying something new. Work with a pa-
tient attitude; many presses perform better when
stroked carefully than when operated in slam-
bang fashion. Develop an interest in both interior
and exterior ballistics; there's lots of handloading
literature around, much of it free from powder
makers, to help you learn more about loads and
reloading. And work with a mature mind, always
realizing that, although shooting is a sport and
that handloading is an enjoyable, money-saving
hobby, you are *indeed* working with potentially
dangerous materials. If you don't go out looking
for trouble, trouble won't come looking for
you! ●

PATTERNING

When it comes to getting the most out of your reloads, the pattern board has the answers

by DON ZUTZ

IT IS a fact that manufacturers do not check the accuracy of patterning qualities of a shotgun in the popular price range. Such individualized attention is given only to those models carrying fancy price tags. True, the guns are proof tested for safety, but that's the extent of it. After that, the hunter or trap shooter is on his own to learn whether a given smoothbore shoots where it's pointed and whether or not it throws the anticipated pattern.

If a hunter does nothing more than fire one pattern to check his gun's accuracy, he is already far ahead of the crowd. More than one man has run through a season of misses before he learned that his barrel wasn't straight! I once had a 3-inch 20 gauge side-by-side which, at 40 yards, was far from centering its patterns on a 40-inch-square sheet of paper. The right barrel sent its main mass past the left side of the patterning sheet when the gun was pointed directly at the center, while the left tube blew its charge off to the right. With a centered hold, my efforts did nothing more than put fringe pellets on paper. You can imagine what fun I'd have had with that SxS on ducks or far-flushing sharptails!

It is also important to fire a test shot or two with trap guns. These specialized shotguns are normally made to place their patterns high to intercept the rising trap target, and failure to learn *how* high a certain gun is shooting can result in many, many misses below or above the clay pigeon, depending on the individual gun's point of impact.

Failure to test for pattern density can also lead

(Right and below) Trap shooters will want to experiment to learn exactly what their loads are doing. Nothing is guaranteed even if a gun is stamped "Full Choke." For instance, this M12 Winchester (below) averaged only 57 percent with Lawrence brand chilled 8s. But when it was fed the same reloads with the harder Magnum-grade 8s (right), it responded by tossing honest full-choke patterns of 70 percent.

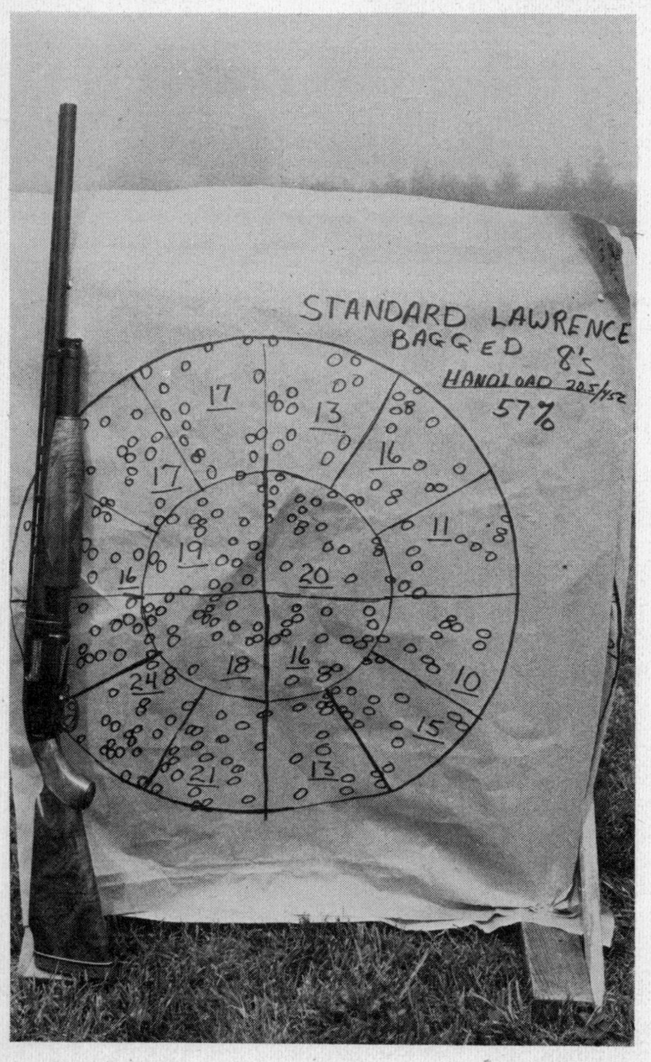

to frustration in the way of missed clay targets or crippled and lost game birds. Here, again, the average hunter or shooter takes too much for granted. He assumes that a gun marked "Full Choke" will invariably throw tight, long-range patterns with any and all loads. So, too, does he assume that open-choked guns will deliver wide, easy-to-hit-with clusters at short range, and that a modified choke will always give good, intermediate spreads.

But it doesn't work that way! This thing called "choke" in a shotgun is nothing more than a constriction left in the barrel at the muzzle, and it is *absolutely no guarantee* that all loads will indeed perform the same when fired through that barrel! Yes, there are myriad differences between loads, and they can respond differently when passing through the various choke tapers and constrictions. In other words, nothing is certain when it comes to shotgun patterning! Just shooting at clays or game isn't a reliable indicator of gun/load performance, either. Even crummy patterns will break some clays and drop some birds. Indeed, you can drop a goose from 60 yards using a cylinder bore riot gun *if* you get in a lucky head shot with just one No. 2 pellet—but that doesn't make the riot gun a bona fide goose gun! Thus, hits on clays and game can often mislead a shooter into believing he's getting better patterns than he actually is. In short, there's no way to judge a given shotgun's patterning ability than by—patterning.

There are two ways in which patterning can be done: the scientific and the practical.

Scientific Patterning

The standard range for checking shotgun patterns stateside is 40 yards. This distance is between the gun's muzzle and the patterning sheet, not between the shooter's feet and the target. The charge is fired at a *blank* sheet of paper or cardboard about 40 inches square. A 30-inch-diameter circle is inscribed around the main concentration of pellet holes only *after* the shot is fired. The easiest way to draw the circle is to use a cardboard overlay along with some careful eyeballing of the perforated sheet. The circle is drawn after the shot because one generally cannot shoot a shotgun accurately enough to put the charge perfectly into a pre-inscribed circle, and also because barrel vibrations may alter the points of impact.

The only exception to the above is the .410 bore, which is normally tested over a 25-yard range with a 20-inch-diameter circle. But the .410, too, is fired at a blank sheet to start, and the 20-inch-diameter circle is drawn thereafter. The .410 obviously doesn't have enough shot to fill out a full 30-inch pattern.

The first step in evaluating the performance of any gun/load combo is finding its actual efficiency, which is also known as its "patterning percentage." This is done by dividing the total number of pellet holes found in the 30- or 20-inch circles by the number of pellets in the original (unfired) shot charge. For example, if we had 350 No. 7½s in a 1-ounce, 20-gauge reload and found 175 holes in the 30-inch circle at 40 yards, it would be a 50 percent pattern. Here is how efficiency ratings are listed for the various degrees of choke:

Choke	Efficiency Range
Extra Full	75% or above
Full	65-75%
Modified	55-65%
Improved Cylinder	45-55%
Skeet	35-45%
Cylinder Bore	35% or less

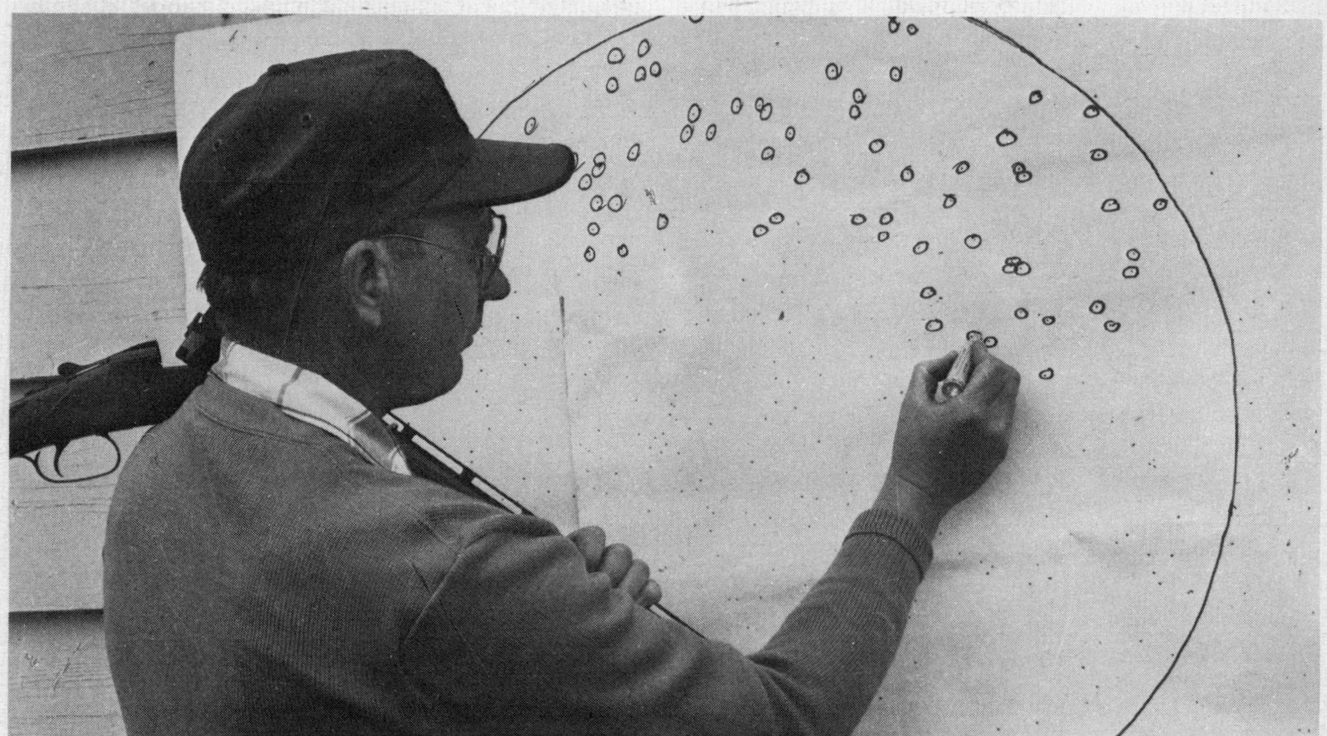

The 30-inch-diameter circle is drawn only *after* the shot has been fired into a blank sheet of paper about 40 inches square. (The circle is drawn around the area of greatest pellet density.) Counting the holes inside the 30-inch circle, and dividing the tally by the number of pellets in the original (unfired) charge gives you the gun's pattern percentage. Many shooters don't pattern their guns—it's a mistake.

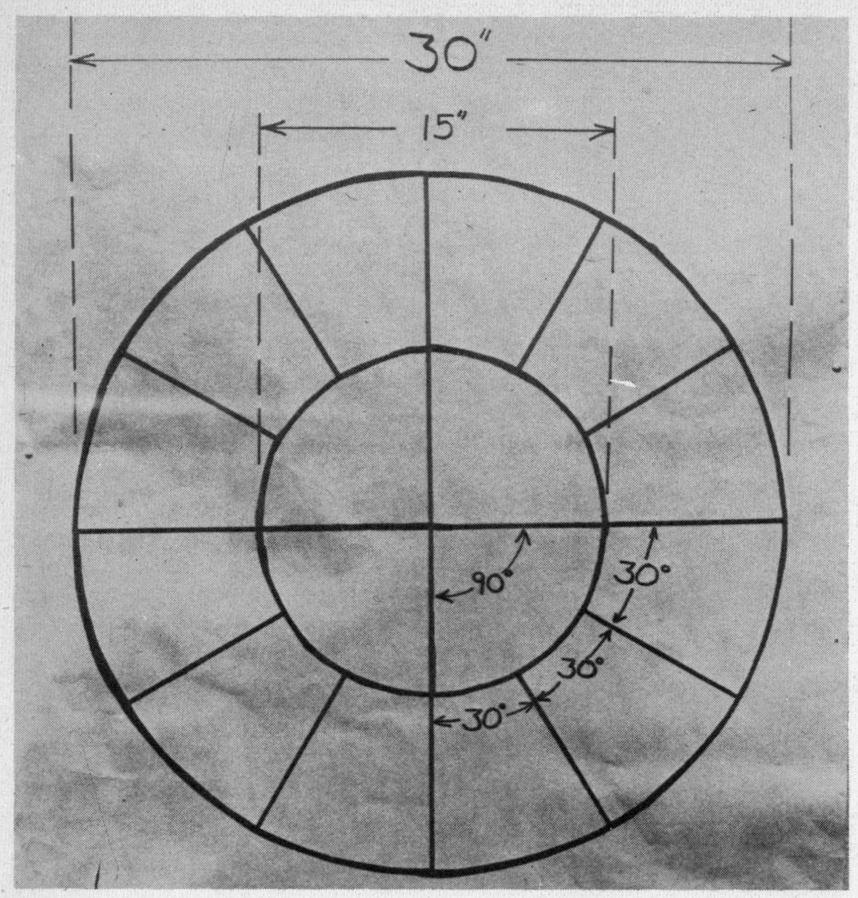

Scientific pattern reading is done with an overlay divided into 16 fields according to these dimensions. Each field has about 44 square inches which gives the shooter a chance to learn how his gun/load combination distributes its pellets.

Our 1-ounce 20-gauge reload, then, was delivering an improved cylinder pattern regardless of what barrel it came from! That's the point: it's the pattern that counts, not what's stamped on the barrel.

The only way to be perfectly accurate about percentages is to know how many pellets, on average, were in the unfired load. Such counts can vary slightly from bag to bag depending on size and antimony content. But to simplify things a pellet-count table is included here.

In my opinion, the hunter or trapman who shoots a few patterns to learn his gun's efficiency is well ahead of the field. Most shooters merely think they know.

And if one wishes to make a further study of his gun/load combinations, he can do so by dividing the standard 30-inch-diameter circle into sixteen individual "fields" like the wagon wheel diagram shown nearby. This type of pattern outline uses a 15-inch-diameter "core" swung on the same center point as the main circle, and that core is then quartered, as is the entire 30-inch circle. Next, the outer rim, or "annular ring," of the circle is further divided into 12 additional fields, each sliced at 30 degrees from the center point.

CHILLED SHOT TABLE

Weight Ounces	½	⅝	¾	⅞	1	1⅛	1¼	1⅜	1½	1⅝	1¾	1⅞	2	2⅛
Weight Grains	219	273	328	383	438	492	547	602	656	711	766	820	875	930
Loads per Lb.	32	26	21	18	16	14	13	12	11	10	9	9	8	8

Size.	Dia. In.	Approximate No. of Pellets per load												
BB	.18	25	31	38	44	50	56	63	69	75	81	88	94	100	106
2	.15	44	55	66	77	88	99	110	121	132	143	154	165	176	187
4	.13	68	85	102	119	136	153	170	187	204	221	238	255	272	289
5	.12	86	108	129	151	172	194	215	237	258	280	301	323	344	366
6	.11	112	139	167	195	223	251	279	307	335	362	390	418	446	474
7	.10	150	187	224	262	299	336	374	411	449	486	523	561	598	635
7½	.095	173	216	259	302	345	388	431	474	518	561	604	647	690	733
8	.09	205	256	307	358	409	460	511	562	614	665	716	767	818	869
8½	.085	240	300	360	420	480	540	600	660	720	780	840	900	960	1020
9	.08	293	366	439	512	585	658	731	804	878	951	1024	1097	1170	1243

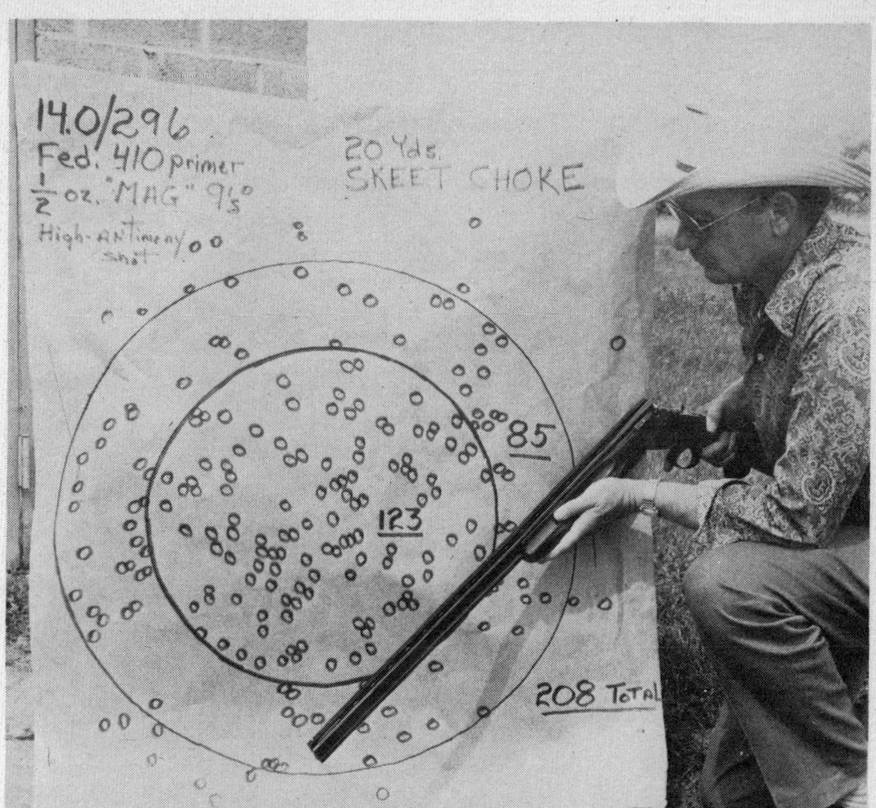

(Right and below) These patterns were shot with the same .410 using basically the same reload. They show how important pellet hardness is. The first pattern below shows a low count with normal chilled (low-antimony) shot, while this second pattern (right) was made with hard, high-antimony shot of the same size which printed a significantly greater density.

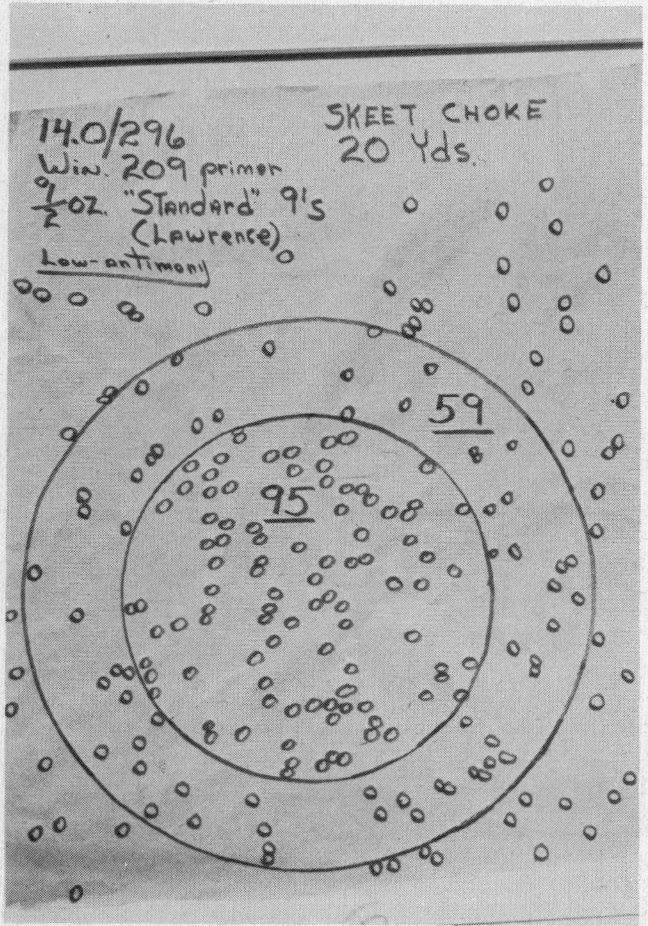

Each of the 16 fields encloses about 44 square inches of area, and the experimenter can use them to determine the pellet distribution characteristics of each load. And different loads do *in fact* scatter their pellets differently from the same gun!

Using the sixteen-field pattern outline, the experimenter can learn his load's ability to print even patterns, which means the uniformity of hits on a field-to-field basis. He can also observe its thickening ratio, which is sometimes referred to as "center density," by finding the number of hits in the core as compared to the number of hits in the annular ring. Another check point is target coverage, meaning a load's ability to put the desired number of pellets into a given area for clean kills. For example, we know that the vital area of a pheasant is roughly 20 square inches, and that target size would fit into each of the 16 fields two times. If we think we need three No. 6s in each ringneck to stop it cleanly, we can eyeball the pattern to make certain we have 6-7 No. 6 shot evenly distributed in each field as a minimum effective coverage.

Although the sixteen-field pattern outline is generally used at 40 yards (38 meters in Europe), the sportsman can move it to whatever range he

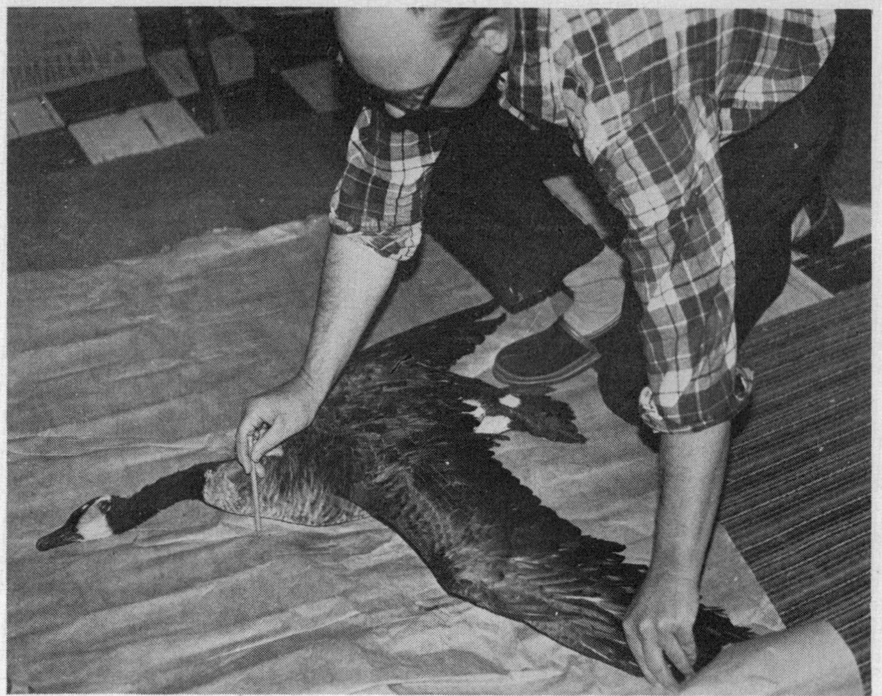

Practical patterning can be done by tracing the outline of actual game birds and using the outline later on patterning sheets.

finds better suited to his average hunting range. This will give him a better idea of what his equipment is doing at a normal working range rather than an industry-established distance. A quail hunter can test at 15-25 yards; a duck hunter at 50 yards; a woodcock hunter can pattern at 12-15 paces; and a trapshooter can fire at 32 yards, which is about the distance he takes clays from the 16-yard line. And that brings us to the practical side of patterning.

Practical Patterning

Many hunters have an aversion to anything that smacks of scientific organization. They are practical fellows with no mind for figures; they like to do things the easy way. Indeed, many

A metal goose silhouette, marketed by Ballistic Products of Plymouth, Minnesota, is useful in checking waterfowl loads. A light coat of plaster of Paris was applied to this silhouette—it clearly shows the strike of the pellets.

Working a clay target or a 5-inch-diameter disc through the pattern will disclose gaps. Surprisingly, a clay target covers much the same area as does the vital area of most game birds.

This 3-inch 12 (right) threw a low center density with low-antimony chilled shot. Its actual efficiency was like that of a modified choke (not a true full choke) at 40 yards. However, (below) when copper-plated (Lubaloy) shot was substituted for the softer, chilled shot, the gun threw the same reload into honest full-choke percentages with a much higher center density. Without patterning, the average hunter may think his magnum reloads are doing better than they are with chilled shot.

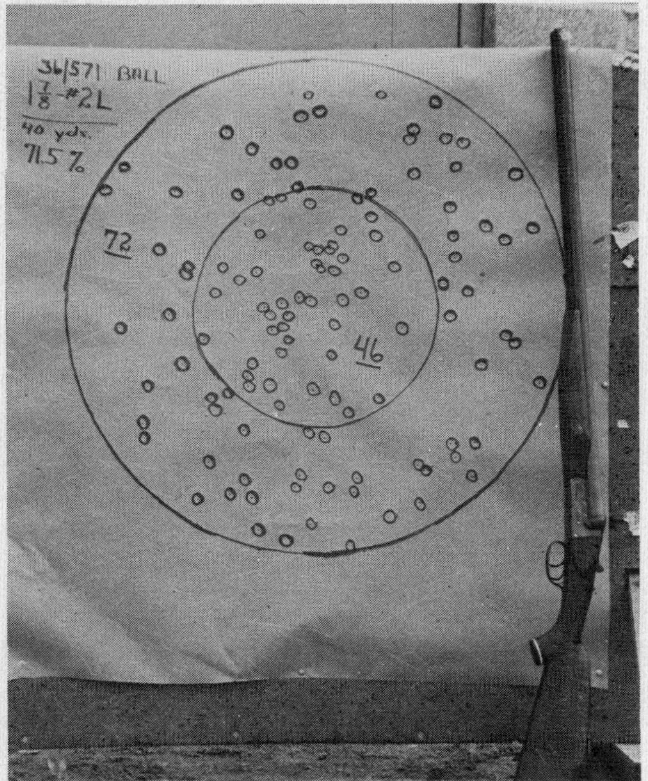

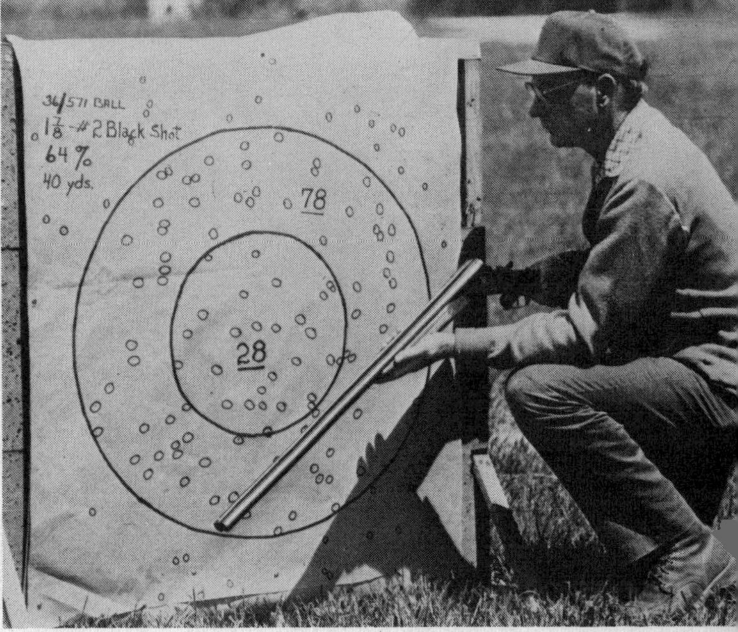

hunters don't pattern their shotguns because they are too lazy to find the paper and to count holes! But there are ways for even these practical fellows to check shotgun performance.

To begin, there's the practice of setting out life-sized targets at various ranges. In general, this constitutes drawing a bird's outline on cardboard. It's easily done. The next time you bag some game, make a tracing of it on paper and keep the outline to transfer to patterning sheets.

cled pattern to find weak spots. It is hardly a misleading check. For if one were to compare the 5-inch disc or a clay target to the vital area of most game birds, he would find that they have much in common. A clay target will normally cover the entire vital area of such upland game as quail, woodcock, dove and grouse. It will also comprise about the same area as a pheasant's breast; ditto for that of a mallard-sized duck. It is also a very good check for effectiveness on outgoing game, as the flat surface of a clay saucer pretty well duplicates the cross section of a game bird flying away from the gun.

When using the clay target or 5-inch-diameter disc to judge pattern effectiveness, the experimenter will want to use the correct shot size and practical range, of course. There's no sense in testing a woodcock gun and load at 40 yards; that should be done inside 20 paces. Nor is there any sense checking a duck gun at extremely long distances if the hunter normally blasts away at

(Above) Hard shot patterns better than soft shot. Lawrence brand "Magnum" shot, left, has a higher antimony content than the same company's chilled shot, at right.

(Right) For the best patterns, pellets should retain their spherical shape. That is best done with pellets like these which are (from left to right) nickel plated, copper plated, and high-antimony lead shot.

Always remember to trace the bird according to the way it appears to the gun: a quail will be flying across or away from the gun and will normally present a side or outgoing shot; a duck or goose will be passing overhead.

Another method is to use metallic silhouettes when available. Spread them with a light plaster of Paris mixture, and the new coat will be dry by the time you can walk from the target back to the firing line. (The goose silhouette on page 42 was obtained from Ballistic Products, Inc., which is mentioned in the article on buffered shot loads.)

Finally, practical patterning tests can be run very effectively by using the so-called "patchiness" test. This is done by running either a 5-inch-diameter disc or a clay target over the encir-

distances of around 40-50 yards.

Thus, patterning need not be a laborious task involving scientific standards and mathematics. A practical approach is possible.

Whether a hunter uses the scientific or practical approach, however, he'll learn a lot about shotgun and shotshell performance. One thing he will observe is that using plain chilled shot often frustrates matters due to the potential for pattern-destroying pellet deformation. He'll quickly understand that the best way to get excellent patterns from his reloads is to use hard, high-antimony shot like Lawrence's "Magnum" grade or Remington's RXP-grade. But most importantly, he'll find those reloads that pattern best and are the least inclined to cripple and lose game.

●

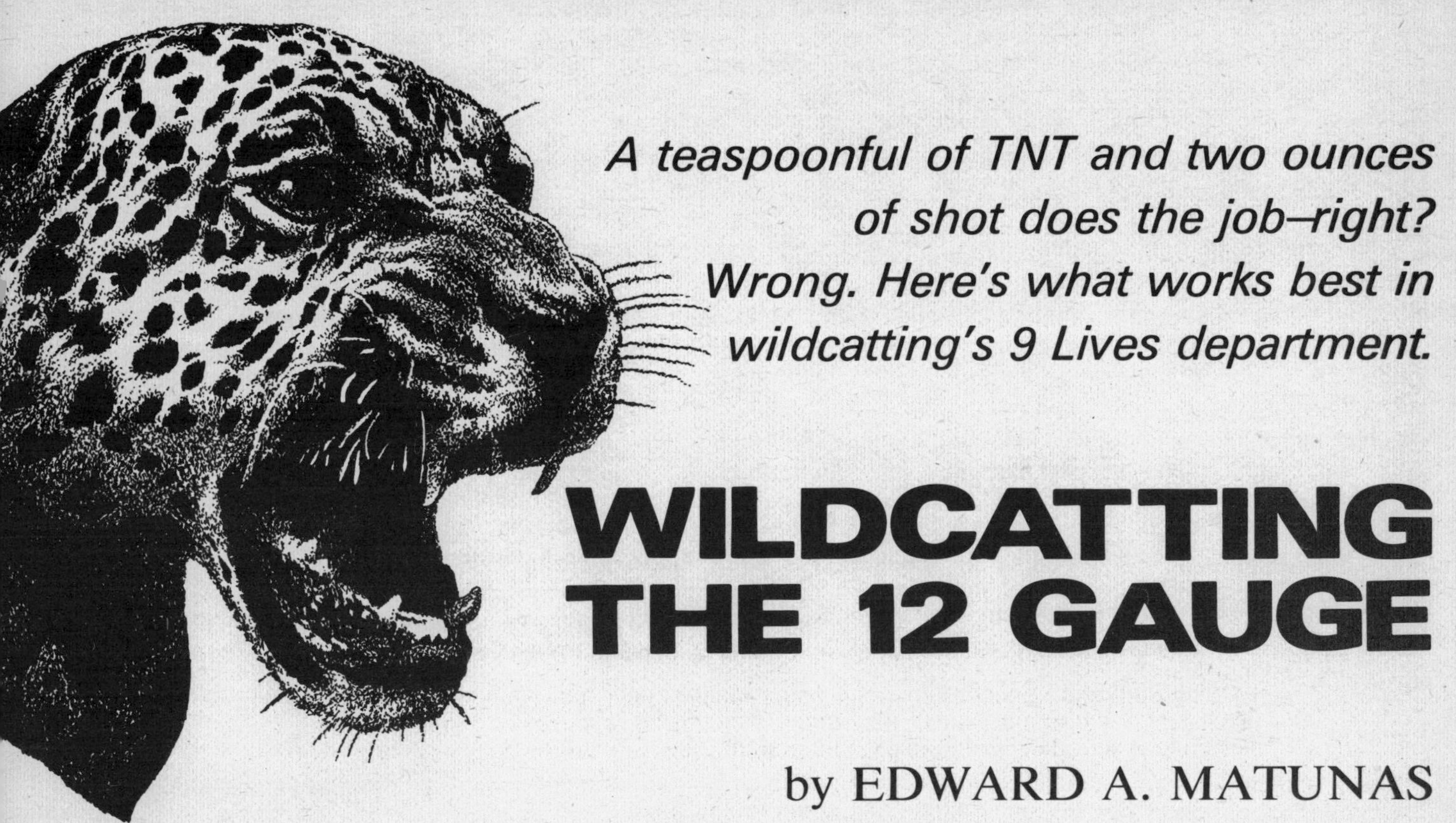

WILDCATTING THE 12 GAUGE

by EDWARD A. MATUNAS

A WILDCAT shotshell? Yes, there is such an animal. Perhaps not in the sense that a rifle or pistol loader would think of, but nevertheless wildcat shotshells are common practice with savvy handloaders. First let's make it clear that, unlike metallic cartridge wildcats, shotshell wildcats have to do with the load put into the case rather than the changing of the case configuration. But is there a need to come up with variations of the already large number of factory loads which are currently available?

To answer this question let's look at some history. Factory loaded, black powder, paper shotshells first became available in (about) 1885. The sale of empty paper shells had been going on for some time prior.[1] In 1889 the Winchester catalog showed six 10 gauge and seven 23 gauge black powder loads. No shot sizes were specified as the customer could select from any of seventeen different sizes (BBB,BB,B,1,2,3,4,5,6,7, 7½,8,9,10,11,12, and Dust). These sizes were offered in both chilled or soft shot, and both eastern and western shot sizes were offered. If my math is correct that's almost 900 different loads! After only four years in the market, the number of choices was already cumbersome.

In 1890 the same catalog went to 20 basic loadings. By 1894 23 basic loads were in use. When one adds all the possible shot size selections this comes to over 1000 different loads being offered. Smokeless powder loads were offered in 1893 to add to the array of possible variations; and, by 1907 the Winchester catalog was showing three types of powder (black, bulk smokeless, and dense smokeless) offered in many brands. Also soft and chilled shot were available in a wide range of sizes. The customer could literally have his shotshell ammunition loaded any way he wanted (within the confines of safety). Due to the great and seemingly endless variety of factory loads offered, the handloading of shotshells declined drastically at that point in history. And, as we know, it did not again become a strong factor in the supply of shotshell ammunition until the 1950's.

During the years 1907 and 1908 the list of available shotshell loads peaked (in the Winchester catalog) at a total of 14,383 different possible combinations. The rest of the industry was in a similar condition. When one considers the possible variations and overlaps from the other ammunition manufacturers, the customer had a

Heavy grouse and woodcock cover demands special loads. A "wildcatting" reloader can put together a 1- or 1⅛-ounce load using soft "drop" shot and drive it at a full 1400 fps. Such a load provides maximum dispersion of the shot and hence is an ideal brush load.

choice between a bewildering 15,000 (approximately) different loads. Now that would be confusing for the very best of us.

Needless to say, this vast array of loads was having a financial impact on the manufacturers. They began a concentrated effort to reduce the number of loads offered and hence increase profitability.

In 1921 the first major steps were taken in greatly reducing the number of loads offered. By 1925 the number had been reduced from the high of about 15,000 to a mere 1,747 load combinations. At that, this listing contained 48 different soft shot sizes, 37 chilled shot sizes and 26 different brand names.[1] At that point, even with the reduction of about 88 percent of the loads available previously, I doubt if many of us could have kept track of even a small portion of what was being offered by the manufacturers. By 1926 the customer could pick from *only* 996 combinations; 1927 saw only 759 loads being offered. By 1931 only a *mere* 343 loads were available. Through a series of continuing reductions the available options were reduced from 343 loads to 156 loads in 1944 and finally only 137 loads were offered in 1947.

A table of these changes follows:

Loads Offered In:	Number Offered:
1889	884
1907-1908	15,000 (approx.)
1924	4,067
1925	1,747
1926	996
1927	759
1930	490
1931	343
1937	283
1939	262
1944	156
1945	141
1947	137

The 137 loads offered in 1947 have grown to about 200 today. For those of you who have an interest in the details of the previously discussed historical information a reprint of a copy of George E. Watrous' *Standardization and Simplification of Shotshells* (54 pages-not bound) is available from PROmat Enterprises, P.O. Box 286, Clinton, CT 06413 ($7.95 prepaid).

I think a prudent person would agree that 15,000 loads is simply too much of a good thing. However, an equally prudent person would agree that the dropping of some 14,800 choices

12 GA. 2-3/4" FACTORY LOADS CURRENTLY AVAILABLE

OUNCES OF SHOT	VELOCITY IN FEET PER SECOND																									
	1135	1140	1145	1150	1155	1160	1175	1185	1190	1200	1210	1220	1240	1250	1255	1260	1275	1285	1290	1295	1300	1325	1330	1350	1375	1400
7/8																										
1																			●							
1-1/8			●							●					●						●					
1-1/4												●											●			
1-3/8																										
1-1/2																●										
1-5/8																										

has undoubtedly resulted in the loss of some fine shotshells. Is there a need for wildcatting shotshells? You betcha!

To demonstrate our point, Table I lists the loads currently available in 12 gauge for the 2¾-inch shell. It shows that there are basically 8 different shot weight/velocity combinations available. Also there are 8 shot sizes (BB,2,4, 5,6,7½,8, and 9) to choose from, but not every shot size is available in every load. Also, one

One of Connecticut State Police's finest, Sergeant Lary Ahearn, with the proof of the worth of wildcatting the 12 gauge. His "custom" 12 gauge 1100 (parkerized) and 1⅜ ounces of shot were partly responsible for this bag of 14 scoter and a lone bluebill. He was ably assisted by the author using a wildcat 12 gauge loading of 1⅝ ounces of shot.

has the choice between plated and non-plated, buffered and non-buffered shot. In addition to these choices there are, of course, slugs, various buckshot sizes, and steel shot. This should be sufficient you say? Then why is it that one of the most popular reloading charge weights for waterfowl is missing from the factory line-up? I refer to the 1⅜-ounce load at 1330 fps. Many waterfowlers have discovered that this load will put more energy into its shot column than the factory so-called 1½-ounce magnums. Yes, the 1½-ounce pattern is theoretically more dense but its 1260 fps velocity versus the 1⅜-ounce reload's 1330 fps velocity severely handicaps the load. Originally, when introduced, the factory 1½-ounce magnum load had the muzzle velocity of 1315 fps. But the factories were unable to maintain this velocity level and keep pressures where they belonged, so down came the velocity standards to 1260 fps. The 1⅜-ounce reload at

12 GA. 2-3/4" FACTORY LOADS CURRENTLY AVAILABLE

VELOCITY IN FEET PER SECOND

(● = dot; ▣ = shaded box denoting an available factory load)

OUNCES OF SHOT	1135	1140	1145	1150	1155	1160	1175	1185	1190	1200	1210	1220	1240	1250
7/8										●				
1	●	●	●	●	●	●			●	●	●	●	●	●
1-1/8			▣							▣			●	●
1-1/4				●				●			●	▣	●	
1-3/8										●				
1-1/2										●			●	
1-5/8														

OUNCES OF SHOT	1255	1260	1275	1285	1290	1295	1300	1325	1330	1350	1375	1400
7/8												
1			●	●	▣	●	●					
1-1/8	▣	●	●				▣		●			●
1-1/4		●		●		●	●	●	▣	●		
1-3/8			●	●		●	●		●			
1-1/2		▣	●	●				●				
1-5/8												

● From DuPont, Hercules and Winchester
Note: Shaded boxes denote available factory loads.

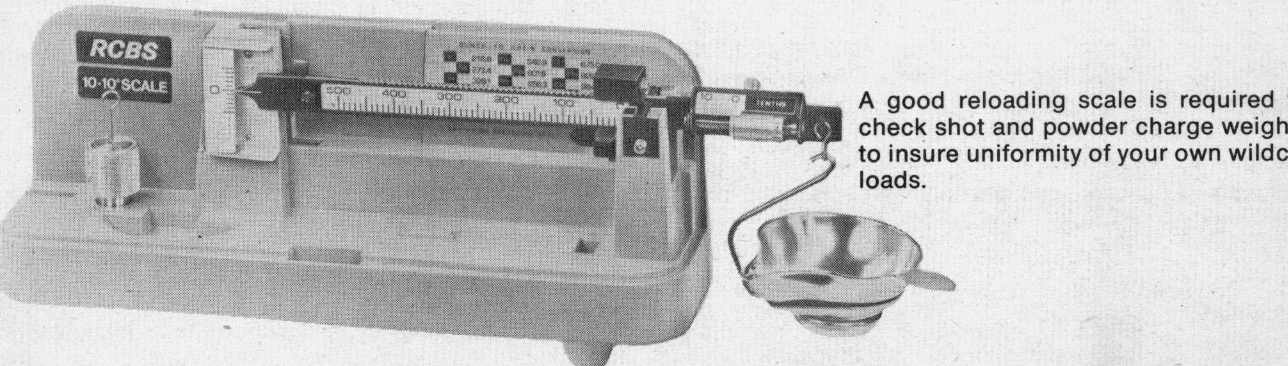

A good reloading scale is required to check shot and powder charge weights to insure uniformity of your own wildcat loads.

1330 fps has a muzzle energy of some 50 ft. lbs. greater than the factory magnum load. And when temperatures drop, the 1⅜-ounce load has even a greater edge. Also, most users of this load are firmly convinced it will pattern better than the factory 1½-ounce magnum load. This author can be counted among those who feel this way.

If we look at Table II we find that the three major powder suppliers list a great number more loads than the basic factory loads (shot weight/velocity). In fact we can find, without too much searching, over 50 different shot weight/velocity combinations; and, if we go to other sources this list expands even further.

It is acknowledged that a fair number of the velocity levels shown are a result of components that choose to turn in different levels than the targeted velocity. However, even the elimination of such loads would leave us with more data than required.

The loads shown in Table III have been selected as those being valuable to the shotgunner. Why? The answers lie in the loads. Let's cover them by shot charge, weight and velocity.

⅞-Ounce of Shot

Most of us are familiar with the ⅞-ounce field and Skeet loads in 20 gauge. A ⅞-ounce 12-gauge

48

12 GA. 2-3/4" FACTORY LOADS CURRENTLY AVAILABLE

OUNCES OF SHOT	VELOCITY IN FEET PER SECOND																									
	1135	1140	1145	1150	1155	1160	1175	1185	1190	1200	1210	1220	1240	1250	1255	1260	1275	1285	1290	1295	1300	1325	1330	1350	1375	1400
7/8										●																
1			●							●					●				●							●
1-1/8			●							●					●						●					●
1-1/4			●									●			●								●			
1-3/8															●						●		●			
1-1/2																●										
1-5/8															●											

Note: Shaded boxes are standard loads duplicating factory loads.
● These boxes are "wildcat" data requirements.

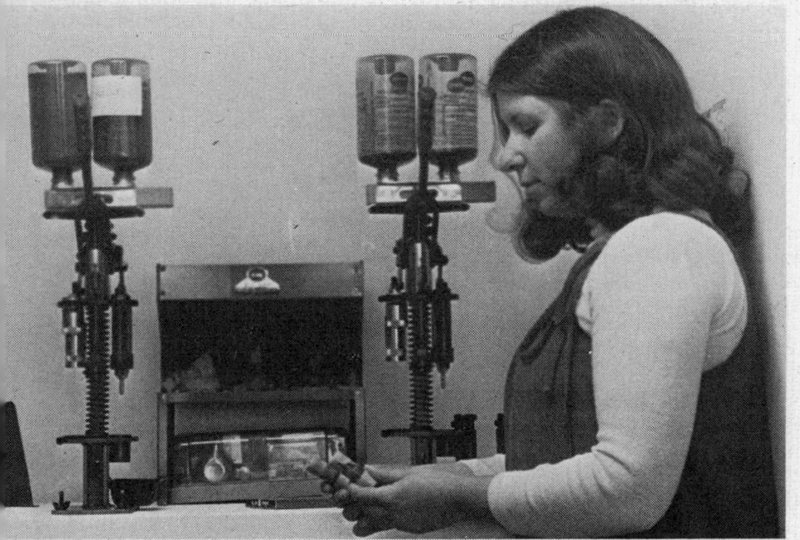

load at 1200 fps allows the reloader the total freedom of using a load as light as the lightest 20 gauge factory offering. This can be a blessing for someone who wants to keep the cost of his shooting to an absolute minimum while retaining a load that will provide excellent results for Skeet and light upland game.

A simple but orderly loading bench is all that's required to produce custom, "wildcat" 12-gauge shotshells.

It also is a fine load with which to start a recoil-shy shooter. Examples here could include a young or new shooter or one of slight stature. As a shooter's tolerance to recoil increases, the load can be increased in shot weight. Thus, only one gun need be purchased or shot from the beginning of a shooter's career right on through his entire shotgun shooting lifetime. With the price of guns today who could argue with the logic of needing to purchase only one good gun?

1-Ounce of Shot

There is a growing interest in 1-ounce, 12-gauge loads. Due to the high cost of shot, more and more reloaders are switching from the standard 1⅛-ounce Skeet and trap loads. Factory 1⅛-ounce target shotshells are loaded to two nominal velocity levels: 1145 fps and 1200 fps. As a result, the 1-ounce reload must possess one of these two velocities in order to keep the shooter's lead constant when he switches to the lighter shot

Often, wildcat powder charges cannot be thrown from standard bushings. You will either have to alter a standard bushing or use an adjustable powder measure such as the pictured Lyman #55, a favorite of reloaders.

charge. The factory 1-ounce loading that moves out at 1290 fps actually has more recoil than a factory 2¾ dram equivalent 1⅛-ounce load. We therefore require a slightly reduced velocity level to keep recoil on a sensible plane. There are factory 1⅛-ounce loads that chronograph out at 1255 fps; so, this velocity level becomes a natural selection.

But what about the 1400 fps loads we are sug-gesting in Table III? This load is for those who want as wide a pattern as possible for use in heavy cover. Nothing makes a better "brush load" than combining high velocity with soft shot. This approach opens up patterns as much as they can possibly be opened. For a short time one of the major ammunition companies made a special international Skeet soft-shot load that gave 1400 fps as a nominal velocity. Nuff said.

1⅛-Ounces of Shot

Once again we need to start out with the recoil-shy shooter in mind. The 1145 fps level will do this nicely. It should be said that *less* than 1100 fps seldom offers good internal ballistics and uniformity. Also such loads tend to provide overly dense patterns and are seldom effective in the field with respect to penetration at game-taking ranges. Keeping velocities to a nominal 1145 fps will keep us away from potential problems; and, this level of velocity also duplicates the light factory Skeet and trap loadings.

Moving on to the 1200 fps mark, we can duplicate the velocity levels of factory, heavy Skeet and trap loads. We might also try to duplicate the factory velocity of 1255 fps (3¼ dram equivalent) as well as the factory 3½ dram equivalent load at 1300 fps. These velocity increases are in approximate steps of 50 foot seconds per load. Quite simply, they are natural steps through which a shooter can develop his recoil tolerance.

Finally we need a load to spread the shot as much as possible for special Skeet applications and for brush work. The 1400 fps mark has been proven to be a workable level for these purposes when accompanied by non-chilled (drop) soft shot. (Velocities over the 1400 fps mark are almost impossible to obtain in combination with good internal ballistics. Patterns also do not seem to continue to open up past this velocity.)

1¼-Ounces of Shot

To maintain the same lead, and to offer the shooter a chance to climb the recoil ladder slowly, it's smart to select the same basic velocities we have used for our 1⅛-ounce loadings. Therefore, as a base requirement, we need loads at 1145, 1200, 1255, and 1300 fps. In order to duplicate factory shotshells we will also need to add 1220, and 1330 fps loadings. These two loadings negate the need for the 1200, and 1300 fps velocity levels as they are very close to our

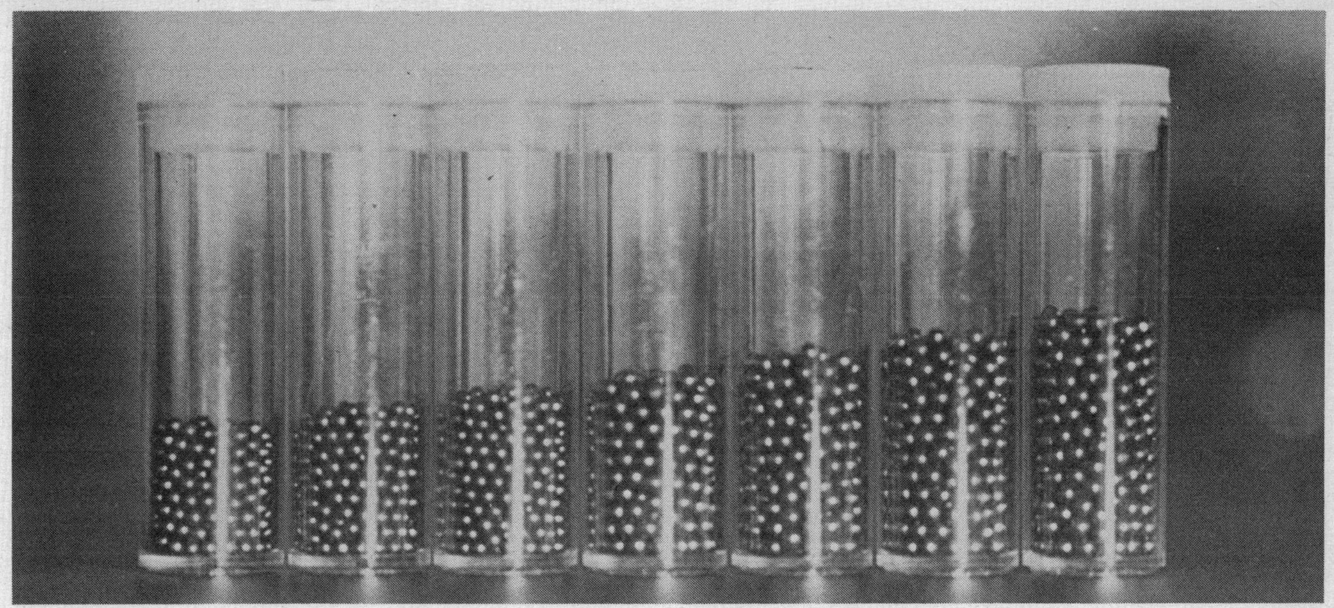

A wide variety of shot weights are available for the 12 gauge wildcatter. Left to right are shown the shot charge options available to you: ⅞-ounce, 1-ounce, 1⅛-ounce, 1¼-ounce, 1⅜-ounce, 1½-ounce and 1⅝-ounce.

previously mentioned base requirement. This leaves us with velocity levels of 1145, 1220, 1255 and 1330 fps.

Because this shot weight is frequently used for long-range hunting and often on large birds, it may behoove us to also select the maximum possible velocity (for this shot weight) for inclusion in our requirements. Safe ballistic practice generally dictates that 1350 fps is about as far as we can go. One could argue whether or not the extra 20 fps over our factory duplication speed justifies another listing. I doubt it. I hesitate to suggest that with most shot sizes this extra margin of muzzle velocity leaves only 10 foot seconds of extra velocity remaining at 40 yards. A convincing argument you say? Or did some say that they *must* have the extra velocity for their long range goose shooting with BB's and #2's, where the velocity will hold up better? At 60 yards, 20 additional foot seconds of muzzle velocity will mean only about 5 feet per second more remaining velocity with #2 shot and possibly 10 feet per second more velocity with BB size shot. Translate that into foot pounds and you can hardly find it. Shot-to-shot variation will cause bigger differences. When you realize that temperature changes can rob as much as 100 foot seconds from your muzzle velocity, the case is closed; the decision final—1330 fps will be our maximum requirement. This will keep your lead constant with factory, high-velocity ammunition and offer other advantages to those who simply want to duplicate their favorite loading.

1⅜-Ounces of Shot

This once was a standard factory offering. There's no doubt that the shooter found 1½ ounces of shot at 1315 fps more appealing than 1⅜ ounces of shot at 1330 fps. However, when the velocity of the factory 1½-ounce magnum load was dropped from 1315 to 1260 fps, no attempt was ever made to reintroduce a 1⅜-ounce load. It didn't take the reloader long to realize that the 1⅜-ounce charge was an ideal heavy, long-range wildcat charge weight.

Again, in order to let the shooter develop his skill by experiencing various recoil levels, and to offer a velocity range suitable for a number of purposes, we need data for several velocity levels. However, with a heavy charge weight of shot it is not practical to load at the lower velocity limits. When a shooter requires this much shot he invariably requires at least a moderate velocity level—1255, 1300 and 1330 fps reloads will cover all possible applications and legitimate desires for most shooters.

1½-Ounces of Shot

There is a need to duplicate this factory load for those who have been satisfied with its per-

12 GA. FACTORY SHOT CHARGE WEIGHTS AVAILABLE (IN OUNCES)

VELOCITY IN FEET PER SECOND

SHOT SIZE	1135	1140	1145	1150	1155	1160	1175	1185	1190	1200	1210	1220	1240	1250	1255	1260	1275	1285	1290	1295	1300	1325	1330	1350	1375	1400
BB																						1¼				
2																1½						1¼				
4															1⅛	1½			1			1¼				
5															1⅛	1½			1			1¼				
6												1¼			1⅛	1½			1			1¼				
7																										
7½			1⅛							1⅛					1⅛							1¼				
8			1⅛												1⅛											
9			1⅛							1⅛					1⅛						1⅛	1¼				
11																										

The factory shot weights, velocity, and shot size combinations are very limited as can be seen from this chart. The wildcatting reloader can load any shot size with any charge weight of any chosen velocity.

formance. Ballistically this load is as good as can be done with current components.

1⅝-Ounces of Shot

There is only one shotshell—the "ACTIV" case by Rainel—in which such a loading is possible while maintaining a velocity level that would make this practical. As this is a special purpose waterfowl load, only the maximum velocity loading need be considered. The muzzle velocity works out to be 1255 fps.

So what have we decided? We have said that the eight factory shot weight/velocity combinations are far too few to cover all our needs. And the current array of available data is too extensive (and confusing) while leaving some requirements unfulfilled. We have decided that some 20 loads will fill our total requirements with respect to shot weight and velocity.

This leaves open the matter of shot sizes. For

SHOT SIZE SELECTOR

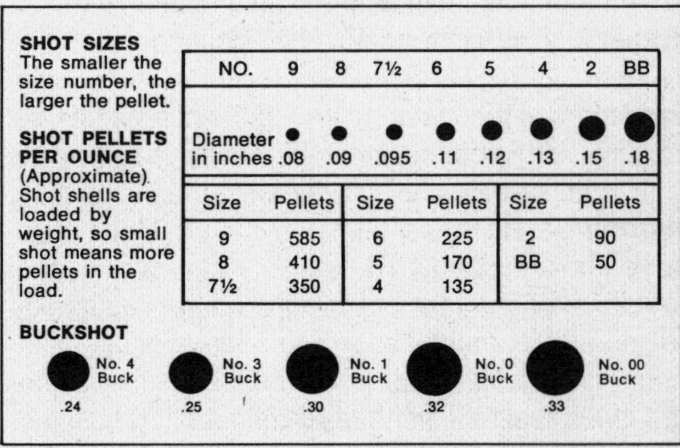

Shot chart is courtesy of Federal Cartridge.

convenience, shot size selection can be further boiled down to a very basic listing. Required are BB, 2, 4, 6, 7½, and 9's. BB's and 2's are for turkey, fox, and geese. Fours are for ducks and pheasant. Sixes are fine for squirrel, rabbit, crow and large grouse; 7½s will do for trap, partridge, and dove. And, finally, 9's will do for woodcock, snipe, quail, rails, and Skeet shooting. This may seem over-simplified for some but I guarantee it will work. No, I do not want to debate differing opinions. If some other shot size seems to be better for you then go ahead and use it.

But where does the "wildcatting" come into play with shot sizes? Well, the factories ignore the fact that all shot sizes can be used in all loads; and, they put out only those loads that seem to fit what *they* have determined to be *your* needs. As every serious long range goose hunter will attest, 1½ ounces of BB's are about as good a goose load as you can cram into a 2¾-inch case. Yet, at least one of the major ammunition suppliers does not offer BB's in anything more than a 1¼-ounce loading. This is a poor substitute for what actually is required. But as a wildcatting shotshell reloader you need not be bothered by such poor marketing decisions. You can go right ahead and load up 1½ ounces of BB's or any other shot size

you may desire in your chosen loads. (Table IV indicates the limitations of factory load/shot-size-selection with one of the major manufacturers. You have the option of any shot size within the charge weights and velocities listed.)

In order to make this article complete, you will need some data to fill all the needs we have outlined. We have selected what we feel are the very best loads to fill the needs outlined. These loads are included in Table V. Put the loads together exactly as shown with *no* substitution of components. *(In that neither the publisher nor the author can control the use of this data, the components selected, the manner in which they are assembled or the firearm in which the loads may be used, neither the publisher nor the author can accept responsibility for the use of this data.)* •

Reference

[1]George R. Watrous, *Standardization and Simplification of Paper Shotshells,* 1948.

Table V

WILDCAT LOADS

12 Gauge 2¾-inch Cases

⅞-Ounce of Shot

Case:	*Winchester Western Compression Formed*
Primer:	Winchester WW209
Powder:	20.0 grains of Winchester 452 AA
Wad(s):	Winchester WAA12 with a 20 gauge Federal ¼-inch fibre filler wad inserted into the shot cup.
Velocity:	1200 fps.
Pressure:	7,300 LUP.
Notes:	The low pressure of this load is less than desirable. In order to avoid the possibility of a blooper, this load should be used in cases that have been fired only once. This will insure a strong crimp. Also, dies should be adjusted to insure loaded cases are no longer than a factory load in the same case. A good, firm, deep crimp is a must. *Never* use this load when the temperature goes below 40° F.

1-Ounce of Shot

Case:	*Winchester Western Compression-Formed*
Primer:	Winchester WW209
Powder:	19.0 grains of Winchester 452AA
Wad(s):	Winchester WAA12 with a 20 gauge Federal ¼-inch fibre filler wad inserted into the shot cup.
Velocity:	1145 fps.
Pressure:	9,000 LUP.
Notes:	It is easier to assemble loads requiring filler wads in the shotcup if all such wads are placed into the plastic wad before you begin to reload.

Case:	*Peters Blue Magic*
Primer:	Federal 209
Powder:	16.0 grains of Dupont "Hi-Skor" 700-X
Wad(s):	Federal 12S3
Velocity:	1145 fps.

Pressure: 8,300 LUP.
Notes: Due to the low chamber pressure this load is not suggested for use under 40° F.

Case: *Winchester Western Compression-Formed*
Primer: Winchester WW209
Powder: 20.5 grains of Winchester 452AA
Wad(s): Winchester WAA12 with a 20 gauge Federal .135-inch card filler wad inserted into the shot cup.
Velocity: 1200 fps.
Pressure: 9,500 LUP.
Notes: Any brand card wad (one .135-inch or two .070-inch) may be substituted.

Case: *Peters Blue Magic*
Primer: C.C.I. 209
Powder: 18.5 grains of Hercules Red Dot
Wad(s): Winchester WAA12
Velocity: 1200 fps.
Pressure: 9,200 LUP.
Notes: A convenient load to put together in that it requires no filler wads and uses easy-to-find components.

Case: *Winchester Western Compression-Formed*
Primer: Winchester WW209
Powder: 22.0 grains of Winchester 452AA
Wad(s): Winchester WAA12 with a 20 gauge Federal .135-inch card filler wad inserted into the shot cup.
Velocity: 1255 fps.
Pressure: 10,500 LUP.
Notes: A good, clean-burning load.

Case: *Winchester Western Compression-Formed*
Primer: C.C.I. 109
Powder: 21.5 grains of Winchester 452AA
Wad(s): Winchester WAA12
Velocity: 1290 fps.
Pressure: 9,900 LUP.
Notes: This load duplicates the ballistics of the factory 1-ounce load.

Case: *Peters Blue Magic*
Primer: Remington 97★
Powder: 19.5 grains of Hercules Red Dot
Wad(s): Remington R12L
Velocity: 1290 fps.
Pressure: 9,400 LUP.
Notes: This load duplicates the nominal velocity of the factory 1-ounce load.

1⅛ Ounces of Shot

Case: *Winchester Western Compression-Formed*
Primer: Winchester WW209
Powder: 19.5 grains of Winchester 452AA
Wad(s): Winchester WAA12
Velocity: 1145 fps.
Pressure: 9,400 LUP.
Notes: This load duplicates the factory 2¾ dram (light) target load in this case.

Case: *Peters Blue Magic*
Primer: Remington 97★
Powder: 17.5 grains of Hercules Red Dot
Wad(s): Remington RXP 12
Velocity: 1145 fps.
Pressure: 9,300 LUP.

Case: *Winchester Western Compression-Formed*
Primer: C.C.I. 109
Powder: 18.0 grains of Hercules Red Dot
Wad(s): Winchester WAA12
Velocity: 1200 fps.
Pressure: 10,400 LUP
Notes: A very popular load.

Case: *Peters Blue Magic*
Primer: Federal 209
Powder: 18.5 grains of Dupont "Hi-Skor" 700-X
Wad(s): Remington RXP12
Velocity: 1200 fps.
Pressure: 10,500 LUP.
Notes: A clean-burning load.

Case: *Peters Blue Magic*
Primer: Federal 209
Powder: 24.0 grains of Dupont SR7625
Wad(s): Federal 12S4
Velocity: 1255 fps.
Pressure: 9,800 LUP.
Notes: The Federal 12S4 wad is not readily available at all retail outlets.

Case: *Winchester Western Compression-Formed*
Primer: Winchester WW209
Powder: 27.0 grains of Winchester 473AA
Wad(s): Winchester WAA12
Velocity: 1300 fps.
Pressure: 9,800 LUP.
Notes: This load duplicates the ballistics of the factory 3½ dram equivalent International Skeet Load.

Case: *Peters Blue Magic*
Primer: Winchester WW209
Powder: 26.5 grains of Winchester 473AA
Wad(s): Remington RXP12
Velocity: 1300 fps.
Pressure: 9,500 LUP.

Case: *Winchester Western Compression-Formed*
Primer: Winchester WW209
Powder: 35.0 grains of Winchester 540
Wad(s): Winchester WAA12
Velocity: 1400 fps.
Pressure: 10,000 LUP.
Notes: A minimum of 60 pounds of wad pressure is required.

1¼ Ounces of Shot

Case: *Winchester Western Compression-Formed*
Primer: Winchester WW209
Powder: 23.5 grains of Winchester 473AA
Wad(s): Winchester WAA12
Velocity: 1145 fps.
Pressure: 9,500 LUP.
Notes: A Winchester WAA12F114 wad may be used for slightly denser patterns.

Case: *Peters Blue Magic*
Primer: C.C.I. 209
Powder: 31.5 grains of Dupont SR4756
Wad(s): Winchester WAA12
Velocity: 1330 fps.
Pressure: 10,600 LUP.

1⅜ Ounces of Shot

Case: *Peters Blue Magic*
Primer: Winchester WW209
Powder: 30.0 grains of Dupont SR4756
Wad(s): Winchester WAA12R
Velocity: 1255 fps.
Pressure: 10,800 LUP.
Notes: A clean-burning load.

Case: *Winchester Western Compression-Formed*
Primer: Winchester WW209
Powder: 32.0 grains of Dupont SR4756
Wad(s): Remington RXP12
Velocity: 1255 fps.
Pressure: 10,300 LUP.

The .410 & the 28

Here's a reloader's look at the smallest of the gauges—their potential and popularity.

by TOM ROSTER

About the Author: Tom Roster is the Reloading Editor for The American Shotgunner, *and Technical Editor for* Skeet Shooting Review.

IF YOU'RE a typical shotgunner you've probably spent the majority of your shooting with the 12 gauge. Maybe you've spent some time shooting the 20, and perhaps even less with the big 10 or disappearing 16 gauge. If you're an uncommon shotgunner you might have developed most of your shooting experience with the 20 gauge or 10 gauge.

But whether you're a typical shotgunner or not, few shooters have developed a great deal of experience with the .410 bore or 28 gauge. These two smoothbores remain shotgunning's smallest and least-used gauges. They also remain relatively misunderstood, hard to find, hard to purchase ammo for, and only infrequently reloaded. Most shooters couldn't tell you much about these two shotshells, and still others couldn't tell you the difference between them. Let's take a look at each and try to unravel the mysteries of both.

The .410

Nearly every shotgunner who first turns to the .410 bore does so from one of two motivations: either he is a beginner and thinks he wants a little gun with little recoil, or he's an experienced shooter looking for a challenge. The two reasons seem mutually exclusive, and to a certain extent most certainly are. But, confusion surrounding the .410 is common; no one really seems to truly understand it, and I have yet to meet a shotgunner who claims to have mastered it.

Many experienced shooters call the .410 the "idiot stick." Others call it the pee-wee bore, still others the .410 gauge. Idiot stick, the .410 is definitely not, unless you're referring to the shooter (rather than the shotgun) trying to cleanly kill game beyond 25 yards. Pee-wee bore the .410 is, as it is currently the smallest shotgun bore available to smoothbore enthusiasts. The .410 has a true bore diameter measuring .410-inch, and is not a gauge in any sense of the word.

I call the .410 "shotgunning's ultimate challenge," for it is the most difficult of all shotguns with which to hit. Just ask any Skeet shooter. And in case you don't know any Skeeters, take the time to pattern test either the 3- or 2½-inch .410 load sometime. Don't bother to go back to 40 yards for your testing efforts though, the .410 just won't make it with anything other than a wide open, very patchy, blown-looking pattern. In fact, you could probably throw a better pattern by hand at 40 yards.

Instead, confine your efforts to a conservative 25 yards with the 2½-inch, ½-oz., .410—30 yards at the outside for the 3-inch, $^{11}/_{16}$ oz. loading. Don't waste your time with the traditional 30-inch patterning circle either. Modesty is the watchword here. Try a smaller 25-inch circle instead. You'll soon discover the .410's inherently poor patterning qualities. You'll also discover that any shot size larger than 7½ is out in the 2½-inch, ½-oz. loading with No. 6s being the big

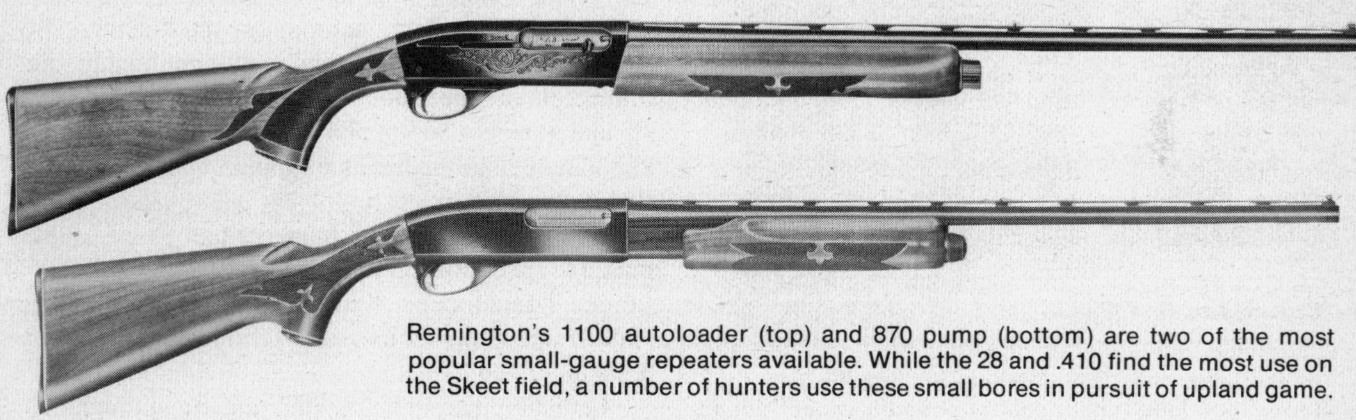

Remington's 1100 autoloader (top) and 870 pump (bottom) are two of the most popular small-gauge repeaters available. While the 28 and .410 find the most use on the Skeet field, a number of hunters use these small bores in pursuit of upland game.

The .410, while extremely limited as a hunting gun, is perfectly at home in clay target games where it provides shotgunning's greatest challenge.

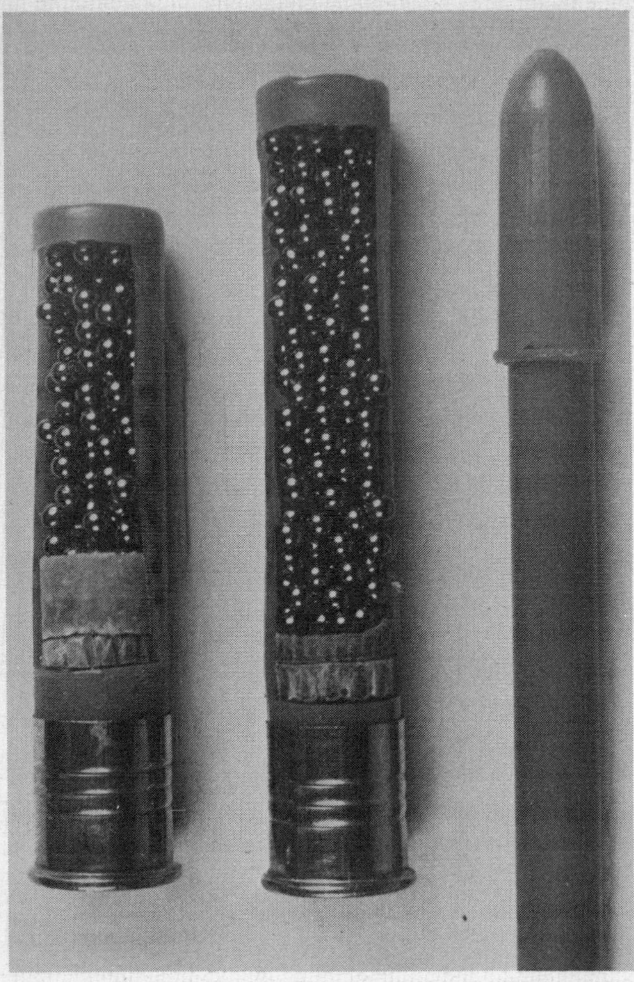

The shot column in any .410 bore loading, be it for the 2½- (left) or 3-inch shell (center), is barely wider than a ballpoint pen (right). In fact, the shot column in the .410 is proportionately longer than its diameter when compared to any other gauge. This results in excessive bore contact and a great degree of pellet deformation.

boys in the 3-inch version. Your final discovery will be that regardless of which components you test, 25 yards is the limit of reliable pattern density for the 2½-inch shell and 30 yards the outer range for the 3-inch loading.

Not only will the effective range prove to be short for consistent patterns with the .410, but as suggested already, the effective pattern diameter will seldom measure larger than 25 inches. The .410, you see, will truly prove to be a pee-wee bore, with its components and range limitations proportionately small. Your pattern testing will prove very useful if you can demonstrate all of this to your own satisfaction, for you will have realized the .410 for what it is: a short-range-only smoothbore, first; a challenge, second.

All too many shotgunners make the mistake of approaching the .410 as just a "little gauge," with an assumed mid-range potential. Not so! The .410 is the shortest range shotgun just as the 2½-inch hull is the shortest shotshell. In addition, its effective pattern spread is much smaller than that of all the other shotguns, and it usually is loaded with the smallest shot sizes. Make no mistake, the .410 is not just a tiny shell and a tiny shotgun, *it's an altogether different shotgun*.

The differences go beyond its short range limitation and its tininess. First, the .410, surprisingly, develops 1145 to 1200 fps velocity levels for Skeet shooting or very small (or very close range) bird hunting. These levels are, of course, standard clay target shooting velocity levels. The .410 also opens its pattern faster than any of the other gauges making it a favorite for some quail hunters. This seems contradictory, for many shotgunners reason that the larger the diameter of the shot charge in the shell, the sooner it ought to spread upon leaving the muzzle. Air resistance helps to spread patterns; and, the larger the diameter of the shot charge, the more the pellets in that charge are exposed to the pattern spreading effects of atmospheric resistance. Therefore, a wide 12 gauge shot charge *should* open sooner than any amount of lead from a skinny .410.

However, the .410 is *different*. It manages to open its patterns sooner, despite the fact that its ultra-skinny shot charge exposes the least pellets to the ballistic and pattern eroding effects of drag. The principal reason is that the slender .410 proportionately exposes the *greatest* number of pellets to bore contact of all the gauges, as a consequence of its *disproportionately long* shot charge. The result: the more pellets in contact with the bore, the more those pellets suffer from bore scrub and exit the barrel as deformed shot. The more a pellet is deformed, the more surface area it exposes to air resistance. This in turn results in the pellet slowing down faster and exiting the muzzle at a greater angle of divergence from point of aim than a round pellet. The end result of any shot charge containing deformed pellets is open patterns. And, since the .410 deforms a greater percentage of its pellets than the other gauges, its patterns open up the soonest.

Another seemingly odd thing about the .410, until it's understood, is the fact that this pipsqueak bore in both 2½- and 3-inch persuasion tends to develop the highest chamber pressure of all the gauges. Thus, it's more difficult to move the 2½-inch .410's shot charges much faster than 1220 fps without generating chamber pressures that exceed 11,000 LUP. The same is true of the 3-inch "Magnum" load. Reloaders who forget this ballistic fact and add more powder for a little extra velocity can build dangerous bombs in the .410 faster than in any other gauge. The reason is that chamber pressure tends to rise as bore diameter decreases. That is, the more a given powder type and charge is confined—put differently: the smaller the area powder gases have to expand into—the higher the chamber pressures tend to rise in generating a given velocity level. Since the .410 has the narrowest bore, and, since its pencil-thin hulls offer very little room for cushion wads and no room for cushioning sections in one-piece plastic wads, the powder gases are more tightly confined than in other gauges.

The .410, however, does have a shotgunning application, but one that is both unique and limited. Anyone looking for an extremely lightweight, challenging short range smoothbore with little or no apparent recoil should consider the .410. But there is one more reason to shoot the .410 and that is best summarized in one word— fun.

It's truly a joy to swing a .410 and break clay targets at short range games like Skeet. At Skeet's typical target hitting distances of 15 to 21 yards, the .410 can handle this chore to perfection. Again, the only problem with it is that you only have a 20-25-inch pattern working for you. But maybe that's not really a problem. Many Skeet shooters and plain, ordinary shotgunners like the challenge of trying to smash clays with the .410. To them, the .410 can only sharpen and refine their lead and pointing. After all, they argue, the man who can really shoot one of these pipsqueaks is truly an expert shotgunner. Believe me, if you shoot the .410 for awhile, the other gauges will soon seem much easier to hit with.

However, for hunting, the word "fun" is out and the word "responsibility" is in. The .410 is a dubious hunting choice at best. Given its small pattern, very light shot charges, ability to handle only small shot sizes, and excessively lengthened shot strings, the .410 produces far too many crippled birds for any true sportsman's liking. I'm always unnerved whenever I encounter a father/

son team in the field and find the junior member toting a .410. The reason given is always the same—light recoil. But light recoil only benefits man, not the crippled birds that fly off to die a slow, lingering death. No sir, in my opinion, federal and state law should prohibit any shotgun smaller than the 28 gauge, or better yet the 20 gauge, for all bird hunting with the possible exception of doves, quail, starlings or small pests.

When used to hunt dove and quail, only the 3-inch Magnum should be employed and shots confined to 30 yards at the extreme. Over pointing dogs, the 3-inch .410 can be deadly on 15 to 25 yard shots at flushing coveys of quail. Here, the .410's fast opening pattern has its greatest application. The same is true for gunners hiding near a spread of dove decoys where incoming shots on braking doves are taken at 10 to 20 yards. But pass shooting doves? Never. Here the 28 gauge ¾- or ⅞-oz. shot charge of 7½s is far deadlier and should, in my opinion, be considered the minimum even for expert shooters.

All in all, the .410 is best used as a clay target gun. Go after a speeding clay target at 15 to 25 yards with the .410 and you've got a very enjoyable challenge. Clay birds don't suffer if you only chip or dust them. But the same kind of hit on feathered game can only spell "cripple."

While remaining an expert's gun, the little .410 has undergone some improvement. More than any other shotshell, it has benefitted from the one-piece plastic wad. Even though all one-piece plastic wads for this bore size contain no cushioning section, they help to prevent the .410's long shot column from contacting the bore. As a result, the plastic wads have improved the .410's pattern density (in 2½- and 3-inch persuasion) about 20 percent in typical over-the-counter guns. In terms of evenness, the patterns have also improved thanks to a resulting reduction of bore scrub. The excessive patchiness that has always earmarked .410 patterns in the past has been brought under control and sometimes even eliminated.

Even though an $^{11}/_{16}$-oz., 3-inch Magnum loading is now available to .410 enthusiasts, I've never found that it patterned worth a hoot. The ⅝-oz. handload, however, can normally be counted on to place as many (if not more) pellets in the 25-inch circle at ranges from 20 to 30 yards than the heavier $^{11}/_{16}$-oz. loading. The lower chamber pressures generated by the lighter load, the extra room gained in the hull for wad column manipulation, and the fact that the ⅝-oz. load is *completely* contained in the 3-inch one-piece plastic .410 wads (as opposed to the ¹¹/₁₆-oz. loading only squeezing 75 percent of its payload into the same wad), all contribute to fewer deformed pellets. The obvious results is an improved pattern with a ⅝-oz. loading. As an added bonus, the ⅝-oz. charge will usually deliver more energy to the target thanks to a higher percentage of its pellets emerging from the barrel undeformed.

Handloading the .410 has become much more desirable and convenient thanks to the one-piece plastic wads and improvements in reloading presses. The major manufacturers offer a total of three 2½-inch and three 3-inch .410 hulls to choose from. By far the most durable and easy to reload are Winchester's Super-X and AA 2½-inch, compression-formed .410 hulls along with the 3-inch compression-formed Super-X hull. They both possess very stiff case walls and flexible crimp areas. This adds up to excellent shell strength and long-term reloadabiity. The Remington .410 SP plastic shells—in both 2½- and 3-inch—are good second choices for reloading. These hulls possess a plastic base wad and good wall strength. The Federal .410 shells made with the Reifenhauser process (again in 2½- or 3-inch) also rank a close second for reloading. Relatively weak walls, however, allow the hulls to buckle if wad column height is not close to perfect.

Four companies manufacture 2½-inch, one-piece plastic wads: Federal, Remington, Winchester-Western and Trico Plastics. Federal assigns its 2½-inch .410 wad a catalog number of 410SC; Remington, SP-410; Winchester-Western, WAA41, while Trico makes no less than three different 2½-inch wads—one for the W-W AA hull, another for the same hull when W-W 296 ball powder is loaded, and still another for the Federal and Remington 2½-inch plastic hulls. Only Remington markets a 3-inch .410 one-piece plastic wad—its product number is SP-4103.

All of these miniscule, one-piece plastic wads resemble one another in that they are merely long, skinny shotcups with an obturating skirt extending down from the shotcup base. In other words, unlike most one-piece plastic wads for the other gauges, .410 one-piecers do not have a cushioning section. They are, so to speak, merely a plastic overpowder wad attached to a shotcup. Remington's .410 wads are the largest in diameter and fit nicely in the Remington and Federal hulls. Federal's one-piece plastic wad is mid-range in diameter and fits all three plastic cases. Winchester's wad is the narrowest in diameter and works nicely in both its internal, tapered, compression-formed shells along with Federal's hulls as well. It's a little too narrow, however, to form a good gas seal in the Remington product.

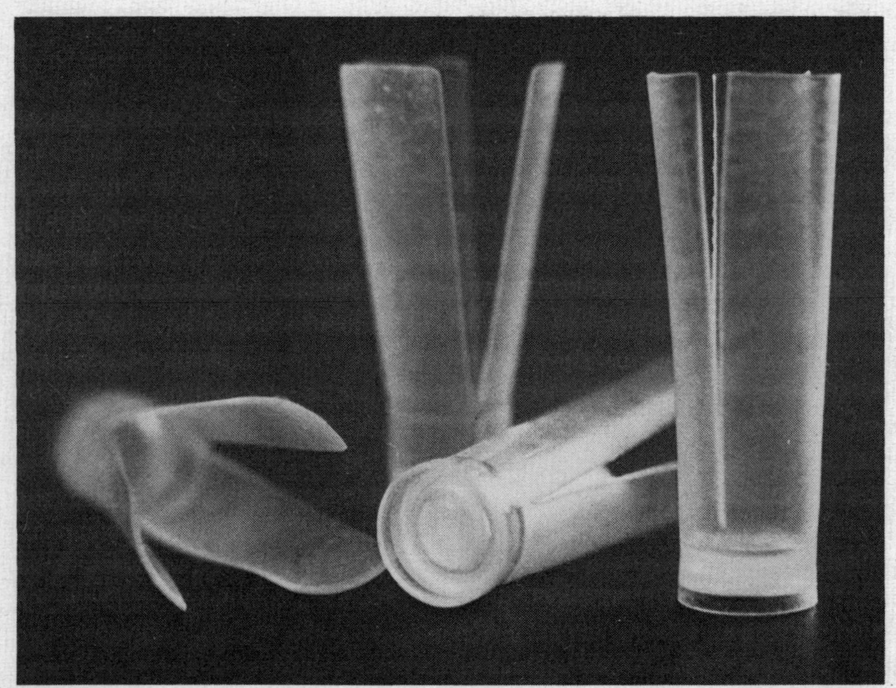

All of the plastic, one-piece .410 wads available for reloading are very similar in design. Unlike the other gauges, one-piece plastic wads for the .410 do not contain a cushioning section. Rather, they merely have an elongated shotcup with an integral obturating skirt to effect a gas seal.

Selected 2½″ .410 Bore Reloading Data

| PRIMER | | CASE | | POWDER | | WAD COLUMN | | SHOT | VEL. | PRES. |
Mfg.	No.	Mfr.	Name	Name	Grains	Mfr.	Designation	(Oz.)	(FPS)	(LUP)
W-W	209	W-W	AA	296	14.0	W-W	WAA41	½	1200	9,800
CCI	209	W-W	AA	296	14.0	W-W	WAA41	½	1200	9,100
CCI	209	Rem.	SP	IMR-4227	17.3	Fed.	410SC	½	1205	10,600
Fed.	410	Rem.	SP	IMR-4227	17.5	Rem.	SP 410	½	1210	11,400
Fed.	209	Fed.	Hi-Power	2400	13.5	W-W	WAA41	½	1200	10,900
Win.	209	Rem.	SP	H-110	15.0	Rem.	SP 410	½	1200	——
Win.	209	W-W	AA	H-110	15.0	W-W	WAA41	½	1200	——
Win.	209	Fed.	Hi-Power	H-110	16.0	Fed.	410SC	½	1200	10,500

Selected 3″ .410 Bore Reloading Data

| PRIMER | | CASE | | POWDER | | WAD COLUMN | | SHOT | VEL. | PRES. |
Mfg.	No.	Mfr.	Name	Name	Grains	Mfr.	Designation	(Oz.)	(FPS)	(LUP)
Rem.	97-4	Rem.	SP	2400	17.0	Rem.	SP 4103	$^{11}/_{16}$	1200	13,000
CCI	157	Rem.	SP	296	16.0	Rem.	SP 4103	$^{11}/_{16}$	1135	8,700
Fed.	399	Rem.	SP	IMR-4227	17.7	Rem.	SP 4103	$^{11}/_{16}$	1145	11,600
Win.	209	Win.	Super-X	296	16.0	Rem.	SP 4103	$^{11}/_{16}$	1145	10,200
Win.	209	Win.	Super-X	296	16.0	Rem.	SP 4103	⅝	1195	10,000
Fed.	209	Win.	Super-X	IMR-4198	23.0	Win.	WAA41	½	1300	9,000
Win.	209	Win.	Super-X	IMR-4198	26.5	Fed.	410SC	½	1425	10,500

There are four popular powders for the .410: Du Pont's IMR-4227, Hercules' 2400, Hodgdon's H-110, and W-W's 296. With the exception of 4227, all of these propellants don't burn as cleanly as shooters would like, but all produce excellent ballistics. Du Pont's 4227 is the bulkiest of the four, and when it comes to reloading 2½-inch shells it seems to load well only in the Remington hull. The other three powders are very dense and produce excellent 2½-inch loads and crimps with one-piece plastic wads. All four powders work well in Magnum hulls.

In terms of primers, Federal and Remington both make a very mild force .410 primer. Federal calls its the 410 while the Remington is called the 97-4, W-W's 209 and CCI's 209 primers are also good, mild .410 primers.

By far, the most popular 2½-inch Skeet load is one using the W-W 209 primer, the W-W AA or Super-X hull, 14.0 grains 296 powder, W-W WAA41 wad and ½-ounce of shot. This number travels at 1200 fps with a chamber pressure of 9,800 LUP. Another winner in 2½-inch persuasion is the W-W 209 primer in a Federal shell along with 16.0 grains Hodgdon H-110, a Federal 410SC wad and ½-oz. of shot for a velocity of 1200 fps. A third 2½-inch favorite calls for the W-W AA hull, 13.0 grains of Hercules 2400, Winchester 209 primer, WAA41 or Federal 410SC wad and ½-ounce of shot.

The Magnum hull is really the best choice for assembling hunting loads. Its extra ½-inch of space allows the proper protection of ½-oz. or ⅝-oz. shot charges, or, for those who prefer, room for so-so protection of the ¹¹/₁₆-oz. Magnum charge. If you want a high speed, ½-oz. .410 load, the 3-inch hull allows the use of slowburning rifle powders which, because of their bulk, do not fare well in the diminutive 2½-inch case.

An acceptable ¹¹/₁₆-oz. load calls for a W-W 3-inch compression-formed case, W-W 209 primer, 16.0 grains of W-W 296, and a Remington SP 4103 wad for a velocity of 1145 fps at 10,200 LUP. By dropping only ⅝-oz. of shot in this load you up the velocity to near 1200 fps at 10,000 LUP. You can also increase the powder charge to 17.0 grains of 296 with the ⅝-oz. load for 1220 fps at 11,000 LUP. A real screamer in the 3-inch Magnum shell calls for a Winchester hull, Federal 209 primer, 23.0 grains of Du Pont IMR-4198, WAA41 wad and ½-oz. of shot for a velocity of 1300 fps at 9,000 LUP. (An even faster load can be found in the above load table!)

Modern reloading presses provide excellent crimps, such as these, even with the tiny .410 bore. With the right equipment, you can turn out a quality .410 or 28 reload.

Reloaders can save themselves a lot of trouble when turning out .410s, if they take care in loading these pencil-thin hulls to develop proper wad column heights to prevent case buckling. Of all the reloading tools, Ponsness-Warren's single-stage Du-O-Matic 375 tool will consistently produce the best .410 reloads. Why? It's a result of the hull being completely contained in a full-length P-W sizing die throughout all steps of the loading process. This feature absolutely precludes case wall buckling and produces a crimp fully the equal of, if not better than, factory .410 crimps.

The 28 Gauge

While the 28 gauge is bigger than the .410 its use by smoothbore enthusiasts is less. In fact, if it weren't for the 28 gauge being included as one of the four gauges shot during registered Skeet competition, its extinction might well have taken place 40 or 50 years ago. And since this tiny bore is not nearly as versatile a game gun as the also rare 16 gauge, Skeet may well be considered the 28 gauge's only friend.

The obscure status of the 28 gauge is really a shotgunning shame. Somehow, over a period of time, shotgunners seem to have decided the .410 bore has more use than the 28 gauge. Witness the fact that there is both a 2½-inch .410 shell normally carrying a half ounce of shot, and a 3-inch Magnum packing an $^{11}/_{16}$-ounce shot charge. But the 28 gauge, like the 16, seems to have evolved only a 2¾-inch shell. Unlike all the other gauges, Magnum shells and guns simply aren't available for the 28.

What's more, try to buy a box of 28 gauge ammo that's loaded with anything other than a ¾-oz. shot charge. At least the 16 gauge is available in factory loads in three different shot charge weights. But the poor 28 is stuck with only two factory loads: a ¾-oz. shot charge pushed by 2¼ drams of powder at the nominal industry standard velocity level of 1295 fps; and a 2 dram, ¾-ounce target load that travels at 1200 fps. And when you do buy a box of 28 gauge ammo, you'll also angrily note that it's more expensive than the .410 load!

Most depressing of all, however, is the fact that the 28 suffers from the myth that it's just an unnecessary duplication of the .410 bore both in payload weight (the Magnum .410 loading of $^{11}/_{16}$-oz, is only $^1/_{16}$-oz. lighter than the 28's ¾-oz. shot charge), and in being a light, tiny shotgun. What's more, .410 advocates will tell you that there are more guns and a wider variety of guns chambered for *their* shotshell than the 28. So, why buy one?

Well, the .410 advocates are right in saying the 28 gauge's *standard* payload is *nearly* identical in weight to the Magnum .410, and that there are a wider variety of shotguns available chambered for the .410 than the 28. But, they are very wrong if they try to argue that the .410 is a better performer on either the clay target range, or in the field. The fact is, the 28 gauge develops a higher velocity level at a lower chamber pressure and turns in consistently better patterns than the .410. It also develops a shorter shot string, is much easier to reload and possesses the volumetric capacity to handle a ⅞-oz. payload—a full ¼-oz. more than the Magnum .410 stuffed to absolute maximum capacity! The 28 gauge, in short, is one hell of a lot better shotgun than the .410 on every possible standpoint of comparison, except price. And if the 28 would gain in popularity, prices would start dropping in line with .410 guns and ammo.

I'm not going to claim that the 28 is *the* best gun for certain upland game situations, and I'm not going to tell you it's the easiest gauge to shoot for breaking clay targets. The fact is that most gunners who turn to the 28 gauge are experienced shooters looking for an understudy for the larger gauges, or searching for a novel, challenging gun to shoot. I am going to argue strongly that anyone contemplating owning a light, little gauge, and debating whether to buy a 28 gauge or a .410 bore, will be far better served by the 28 gauge, especially if he is a reloader.

First, the 28 is quite a bit easier to hit with, day in and day out, than the 2½-inch .410. Most certainly, the 28's ¼-oz. heavier shot charge helps in this respect, as does its larger bore diameter, both of which contribute to denser patterns.

thin, especially in the pattern's fringe area. Thus, the .410 shooter throws a cloud of shot at the target which is most certainly as large or larger than the cloud thrown by other gauges, but is so thin the target often passes through untouched. In effect, the .410 casts a large enough net, but the mesh is too large for the fish it tries to trap.

The fact is, given equal weight shot charges of the same quality and size of shot (and the same chokes and barrel lengths), the 28 gauge, or any other gauge for that matter, will always deform fewer pellets than the .410. As a result, the larger gauges will always produce better quality patterns. In turn, the shooter with the 28 gauge will

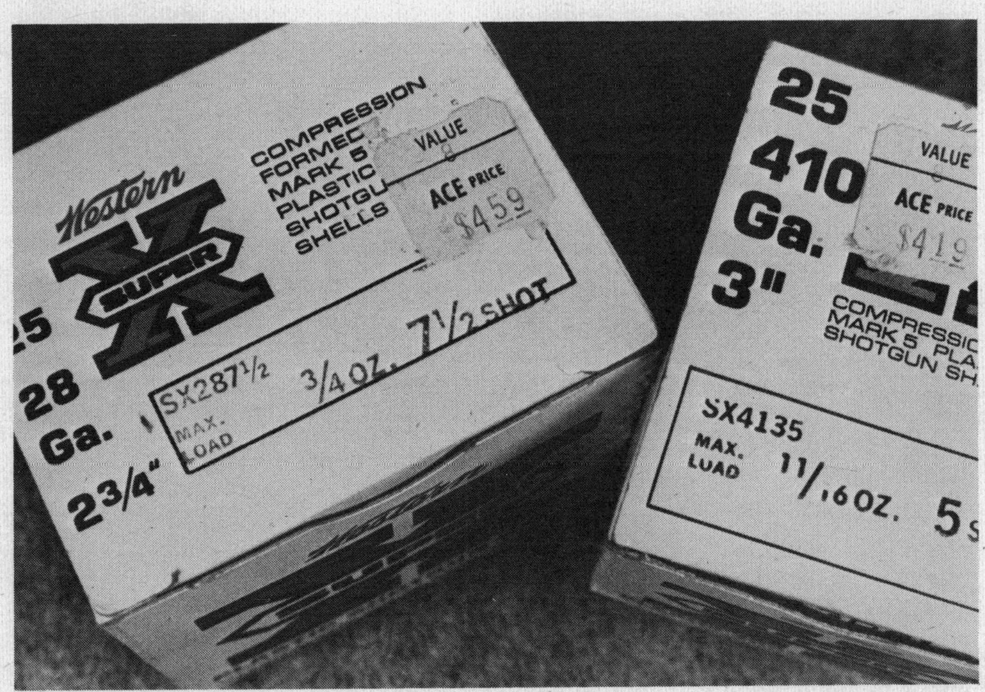

Regardless of where you buy them, the 28 gauge ¾-oz. loading usually costs more than the slightly lighter 11/16-oz., 3-inch .410. Reloading makes economic sense.

How does the 3-inch .410 holding only a 1/16-oz. lighter shot charge than the standard 28 gauge load of ¾-ounces measure up in terms of hitting? Unfortunately, the Magnum .410 load of 11/16-ounces is not employed at Skeet, so no official hitting record exists to draw upon. But I know from observing and directing informal shooting comparison tests that the 28 will consistently turn in higher scores on the Skeet range.

But, shouldn't the .410, logically, be the shotgun that's the easiest to hit with at 25 yards or less? The answer here, paradoxically, is no. For while the .410 does indeed open its pattern spread the quickest, the efficiency of the density of that pattern is usually patchy, inconsistent and very

break more clay targets and bag more birds than with the .410, assuming, of course, that he is accurate in casting his net.

Why? The answer is pellet deformation. The problem is that the .410 must simply have a much longer shot charge than the larger bored 28 gauge in order to contain the same volume of shot. If you want to store a given volume of shot in a cylinder, that cylinder can either be short and fat, or tall and skinny as long as it possesses the total internal area needed to store the volume of shot in question. In the 28 gauge and .410, we are attempting to load ¾-ounce of shot, more or less. The 28 holds that shot charge in an area that is only slightly (1½ times) longer than it is wide.

But, the .410, being so narrow and thin, must store almost the same shot charge in an area that is more than five times as long as it is wide. In short, the 28's shot charge is abbreviated and squat; the .410's is long and skinny.

In the 28 gauge, fewer pellets contact the bore because more pellets are resting in the interior of its shorter, squattier shot charge. Thus, the 28 gauge insulates a higher percentage of pellets

Because of its greater internal capacity, the 28 gauge 2¾-inch hull (right) offers a more conventional shot column for the same weight shot charge than the pencil-thin, 3-inch .410 hull (left). The conventional nature of the 28's shot charge also allows for more protection of the shot column via a shot wrapper which completely contains the shot charge. (Also note the generous cushioning section.) Both protection features are quite lacking in the 3-inch, .410 loading. End result—great velocity levels and superior patterns in the 28 gauge.

from bore-scrub deformation than the .410.

In a nutshell, this is why both of the .410 loadings are so much inferior to anything tossed out of a 28. The .410 will always produce the most deformed pellets of the two guns because it will never be able to protect its pellets as well, nor launch them as gently. Further, it will never be able to launch its shot charge as fast as the 28 gauge simply because its narrow bore will always cause chamber pressure to rise faster. Thus, the 28 gauge can easily push its ¾-oz. shot charge at a whopping 1295 fps muzzle velocity, while the .410 struggles to move a slightly lighter shot charge at 1200 fps and still develop safe peak chamber pressures.

But don't take all this business about patterns on faith. Pattern test a ¾-oz. 28 gauge load against the $^{11}/_{16}$-oz. .410 load with both employing the same shot size and fired through the same barrel length and chokes. You'll find that at 20 yards and beyond, the 28 will usually deliver the more even, dense patterns of the two. The 28 patterns will also show far fewer flyers *and* will produce the densest pattern centers and fringes. You'll also quickly find both guns handle 6s, 7s, 8s, 8½s and 9s the best. Finally, you'll discover both guns run out of consistent killing pattern density for small upland birds at 30 yards, with the .410 actually struggling to make it to 25 yards.

In summary, the 28 is the best of the tiny gauges. It produces even, excellent killing patterns of small shot to an honest 30 yards. And it does so with a 1295 fps velocity level that packs excellent killing energy into each pellet. What's more, if you want to stretch the 28 gauge to 35 yards for over-decoy duck shooting with 6s or 5s, you can do it nicely by handloading ⅞-ounce shot charges at 1220 to 1250 fps velocity levels. You'll still find enough room left in the hull for a good wad column and complete shot charge protection by a full-length shot wrapper. As a result, your ⅞-ounce patterns will be even, and more densely fleshed out by added, *undeformed* pellets.

Reloading the 28 gauge, like the .410 bore, is now largely a matter of utilizing one-piece plastic wads. Just as card and fiber wads have become extinct for the .410, so too have these types of components become extinct in the 28. All three major ammo makers offer 28 gauge one-piece plastic wads. Federal calls its 28 gauge wad the 28S1, Remington the SP28, and Winchester the WAA28. All three are designed to fully protect a

Selected 28 Gauge Loads

| PRIMER | | CASE | | POWDER | | WAD COLUMN | | SHOT | VEL. | PRES. |
Mfr.	No.	Mfr.	Name	Name	Grains	Mfr.	Designation	(Oz.)	(FPS)	(LUP)
W-W	209	W-W	AA	571	20.5	Win.	WAA28	¾	1260	11,000
Fed.	209	Fed.	Plastic	Blue Dot	20.0	Rem.	SP 28	¾	1295	10,900
Rem.	97*	Rem.	Target	Unique	15.0	Rem.	SP 28	¾	1295	10,600
Fed.	209	Rem.	Target	SR-4756	16.0	Rem.	SP 28	¾	1195	9,800
Win.	209	Rem.	Target	SR-7625	14.5	Rem.	SP 28	¾	1195	9,200
Fed.	209	Fed.	Plastic	SR-7625	14.5	Fed.	28S1	¾	1205	10,400
Win.	209	W-W	AA	SR-7625	14.5	Win.	WAA28	¾	1210	11,400
Fed.	209	Fed.	Plastic	Unique	13.5	Fed.	28S1	¾	1200	11,600
Rem.	97*	Rem.	Target	Herco	14.0	Rem.	SP 28	¾	1200	8,700
Win.	209	W-W	AA	Unique	13.0	Win.	WAA28	¾	1200	9,400
Fed.	209	Fed.	Plastic	SR-4756	17.0	Fed.	28S1[1]	⅞	1220	11,000
Win.	209	Fed.	Plastic	HS-6	18.0	Win.	WAA28	⅞	1178	10,500
Win.	209	Fed.	Plastic	HS-7	23.5	Fed.	28S1	⅞	1210	11,000

[1]Cushioning section must be cut from these wads to allow successful crimps.

¾-oz. shot charge. All three possess generous cushioning sections which help greatly in minimizing the deformation of lead pellets from setback during ignition.

All three companies also make plastic 28 gauge hulls in 2¾-inch length only. The Winchester AA or Super-X hull is of unitized construction made by Winchester's compression-formed process. Both the Federal and Remington 28 gauge hulls are of the two-piece design. The Federal hull, which has the most internal volume of all these hulls, has a paper basewad, while the Remington hull uses a plastic basewad. The 28 gauge Remington target hull is recommended for reloading as it uses the 209-sized primer pocket; however, their field shell has a fiber basewad and 57-sized primer pocket.

The 28 gauge will handle a variety of slower-burning powders and 209-sized primers. In our loading table, both ¾- and ⅞-oz. loads are listed. The ⅞-oz. loads require that the reloader cut the cushioning section from the one-piece plastic wad listed for these "magnum" loads in order for the heavier charge to fit into the hull. That leaves a plastic over-powder wad and plastic shotcup for a wad column. Minus the cushioning section a greater percentage of pellets will be deformed by setback. But some shooters like the ⅞-oz. charge for filling out patterns at close range.

As stated previously, the outer range for clean kills on game with the 28 is 35 yards. You could stretch this to 40 yards only by using extra-hard, high antimony (or plated) lead shot. But the question soon arises: If you want 40-yard performance, why aren't you using the 20 gauge?

When shooting a 28, as can well be imagined, a light, short-barreled 6 to 6½ lb., autoloader, pump or over/under is a delight to carry in the field and swing in the close quarters of heavy cover. The little 28 gauge recommends itself for precisely any field hunting situation where a premium is placed upon portability, quickness of swing, and close-range patterning potential from the shotgun. And for those who just want to "play," the 28 offers a whole new world of reloading and shooting experiences.

In 28 gauge, the Skeet/Skeet or IC/M choke combo for side-by-sides or over/unders is strictly a 25-yards-or-less affair for clean kills on quail, dove, woodcock or grouse. The M/F combo, however, enables the 28 to reach out to a full 40 yards with ¾-ounce, or better yet, ⅞-ounce handloads of copper- or nickel-plated 6s or 5s for ducks over decoys, close-range pheasants or close-flushing chukars.

Finally, if for no other reason than you may be searching for an ultra-low recoiling, close-range shotgun, the 28 is by far the better choice over the .410. As experienced shooters will tell you, the little 28 just shoots better and kills better than it ought to. For the good shooter, the 28 gauge will always remain a delightful challenge.   ●

THE PSYCHOLOGY OF Skeet and Trap Reloading

Proper handloading techniques cannot improve a shooter's score – only shooting can!

by ART BLATT
Field Editor, *Guns & Ammo Magazine*

WHY DO competitive shotgunners handload their ammunition? Do they actually reduce their shooting costs substantially? Possibly. Can one actually recreate a loaded shotshell equal to or better than a factory-loaded shell? Unlikely. Can a super-serious and fastidious handloader create a special shotshell load that will enable him to break a better score than a normally-produced reload or even a factory-loaded shell? Hell no! *There's never been a shotshell devised that will break or even chip a target if the shooter doesn't point his scattergun properly.* In over 20 years of competitive trap and Skeet shooting, I've never hit a target by shooting along side of it, under it, over the top of (and certainly not by shooting behind) it. Therefore, regardless of the certainty of the home-grown handload, if you point left and the target flies right, there's no magic or heat-seeking shot swarm which will home in on the target by itself.

Proper handloading techniques cannot improve a shooter's score—only shooting can up one's average. There are no shortcuts to becoming a proficient tournament shooter—it takes years of hard, dedicated work and thousands of rounds of ammunition.

So why, then, do competitive trap and Skeet shooters tie up hundreds of dollars in reloading equipment, spend countless hours at a loading bench and make thousands of shells year after year? Most shooters/handloaders will answer— "economics!" Unfortunately, people who believe this answer are shooting under the delusion of "misguided" economics and I'll prove it to you.

Depending on the area in which you live, it

Today's plastic wads (left to right) from Remington, Winchester and Federal are designed specifically for their own proprietary cases. Shot-to-shot consistency is the competitor's edge—you won't get it by mixing and matching components.

costs between 8¢ and 12¢ to reload a 12 gauge shotshell with 1⅛ ounces of "hard" shot—and this does not include the initial investment of the empty hull. For comparison purposes, let's take an average and state that it costs $2.50 to reload a box of shells, or 10¢ per round. This formula—on the surface—seemingly makes reloading a "profitable" enterprise as a case of Winchester AA shells sells for about $80 or $4 per box. If the shooter saves all his plastic empties, there are countless buyers willing to purchase them at $4 to $5 per hundred which would actually reduce the cost of a case of shells by $20 to $25. The bottom line for a case of shells would set a shooter back between $55 and $60. Earlier, we stated that it costs about $50 per reloaded case of shells, so the handloader is saving between $5 to $10 per case—or is he?

Reloading equipment isn't inexpensive. High-speed shotshell loaders range from about $300 to $750 and it takes a pile of use to redeem one's investment. And, how about an inventory of wads, primers, powder and shot? Any serious handloader can quickly tie up about $1,000 in equipment and components. If this same $1,000 was set aside in a high-yield savings account, the interest earned would equal the cost difference between reloading shotshells and purchasing factory fodder; and, finally, if the handloader decides to sell his equipment, he would be indeed lucky if he could recover 40¢ on each dollar invested. So, from the purely financial aspect of reloading, we can ultimately prove that reloading is a poor investment. So why then do we still continue to load shotshells? Because, it is a relaxing way to get away from the pressures of modern society. A few hours spent in the garage or basement concocting a case of shells from a wide assortment of ingredients is a satisfying chore. And let's face it, reloading *is* a chore. Pulling an operating handle a few thousand times in a few hours can be tiring and we'd all much rather have a topless go-go dancer do our work while we oversee the operation—right?

The key word to quality handloading is *consistency*. Regardless of the load that a shooter settles for, it must be consistent from one loading

(Above and right) Burning up ammo requires lots of cases. The rules of most clubs state that once a hull hits the ground, it belongs to the club. A simple snap-on device like the one shown is inexpensive and serves to provide you—not the club—with the hulls you'll need.

When reloading, be sure to follow the recommendations set down by the manufacturer. The new Eclipse shotshells shown here come with factory loading info. The author used their recommendations in making up some loads that worked perfectly. He also turned out some Eclipse reloads using other components—they didn't work too well! *Follow the manufacturers' instructions!*

session to the next. Remember, there's no shotshell load that will shoot around corners or dip in the middle of its flight path when the elusive clay target hits a chuckhole in the air. There will be times—if you shoot long enough—that God's breath will snatch a target away from you. It's not your fault. It's part of either game—trap or Skeet—if you participate when windy conditions prevail. The most practical and easiest method to produce best-quality handloads is to follow the factory's recommendations. If you prefer a certain brand—be it Federal, Winchester or Remington—stick with the factory components. If you like the way Peters Blue Magic hulls work in both your shotgun and loading press, use only factory-manufactured or recommended components. This includes wads, shot and primers. If you prefer Winchester AA hulls, then one would achieve excellent results using Winchester components.

Handloaders who deviate from factory recommendations are not taking advantage of the factory's expertise and knowledge. These huge companies hire full-time ballisticians and use test equipment (that is not available to the shooting public) to both prove and *disprove* all types of

shotshell handloads. These munitions makers have been successfully turning out millions of shotshells for decades and with little or no problem. Can any of us handloaders make a similar claim? So, instead of pooh-poohing factory instruction sheets and making a half-baked attempt to develop different loads, stick with the numbers provided by the factories.

(Right) Federal paper-tube hulls make excellent reloads but their life expectancy is quite a bit shorter than their plastic counterparts. After two or three firings, the paper tube usually separates from the metal head. If you expect more from your components than they can provide, you'll be inviting disaster during a match.

O.K., let's assume that you have a batch of choice, clean empty cases with matching components—save for shot. What size shot is best for 16-yard trapshooting? Let me share a couple of incidents with you and you can make up your own mind. Over 20 years ago, I used to be extremely nit-picky about handloads. I had developed (?) four special concoctions for trapshooting—one load for singles (16 yards) 2¾ drams, 1⅛ ounces of No. 8 shot and another for handicap (24 yards) 3 drams, 1⅛ ounces of No. 7½ shot. For doubles, I came up with a very light 2¾ dram load of 8s for the first shot and a heavier 3 dram load of 7½s for the second barrel. For almost two years I faithfully stuck to these "perfect" loads and enjoyed moderate success. At one particular trapshoot I accidently grabbed my "handicap" loads and proceeded to break my first 100 straight at 16-yard targets. I noticed that during this event, I had chipped quite a few targets—more than normally. However, the fact that I also recorded my first 100x100 overshadowed my convictions regarding handloading of shotshells. Using the "wrong" load went against everything holy and sacred about handloading for a specific purpose—or was it simply "my day?"

A few years ago, while attending the California State trapshoot in Kingsburg, California, I made another astonishing realization: Some months earlier, I had purchased a case of Remington RXP 2¾ dram shells loaded with 1⅛ ounces of No. 9s. This was definitely a Skeet load and it was used to test some Skeet guns. I had 8 boxes left and as the weather was calm and dry, I decided to use these shells in the opening day event—200 singles targets. My squadmates told me I was making a big mistake and that "light nines" just wouldn't get the job done. I ran 182 straight targets until the trap puller called my first and only "lost" of the day to record an excellent, and somewhat surprising 199x200 for the event. Is shot size all that important?

Two years ago when I was Associate Editor for *Guns & Ammo* magazine, fellow staffer Dave Hetzler and I participated in a unique shotshell reloading/shooting test. We loaded and fired 10 shells each of Winchester AAs, Peters Blue Magics and Federal Champion IIs. Every shot was fired over an Oehler Model 33 chronograph to determine muzzle (instrumental) velocity and each shell was loaded and fired until it became

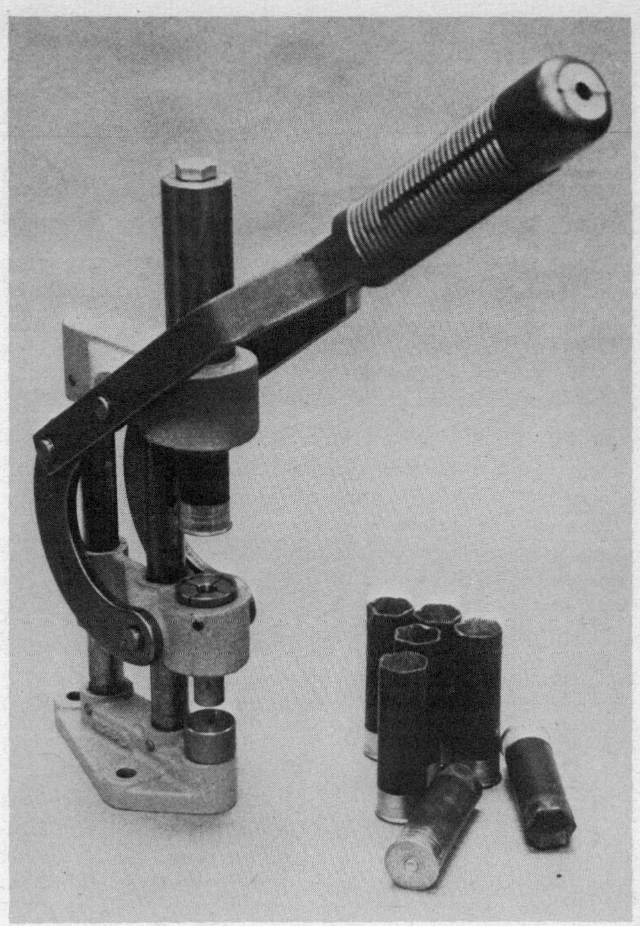

If you use a pump or autoloader, you can lose your concentration quickly if a jam takes place during the heat of competition. A tool like the RCBS Shotshell Reconditioner helps eliminate jams as it insures properly sized case heads.

absolutely useless, i.e., when the front of the mouth was completely shot away and no crimp could be formed or if the primer pockets became too enlarged to hold a primer. Cases that were split—some from neck to base—were used as pressures didn't seem to drop drastically even with gaps in the hull. We later talked to a ballistician at Federal and he explained why we didn't lose a great deal of pressure. When the powder is ignited and during obturation, the skirt on the plastic wad effectively seals the split in the case when exiting the hull. Very little pressure (hence, velocity) was lost through the split in the case, although these enlarged cases were difficult to chamber in a single barrel Perazzi trapgun. We continued to load and fire all the test hulls until the Winchester AA hulls would no longer hold a crimp. The Blue Magics "petered-out" after 21 firings. The Champion IIs succumbed after 19

Handloading alone is not the answer when it comes to running 100 straight. There's no substitute for practice; and, the best practice is shooting in competitive events.

firings while the AAs lasted until the 37th firing. Every hull in this test was in deplorable condition, yet they all produced muzzle velocities within 10 percent of factory ammo. And, they also patterned within 8 percent of factory ammo. At the conclusion of this exhausting 3-day test, we decided to load up 25 of the most miserable looking hulls and see how they would do in "battle." We went out to a local trap and Skeet range and tried to round up some volunteers to help us "test" our ammo. Shooters shied away from us like we had the plague and many mumbled that we were going to blow up a nice, relatively new trapgun. Unquestionably, I was bearing down and concentrating more intently than normal as I wanted to break a big score. Guess what? Right, a perfect 25x25 was recorded. I was absolutely thrilled!

Those in attendance simply shook their heads in disbelief to what they had just witnessed. Again, I wish to drive home an important point: There's *no substitute for shooting practice,* regardless of the quality of shell being fired.

Another sacred cow is the pattern board.

Nearly all those who load use the antiquated pattern board as their supreme testing device. Like many other "proven facts," the pattern board does not include, nor can divulge, the most important aspect regarding shotshell patterns; that is, how many pellets are *eligible* to strike a flying clay at a given distance. We cannot measure *shot string* with a pattern board. At 40 yards, is a shot string 8, 12 or 15 feet in length? What is better, to have a long or short shot string? Can shot string lengths be tailored to serve a shooter's purpose by handloading? For my shooting, I prefer to have a long shot string for handicap trapshooting and a short string for Skeet shooting. In trap, where the target is always going downrange, I want the extra margin of performance and tolerance of having pellets stretched out to 15 feet or so. The opposite is what I'd prefer for short-range Skeet shooting as I want a round cloud of shot surrounding the target. Up to now, there's no inexpensive equipment available to the average shotgunner to accurately measure shot string length at various ranges. So we shotgunners are left to fend for ourselves and prove our loaded shotshells on flying targets.

Another fallacy connected with the pattern board is determining a shotgun's point of impact. Normally, a black spot is set in the middle of the pattern paper and we step back 40 paces to touch one off. At the time of firing, we consciously take a "death grip" on the gun, cheek it as tightly as possible and then shoot. However, during an actual shooting event, we are holding the shotgun differently—usually looser and with the head and eyes more erect than the unnatural position we assume at the pattern board. The results we achieve on the pattern board "appear" to be right on—a 50/50 pattern. However, when we are shooting either trap or Skeet, our line of sight is actually higher than what we artifically created at the pattern board.

There have been numerous occassions when shooters have fired some excellent scores with a pet gun and then made the mistake of shooting it at a pattern board. The result of seeing that favorite smoothbore produce irregular patterns is usually unsettling at best. If you have developed shooting confidence and faith in a particular gun, don't shoot it at a pattern board. If you do, you'll probably either sell that gun or your high scores will quickly plummet. *A person's mind can play funny tricks when it comes to shooting.*

And speaking of mind-boggling occurrences, have you ever had a "blooper" go off during a competitive event? We've all had one or two. As the first blooper is fired. I can assure you your mind will concentrate on the rest of the shells in your pouch. This is another negative aspect regarding handloading for competition.

Recently, there's been quite a bit of conversation about 1-ounce trap and Skeet loads for 12-gauge shotguns. The 1-ounce proponents claim many advantages of reduced "felt" recoil, lower shooting costs and better patterns. I agree with the first two claims, but totally disagree with the third "virtue." If we are governed by rules and regulations from both the ATA and NSSA which allow 1⅛ ounces of shot, no larger than No. 7½s, why not play the game to the hilt. Why should we purposely handicap ourselves? The game is difficult enough unless you have a 100 percent average. The 1-ounce load is great on upland small game like quail and dove, but for breaking targets, load all the shot you can legally use.

How about shot sizes? Let's borrow a quote from a fabled white hunter who was asked by his client, "Why do you carry a 600 Nitro Express?" The professional replied, "Because they don't make a 700 Nitro Express!" The same holds true for both trap and Skeet shooting—bigger is better in the long run. How many targets have we all shot at *and hit* even though they continued on their merry way leaving a puff of dust in their wake? Most of the time this common occurrence happened because the shooter felt that he made a mistake and either mispointed his gun or was using the wrong load. Often, the culprit in this scenario is the target. Ten years ago, practically

The Beco Shell Scope enables the handloader to view through a plastic shell—with the aid of a high-intensity light—to see if the wad is "tipped" or to check and make certain that the shell contains powder and shot. It's a handy little device that helps assure top quality and consistency in your reloads.

Is hard shot better than soft shot? You bet! High antimony content (about 6 percent) helps to reduce pellet deformation while exiting the shotgun barrel. Even though "hard" shot is more expensive, it's worth it in the long run. There's nothing worse than watching a shot charge raise dust off a flying claybird—it can ruin your concentration, as well as your score.

The Ponsness-Warren Model 800B is a quality reloading press capable of turning out large quantities of shotshells in a short time. A single operator can easily average 500 shells per hour—complete with a coffee break.

all day targets were left in their natural black color. Today, most target manufacturers and gun clubs offer colored targets. All of these colored targets are painted in various hues of white, green, orange, yellow or red. I hate to break the news, but, the painting process reinforces the target and makes it harder to break during the manufacturing process, the packaging, the transportation and *in the air*. Today's harder targets have helped gun clubs to reduce their operating costs by lowering the "breakage" factor and target manufacturers have eliminated a large portion of the protective packaging requirements. To overcome the target hardness problem, you should use the largest size shot legally available (7½s) for both Skeet and trap shooting. A single No. 7½ pellet has 30 percent more energy at 40 yards than a single No. 8 pellet. Believe me, today's targets require a good deal of energy to break them.

For over a decade, I've advocated the use of a maximum load for both trap and Skeet shooting: 3 drams equivalent with 1⅛ ounces of 7½ shot. I use this same load for all competitive 12-gauge shooting, be it Skeet, 16-yard singles, 27 yard handicap or a pair of shots on doubles. I *know* what this particular load will do—it eliminates all the variables and I never have to change the setting on my Ponsness-Warren 800B. (Yes, believe it or not, I reload too!) I use one brand of shell, wad, primer, powder and shot and I've noticed a steady increase in my shooting averages.

From a base of 20 years of competitive shotgunning experience, I've come to the conclusion that reloading has, if nothing else, a couple of things going for it. First, it offers (to some shooters) a psychological edge, albeit a misconceived edge. Secondly, that "misconceived edge" provides the shooter with a perceived sense of "dollars saved" and "more shells to shoot."

These two "shooter perceptions" psychologically force the shooter into a position of shooting, shooting, shooting. The Russians have a saying that goes, "The Father of Education is discipline, the mother of learning is *repetition*." I won't argue, especially where "repetition" is concerned.

As a Skeet and trap shooter, you can be assured there is no magic in reloading and no Holy Grail of handloads. If you reload a lot, you will *shoot a lot*—therein lies your psychological edge. When you stand in front of your press, you don't have to genuflect, you only have to turn out loads that are *consistent* and take *every advantage* of the commandments carved in stone by the ATA and NSSA. That, my friends, is the psychology of Skeet and trap shooting. ●

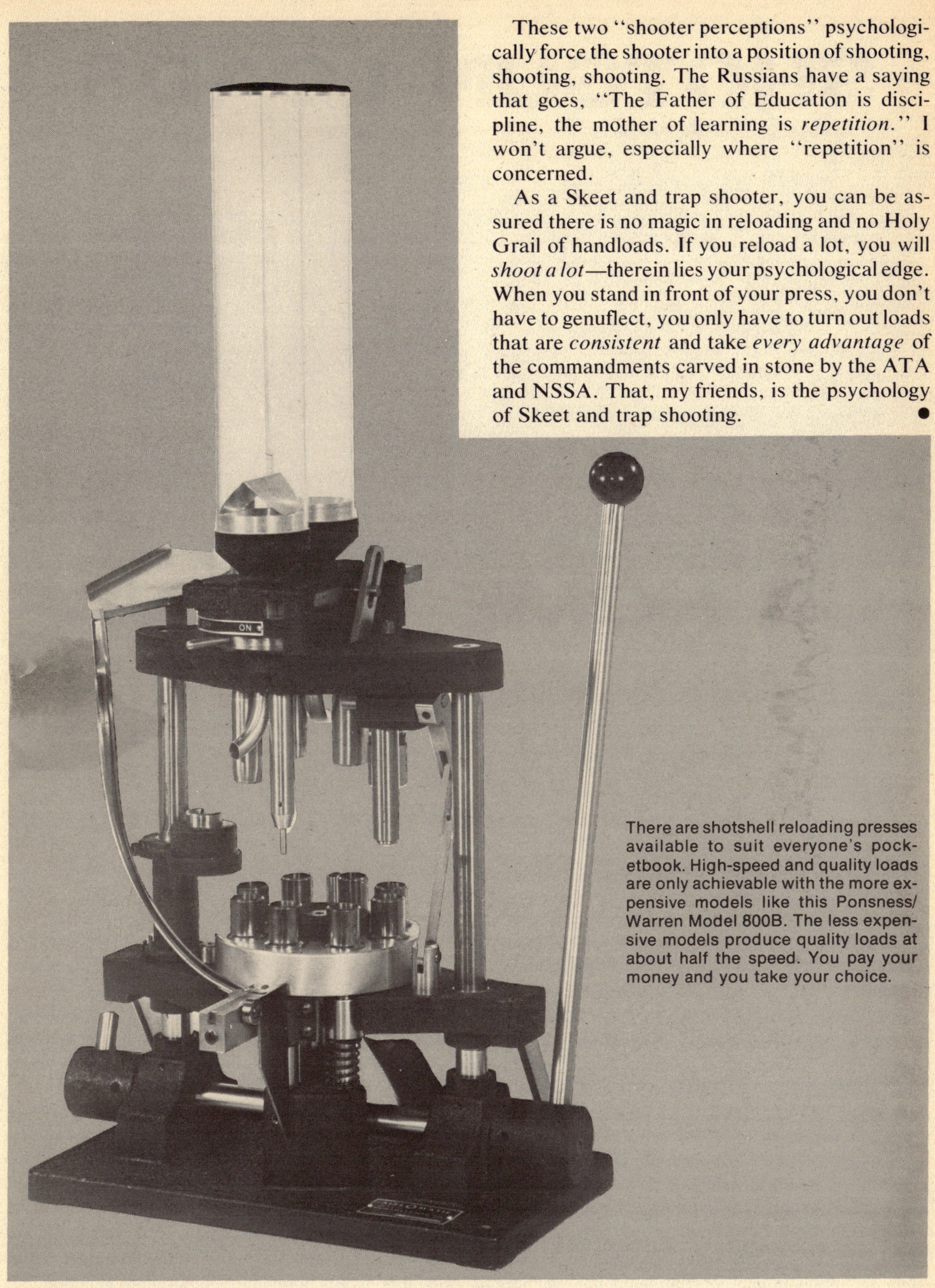

There are shotshell reloading presses available to suit everyone's pocketbook. High-speed and quality loads are only achievable with the more expensive models like this Ponsness/Warren Model 800B. The less expensive models produce quality loads at about half the speed. You pay your money and you take your choice.

SHOTGUN LOADS

FOR HOME DEFENSE

by DICK EADES

A fistful of buckshot may not be the best choice when turning out home defense reloads. But here's what does work.

AT LEAST once a month, someone asks, "What kind of gun should I buy for home defense?" More often than not, I get a skeptical look when I recommend a shotgun. More specifically, I recommend a *big bore shotgun,* as big as the person who wants the gun can reasonably handle. For defensive use, no smooth bore smaller than 20 gauge should even be considered.

Most non-gun-enthusiasts who want a gun to keep at home seem to expect to be told to purchase some sort of handgun. In fact, the question as to which gun to buy is often just a query as to caliber. "Should I buy a .25 or a .38?" Frankly, under conditions of stress, almost any firearm is more practical than a handgun. There's a mys-

tique surrounding handguns that persists despite their very limited utility in the hands of a novice.

Before some dyed-in-the-wool pistolero comes looking for me with blood in his eye, let me elaborate on that last statement. Sure, an *experienced* handgunner can rely on his pistol or revolver anytime he has need of a weapon. If he is proficient with it, he can stop almost any animal on two or four legs in a matter of seconds. A handgun is easily portable, can be kept concealed until it is needed and is by far the most convenient type of firearm to keep close at hand. Unfortunately, few people are natural pistol shots. Top handgunners usually got that way by countless hours of arduous practice, spread over a number of years.

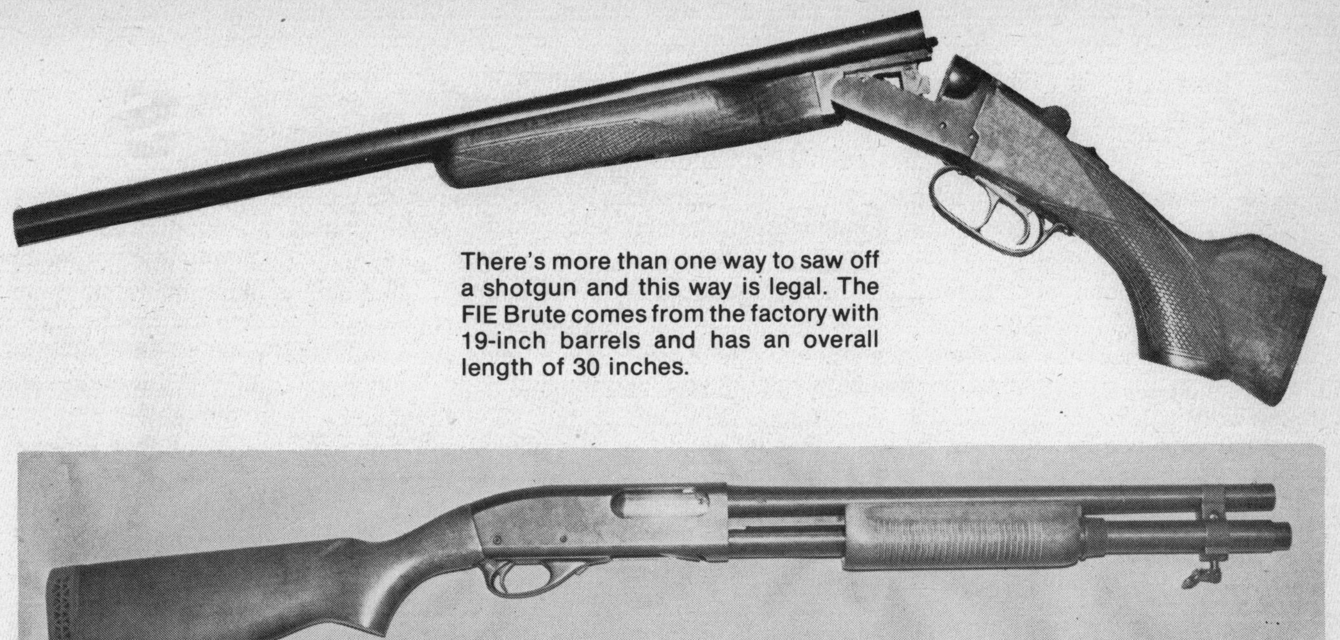

There's more than one way to saw off a shotgun and this way is legal. The FIE Brute comes from the factory with 19-inch barrels and has an overall length of 30 inches.

A slide action riot gun, like this Remington 870 with extended magazine tube, holds six 12-gauge shells and should serve to intimidate almost any prowler.

For the inexperienced shooter, a shotgun is a far more practical defensive weapon than either a rifle or handgun. For the homeowner who hopes to protect himself, his family or his property, the shotgun is an ideal choice. True, it isn't as portable as a handgun. It isn't readily concealable, either. As for portability when it comes to home protection, fear not—you won't be carrying it very far. It's just possible that the display of a shotgun would discourage an attacker. A concealed handgun offers no such fringe benefit. Finally, so long as the shotgun is kept in an easily accessible spot, there's no need to carry it around. Few instances requiring the use of a firearm for defense develop without some sort of warning. The sound of forced entry or strange voices warn of intrusion and permit time to pick up a conveniently stored shotgun.

After I have convinced a prospective gun purchaser that he really should choose a shotgun, I must usually sell him away from the use of buckshot loads for it. Buckshot is fine for police or military use. It may also have a place for hunting in some areas but it is impractical for home defense. Any threat that occurs in the home will demand the use of a firearm at ranges measured in feet, not yards. A firearm that will neutralize an assailant across a large room should be sufficient. For home use, small shot out performs buckshot in many ways.

The case against buckshot for home defense is simple and clear cut. Buck loads contain very few shot, each large enough to do considerable damage when they strike. In a confined area, such as an ordinary room, buckshot is likely to do as much damage to the surroundings as to the intended target. Most homes are walled inside with gypsum filled wallboard or sheetrock, the thickness of which varies with local building codes. However, it's unusual to find residential walls built of board thicker than ½-inch.

A 12-gauge load of 00 Buckshot contains 12 pellets, each weighing about 53 grains. Each pellet is roughly .320-inch in diameter and departs the muzzle at approximately 1150-1200 fps. At short ranges—15 to 25 feet—the pellets will penetrate six or more thicknesses of common wallboard over 2″ X 4″ pine studs. Buckshot pellets can be expected to pass through three such walls before their energy is expended. Such excessive penetration would pose a hazard to other occupants of a house if a buckshot load should be fired inside.

Small shot, such as that used for Skeet or trap,

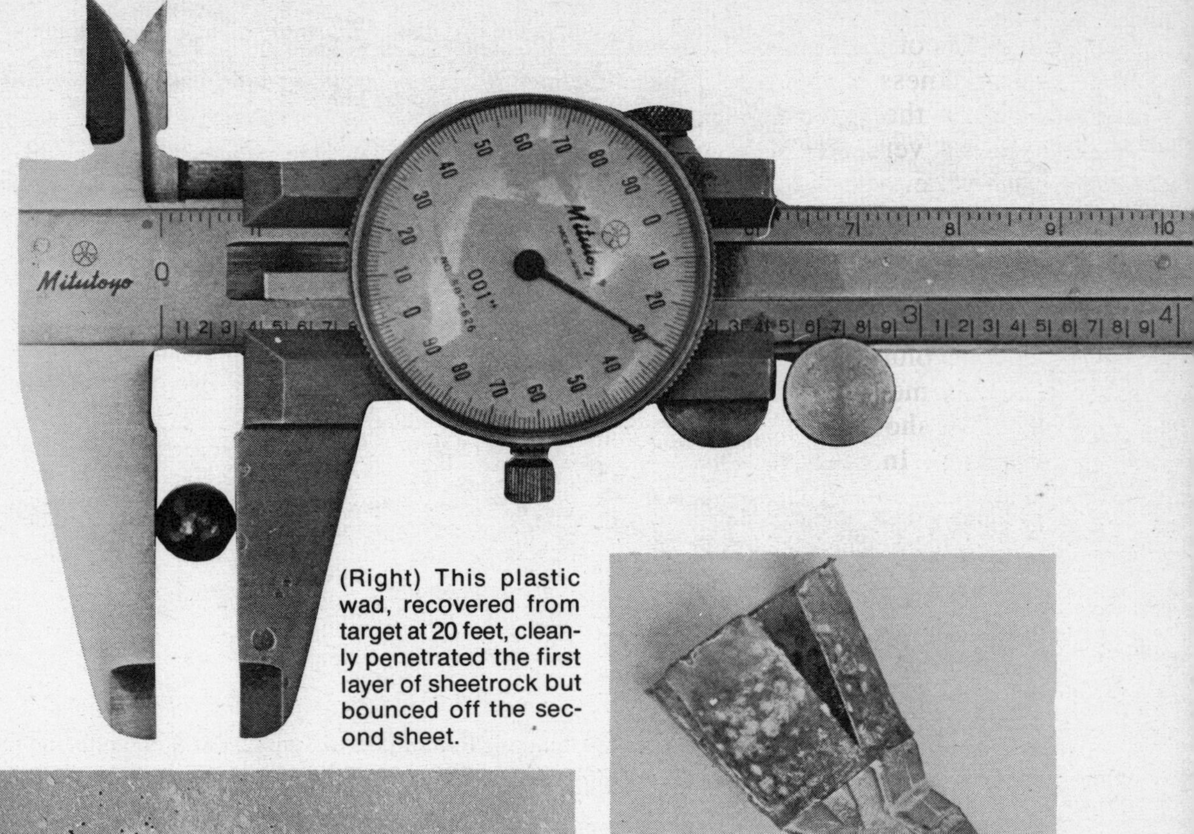

Double-aught Buckshot measures .330-inch in diameter and has too much penetration potential for average home use. Smaller shot—No. 8 or 9—will do the job quite well.

(Right) This plastic wad, recovered from target at 20 feet, cleanly penetrated the first layer of sheetrock but bounced off the second sheet.

(Left) This piece of wall board was ventilated at a range of 20 feet by 1-ounce load of No. 8 shot. The hole measures about 3½ × 4½ inches with very few shot outside a 5-inch circle. Shot was fired from an IC barrel. No shot penetrated third thickness of board and most were stopped inside the second thickness.

has no such penetration problem. A standard Skeet load of No. 9 shot fired at 20 feet will cleanly penetrate only one thickness of ½-inch sheetrock. The second thickness will be damaged but very few pellets will make their way completely through it. A third thickness of wallboard completely stops No. 9 pellets with most of them bouncing off the smooth paperboard outer layer. Even those passing through the paper layer have too little retained energy to do much damage if they should strike a person after passing through the first and second sheets of wallboard.

Effective range and penetration of shot varies almost directly in proportion to the size of shot used. At extremely short ranges, choke seems to have little if any effect on penetration although it makes a remarkable difference in pattern size at even a few feet.

At short range, velocity is high enough to insure damage from any size shot. During tests on sheets of wallboard, even the plastic wads used in modern shotshell loads passed through one thickness every time. In no case did the wad do more than dent the second thickness of board. One small sample of factory-loaded shotshells employed cork wads as a cushion; even small fragments of the cork were deeply buried in the first thickness of sheetrock. One must conclude that even the lightest projectile (smallest shot) would be very effective against an intruder at close range.

The reloader will find another advantage to small shot versus buckshot. The metering chamber or measure of a shotshell loading machine is designed to produce uniform charges of small shot by volume. The space occupied by small shot in a measuring device will hold the same weight of shot, plus or minus a few grains, time after time. In order to handload buckshot, you

single No. 9 shot as 2.4 foot pounds with an initial velocity of 1200 fps. Using this formula, it doesn't take too much arithmetic to multiply the total number of shot in a shell times the energy of each pellet to arrive at total shot-charge energy. For example, a 12-gauge Skeet load of 1⅛ ounces of shot contains about 710 pellets. To calculate total energy, multiply 710 times 2.4. The answer to that one is 1704 foot pounds. Since a .44 Magnum cartridge fired from a 6-inch barrel generates only about 1100 foot pounds of muzzle energy, it's easy to see that a shotgun loaded with small shot is a rather nifty "house broom."

Although any load of small shot makes an ef-

From left to right: 12 gauge, 3-inch Magnum loaded with 00 buckshot; Winchester AA Skeet shell with No. 9 shot and Federal 20 gauge with No. 7½ shot. Of the three, the Skeet load is most practical for home defense.

will probably find it necessary to literally "handload" the shot charge, then return the shell to the machine for crimping.

Handloads for defensive use may be constructed from ordinary components used by most target shooters and hunters. If you are a Skeet shooter who customarily uses modest loads of Red Dot or Green Dot powder behind 1 to 1⅛ ounces of shot, there's no need to rush out for additional bushings. A normal load of 1⅛ ounces of No. 9 shot in a 12-gauge shotgun is just as good for discouraging a prowler as for smashing clay targets.

One ballistics table lists the muzzle energy of a

fective weapon of your favorite shotgun, there are ways to increase performance. It's not necessary to become an authority on exterior ballistics to learn what factors affect shot patterns. Choke, of course, is the most common method of regulating pattern size. Full choke usually assures holding the smallest pattern at any realistic range while a true cylinder bore gives the widest dispersion of shot. It has also been proven that heavy shot loads produce a wider spread than light loads. The difference is not great but it does exist. An average 12-bore, full choke shotgun using a 1-ounce load of No. 8 shot will print a pattern about 9 inches in diameter at 30 feet. The

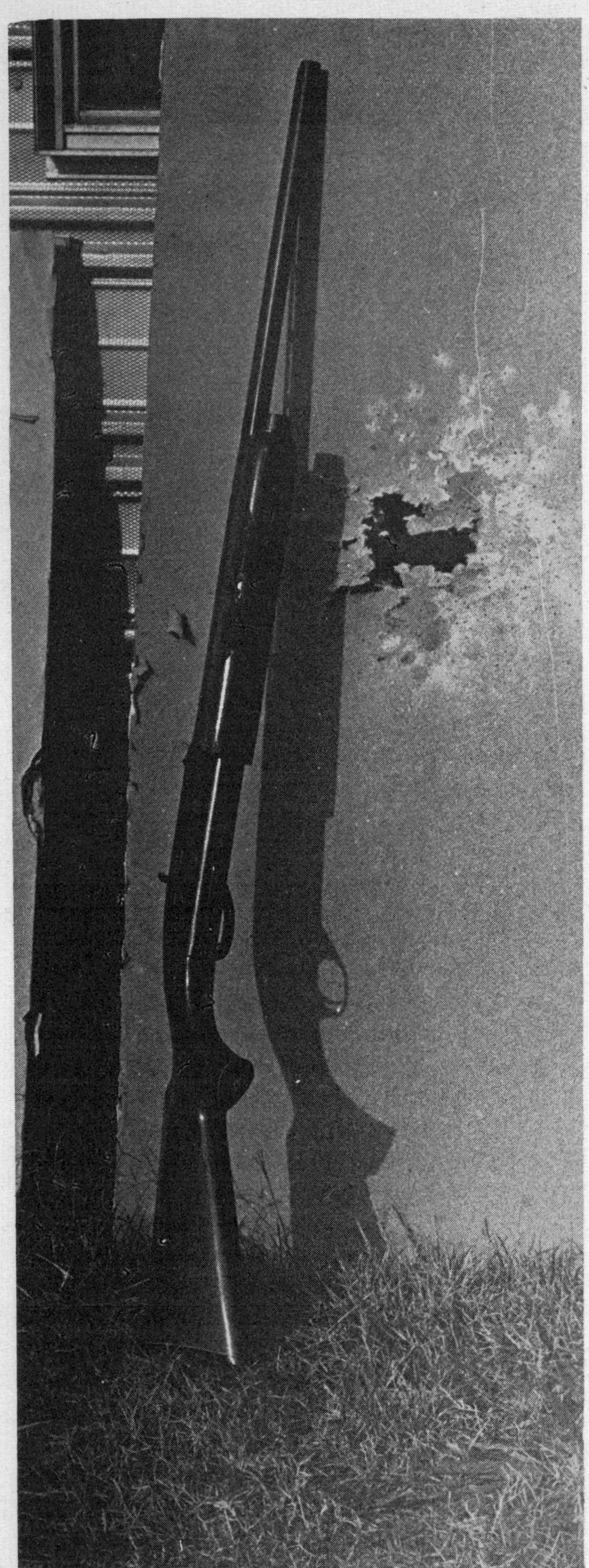

Remington 1100 20 gauge with Improved Cylinder made this impressive hole in wall board at 20 feet. Load was 1 ounce of No. 7½ shot.

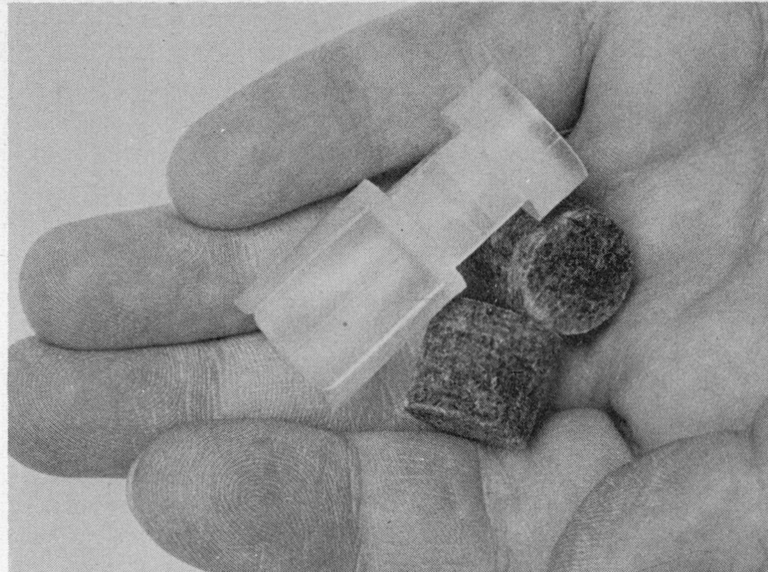

Old-style, one-piece wads produce larger patterns at any range than newer plastic wad with built-in shot protector. Your reloads should be built for dispersion, not density.

same gun, with a 1⅛-ounce shot charge will pattern about 10 inches at the same distance while an increase to 1⅜ ounces will produce a 13-inch pattern. Variables in barrels, degrees of choke and loading will change pattern sizes from those mentioned above but the trend to wider patterns from heavy-shot charges will remain constant.

Shotshells loaded *without* plastic shot protector sleeves or wads will also print wider patterns than those loaded *with* shot protectors. In this case, the wider dispersion is caused by a greater percentage of deformed shot in the charge. Most hunters load to keep deformation of shot to a minimum since they want uniform, dense patterns. For home defense loads, wide dispersion may be more desirable than uniform patterns.

Spreader loads have been available in factory shotshell loads for years. They are also called "brush loads" or "special upland loads." The handloader can easily duplicate them. All of the above loads depend on the use of card inserts in the shot column to interfere with normal flight and spread the shot as it emerges from the muzzle. One type uses two or three thin card wads similar to those employed as over-shot wads in old, rolled-crimp shells. They are layered into the shot charge to divide it approximately into quarters as the shot is inserted into the hull. The other uses card stock to quarter the shot charge verti-

Silhouette target took one load of 00 Buck and a 1¼-ounce load of No. 9 shot from a cylinder bore gun. The large hole in right edge of "5X" ring was made by the wad.

cally in the shell. In application, the card stock is fitted into the hull to form an "X" from the over-powder wad to the base of the crimp and shot poured into all segments of the "X" before closing the crimp.

Spreader loads will work to increase pattern size from any shotgun, regardless of choke. Actual change is unpredictable from gun to gun but you can rely on a substantial increase in pattern size. A full-choke barrel will usually print patterns between modified and improved cylinder with spreader loads, while cylinder-bore guns often show a 25-30 percent size increase.

Handloading shotshells for defensive use differs little from loading for hunting use except that a failure to fire could have much more serious results. If a shell fizzles on a covey rise, it may mean the loss of a quail or two. An oversized hull that won't quite chamber might even delay your hunt until you can get tools to clear a stoppage.

The same symptoms in a defense load could lead to loss of property or even life, depending upon the charitable nature of an assailant. With this in mind, there's no place for sloppy techniques in loading for defensive purposes.

Each hull should be deprimed, then carefully inspected before loading. This may result in an extra step if progressive loading equipment is used but it's worth the time invested. Check the hull for debris inside that could block the primer flash hole and for incipient breaks in the case wall and head. When possible, use only once-fired hulls and segregate them from your practice loads.

Constant visual checks should be maintained while loading is in progress, being especially watchful for uniform height of powder charges and wad seating depth. If modern reloading machines have a shortcoming, it's the occasional trait of failing to drop a full powder charge. After reloading is completed, an external inspection

Before loading, hulls should be inspected for tears, incipient cracks and debris that could block flash hole. New, or once-fired empties are your best bet.

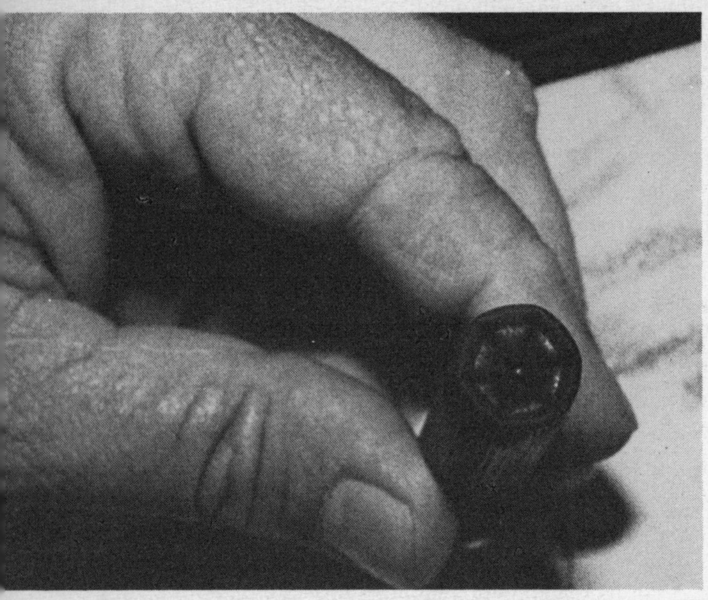

Reloads should be inspected during loading operation. Check crimp carefully.

should be made of each shell. This time, each crimp should be inspected, looking for improper closure or uneven folds. The case body should be smooth and free of bulges; and, the rim should be the same thickness around its circumference and exhibit no indication of stretching or cracking.

The ultimate test, aside from firing, is to check each round through the action of your shotgun. For this purpose, be sure that your test is made outside with the muzzle pointed in a safe direction. Simply load the magazine and work each shell through the feeding, loading, extraction and ejection cycle. Some autoloaders are difficult to manipulate with sufficient force to eject a loaded shell but most can be made to perform if handled carefully. There are a few that are designed to prevent cycling manually. If your favorite autoloader happens to be one of these, check each

Loading with a progressive machine is a fast way to produce a large quantity of shells; however, high-volume production is not usually needed for home protection reloads.

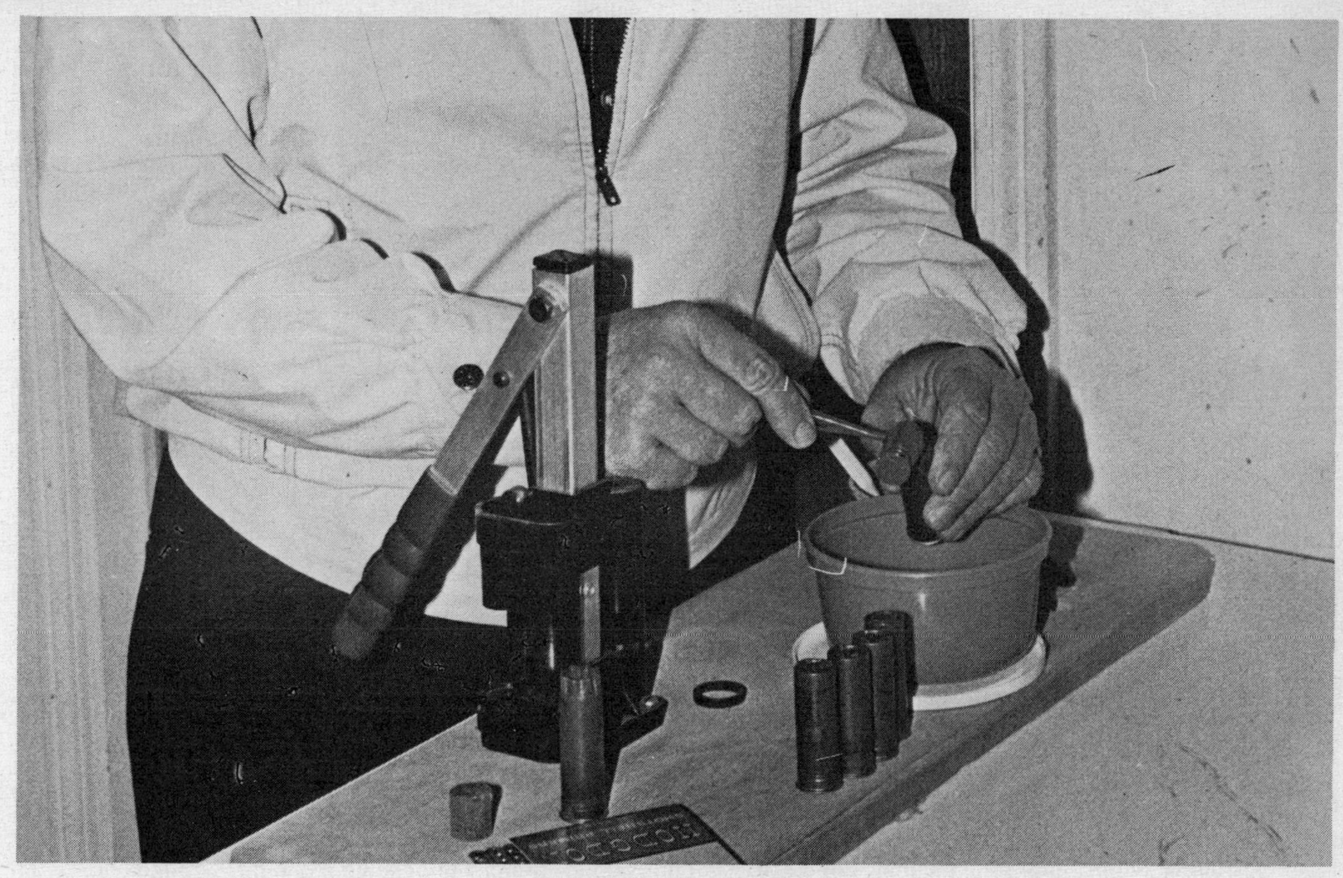

The least expensive loader on the market, Lee Precision's Load-All Jr., produces top quality reloads and permits detailed inspection at all stages.

shell for chambering and extraction. Guns equipped with magazine cutoffs that can't be defeated for test purposes will almost invariably handle any shell that can be manually chambered.

Non-handloaders who want to build their own shotshells for home use can get into the act with very little expense. It's not necessary to purchase a fancy progressive loader for the limited number of shells required. Lee Precision, Inc., of Hartford, Wisconsin, 53027 offers a machine called the Load-All Junior for about $15 that is capable of producing top quality shotshell reloads. The price tag includes all that's needed for loading except primers, wads, shot and powder. While the Load-All Jr. may not be a practical machine for the target shooter who expends hundreds of shells each month, it will turn out a box of shells in less than ½-hour.

Shooting Times' Reloading Editor, Frank Petrini, has an excellent article in this book that fully outlines reloading on a budget—the Lee Load-All and Load-All Junior are well covered. I would suggest you read it. At the same time I would also suggest you see Tom Turpin's article—again, in this book—on spreader loads. Tom will show you how it's done. If I've managed to get you away from buckshot, and on to the smaller stuff, then I've done my job— perhaps we've even managed to save an innocent life.

If you are serious about home defense, a scattergun with small shot loads is the most effective firearm available. In addition to its efficiency, it poses a visual threat sufficient to stop many unpleasant incidents before they start. Some years ago, I witnessed the transfer from a police armory a number of rickety old pump guns which were being replaced by new, slick models. The department armorer stood by, almost in tears. I couldn't understand his feelings and asked why he hated to see the old guns go. His response was candid. He said, "When an officer stands at the end of a dark alley and shucks the noisy action of one of these old clunkers, everything within hearing stops—*immediately!*" •

Roll Your

Tight chokes don't have to mean tight patterns. Spreader loads are the answer.

by TOM TURPIN

AMONG SHOOTERS and hunters, the mystical pot of gold at the end of the rainbow seems to be the "all around" gun. Literally volumes of material have been published on the subject, not to mention hours of conversation around the campfire devoted to the issue. Although many different methods have been tried, nothing has materialized that is totally satisfactory. In all probability, a totally satisfactory solution will never be developed.

In the field of shotgunning, many ideas have been pursued to provide the one-gun shooter with a suitable firearm for all the scattergun games. Perhaps the closest that we have come to the attainment of that goal is the adjustable choke device, of which there are several types on the market. One type uses an adjustable collet at the muzzle which can be adjusted by simply turning the device. Turning in one direction increases the constriction at the muzzle—turning in the other

Own Spreader Loads

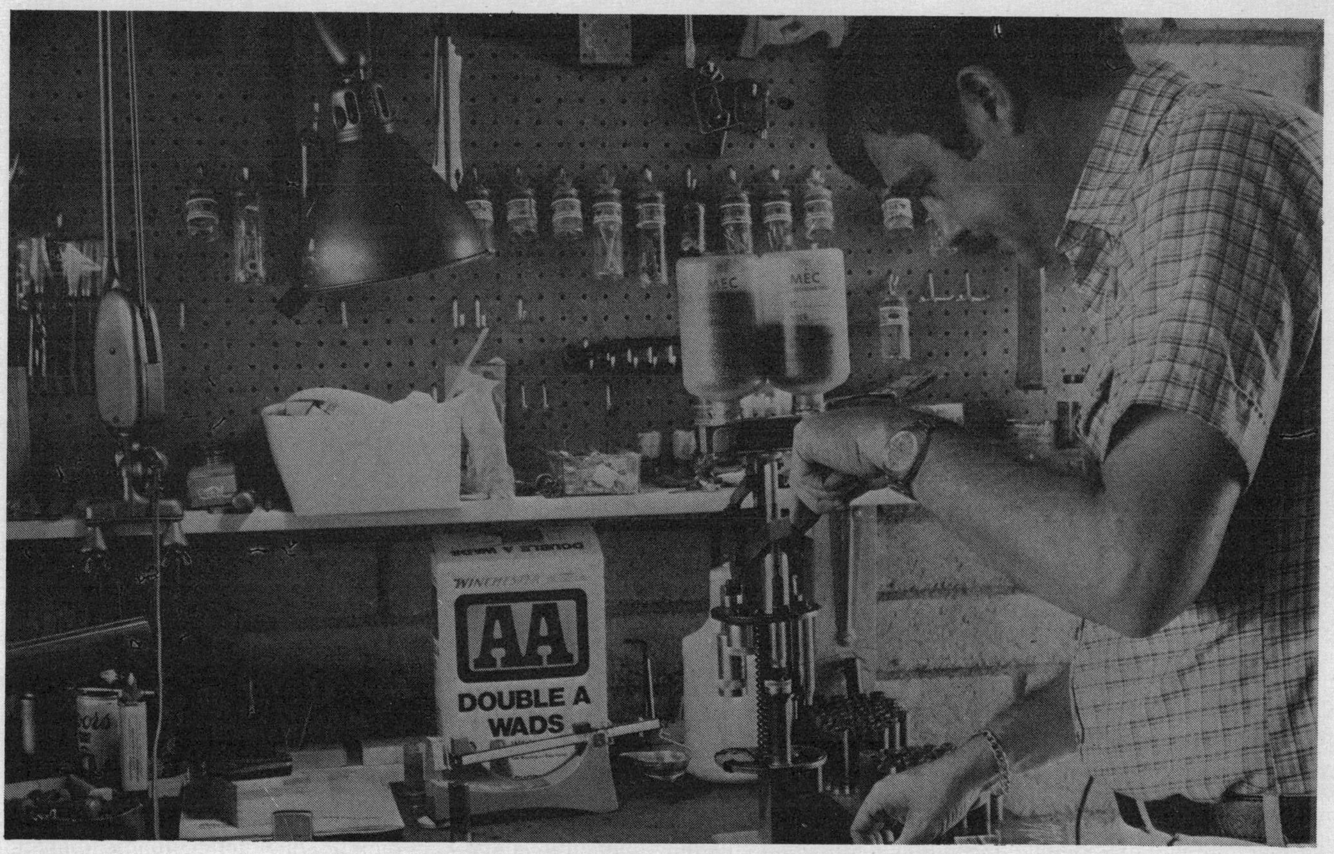

An elaborate reloading setup is not needed for making your own spreader loads. Here, the author is using his MEC 600 Jr.

direction decreases the constriction. In effect, one can change the choke of his gun with a twist of the wrist! Another type that enjoys some success uses removable tubes to change the choke. While this type is not as fast as the collet type, it seems to be equally successful in the market-place.

I even recall a few years ago, perhaps it was even more than a few, there was a collet type adjustable choke on the market that changed settings automatically. It was started with the first shot set at improved cylinder choke; and, when it was fired, the device automatically switched to modified choke for the second shot and to full choke for the third.

Even though both the collet and the removable tube-type choke gizmos work quite well, there is an extremely large segment of the shooting population that does not like them. I suspect the primary reason for the dislike is cosmetic, and

not a lack of efficiency. I recall one of my shooting friends making the statement that these choke devices reminded him of " . . . shooting with a beer can attached to the muzzle of his gun." It's safe to say that many of the adjustable chokes currently on the market are not attractive to a lot of shooters.

There is, however, another method of changing the performance of the shotgun without resorting to the addition of choke tubes, adjustable collets and the like. It has long been known that a given gun will perform differently with changes in ammunition. Even though a gun might be marked full choke, there is certainly no guarantee that it will provide full-choke patterns with all ammunition. In fact, it is not unusual for a given gun to provide improved-cylinder patterns with one load, and full-choke patterns with another. Regardless of what might be stamped on the barrel, the only true indication of the performance of the

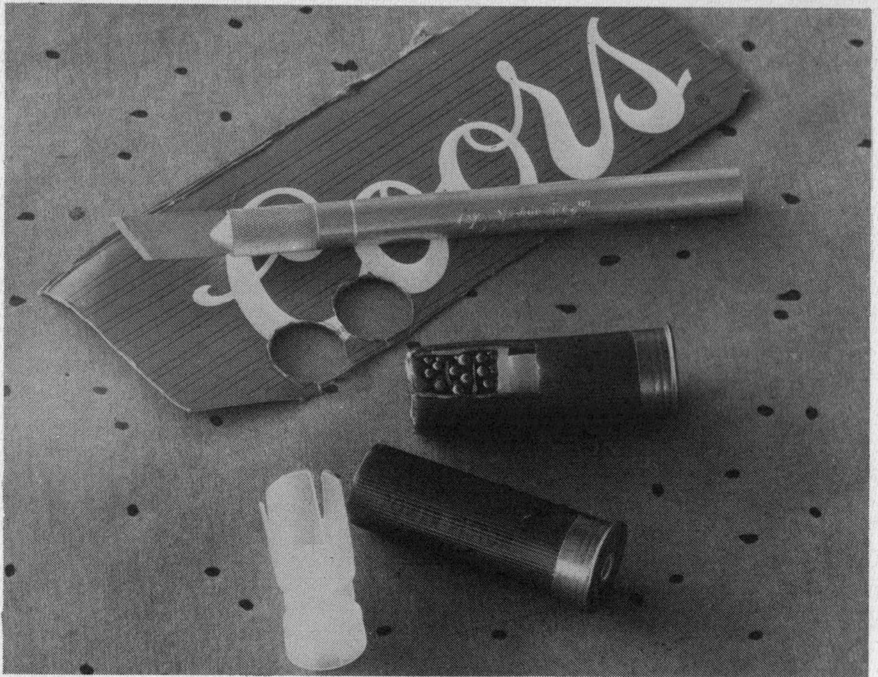

The round-wad type of spreader loading is illustrated here. Note that the cardboard dividers separate the shot into three compartments.

gun is determined at the patterning board. I highly recommend that anyone who is interested in the performance of his scattergun, take it to a patterning board with various loads, and try them all. That alone might very well solve some of the "one gun" problems. (In fact, I highly recommend you see the article on patterning by Don Zutz elsewhere in this book.)

If patterning your gun with various loads does not result in a load that provides sufficient spread for upland hunting, Skeet shooting, or other shotgunning needs requiring more open boring, do not despair! There is something else that can be done to open up the gun's performance. You can turn out your own tailored spreader loads!

Spreader loads are not new. The Belgians at one time loaded a shotshell with square shot! The principle involved was that the square shot would not "lump" together as tightly when traveling down the bore, and when exiting the bore, would have considerably more wind resistance, causing the shot to spread over a wider area (more quickly) than did the traditional round shot. I think there was also an Italian load that utilized a flattened type of shot, on the order of tiny discs rather than round shot. I have never used them, and cannot comment on their effectiveness.

In the absence of square shot and lead discs, there is another approach to convert the tightly-choked scattergun for situations requiring more open chokes. This approach involves adjourning to the reloading bench, and loading up a batch of spreader loads. Manufacturing your own spreader loads is neither difficult, nor does it require any specialized equipment other than a standard shotshell reloader. My own particular reloading tool is a MEC 600 Jr., but any of the tools will work fine.

There are basically two methods of making spreader loads. The first involves the construction of a cardboard "X" to insert in the shotshell, dividing the shot column into four sections. This separation of the shot column facilitates the spreading of the shot column once it leaves the muzzle. The other method also separates the shot column, but does it through the use of small cardboard circles which are alternated with layers of shot in the shell. Both methods work very well, and either will get the job done. I personally prefer to use the "X" method, but only because I find it easier to do. As far as effectiveness goes, I have been unable to detect any significant differences between the two methods.

I recommend trying both methods and selecting the one that best suits your reloading style. With your own particular load and components, it may be that one method will prove to be more effective—in *your* gun—than the other. Again, with my loads, I have been unable to detect any significant differences. Both of these methods are rather simple to do, and require no special tools or equipment. Some thin cardboard, a straight-edge, and a sharp knife or scissors are all that will be needed.

Any thin cardboard stock can be used to make the separators. As an astute observer will note in the accompanying photos, a 6-pack container which originally held a popular brand of beer was the source of my cardboard stock. It has the added advantage of being free, provided you intended to buy the beer anyway! Another excellent material is business card stock. As long as the stock is stiff and not too thick, it will work fine.

Using the base of the wad column as a template, the cylindrical spreader wads can be easily made from a six-pack beer container.

Although a bit counterproductive for spreader loads, I use the one-piece plastic shot cup/wad column in all my shotshell reloading. It is well known that the plastic shot cups tend to tighten patterns. I guess I have just gotten lazy in my old age, as I take the easy route. The pattern board shows clearly that the spreader loads do their job quite well, regardless of the use of the plastic shot cups.

To make the cardboard "X," simply measure the length and width of the shot cup, and cut strips of cardboard slightly undersize from the width of the shotcup. Once that is done, cut the strips to the exact depth of the shot cup. Then, measure the width of each strip to find the center. Using a sharp knife, cut a slit in each strip at the center line, to slightly more than half its length. After that, it is a simple matter to fit the two strips together, forming the "X" cardboard shot separator.

Once the "X's" are made, load the shells in the normal manner until the step is reached where the shot is dropped. At that point, insert one of the "Xs" into the wad before dropping the shot. This will divide the shot cup into four separate compartments; and, since the cardboard takes up some of the volume capacity of the shot cup, it may be necessary to remove a small amount of the shot prior to crimping. Once the crimping operation is completed, set the shell aside or place it in a box marked for spreader loads. Don't get the spreader loads mixed up with your regular loads.

The other method of making spreader loads is almost as simple to do. Instead of cutting the cardboard stock into strips, it is cut into circles. The base of a one-piece wad can be used as a pattern to draw the circles on the cardboard, and scissors used to cut them out. Make two of these circles for each shell to be loaded.

Again, as with the "X" method, load the shell normally until the shot dropping stage. At this point, I drop the shot into the small pan that comes with a RCBS powder scale. Most any other container can be used however. I pour

The "X"-type of spreader load is made by forming a cardboard "X" which serves to separate the shot charge into four compartments.

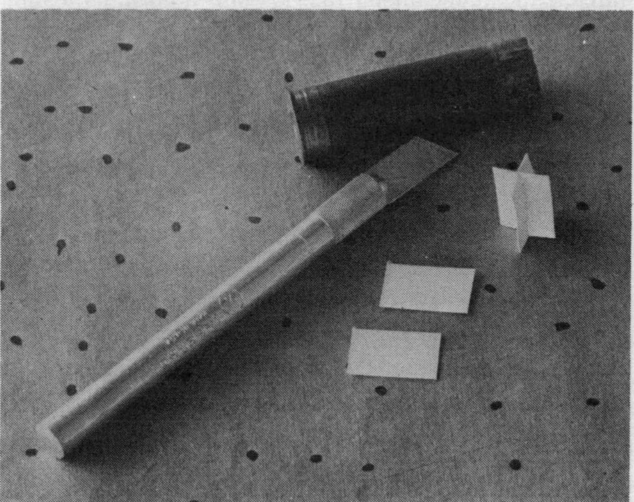

The right barrel of the author's Parker trap gun produced 79 percent patterns without the spreader load, and 57 percent patterns with it. Bear in mind the only difference between the two loads was the addition of the cardboard "X" in the shot column. Spreader loads are ideal on close flushing game in dense cover.

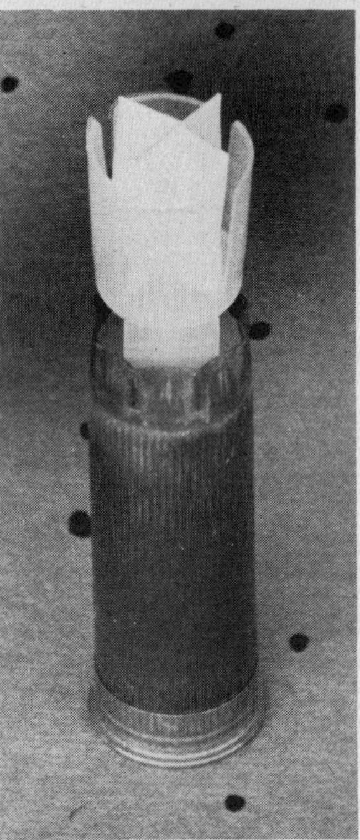

This shotshell has the cardboard "X" fitted into the one-piece plastic wad, and is ready to be filled with shot. The spreader itself may displace some shot, so be sure to hand-fill each wad with shot.

about ⅓ of the charge into the shot cup, and place one of the cardboard dividers on top of it. Another ⅓ of the shot is then poured in and topped with the second divider. Finally, the remaining ⅓ (or slightly less), is poured in and the shell crimped. This completes the load.

All that remains to be done is to adjourn to the patterning board to check the results. To prove emphatically how well the spreader load works, I like to make up identical loads, with and without the cardboard partitions for the patterning session. I think you will be surprised at just how well this simple addition to the shot column will "open up" a tightly choked gun. My own Parker double trap gun has 32-inch barrels choked "full-and-fuller!" A light game load that I often shoot in this gun uses 17½ grains of 700X powder and 1 ounce of No. 4 shot. Without the cardboard partitions, this load patterns 78-79 percent in the gun. By merely adding the partitions, I am able to achieve patterns in the 58 to 59 percent range. Effectively, the old Parker can be instantly changed from a shotgun that delivers very tight full choke patterns to one producing wide modified patterns.

Making up a batch of spreader loads is not as good as acquiring a new gun or a new barrel choked in more open borings. Of course, it doesn't cost nearly as much either! If you are one of those gun nuts that is only looking for an excuse to acquire another gun, then by all means hide this article from the better half, and go ahead and buy one. On the other hand, if you need a more open bored gun to improve your upland game shooting percentages, then I recommend you investigate spreader loads—they are not a panacea, but they are a big step in the right direction.

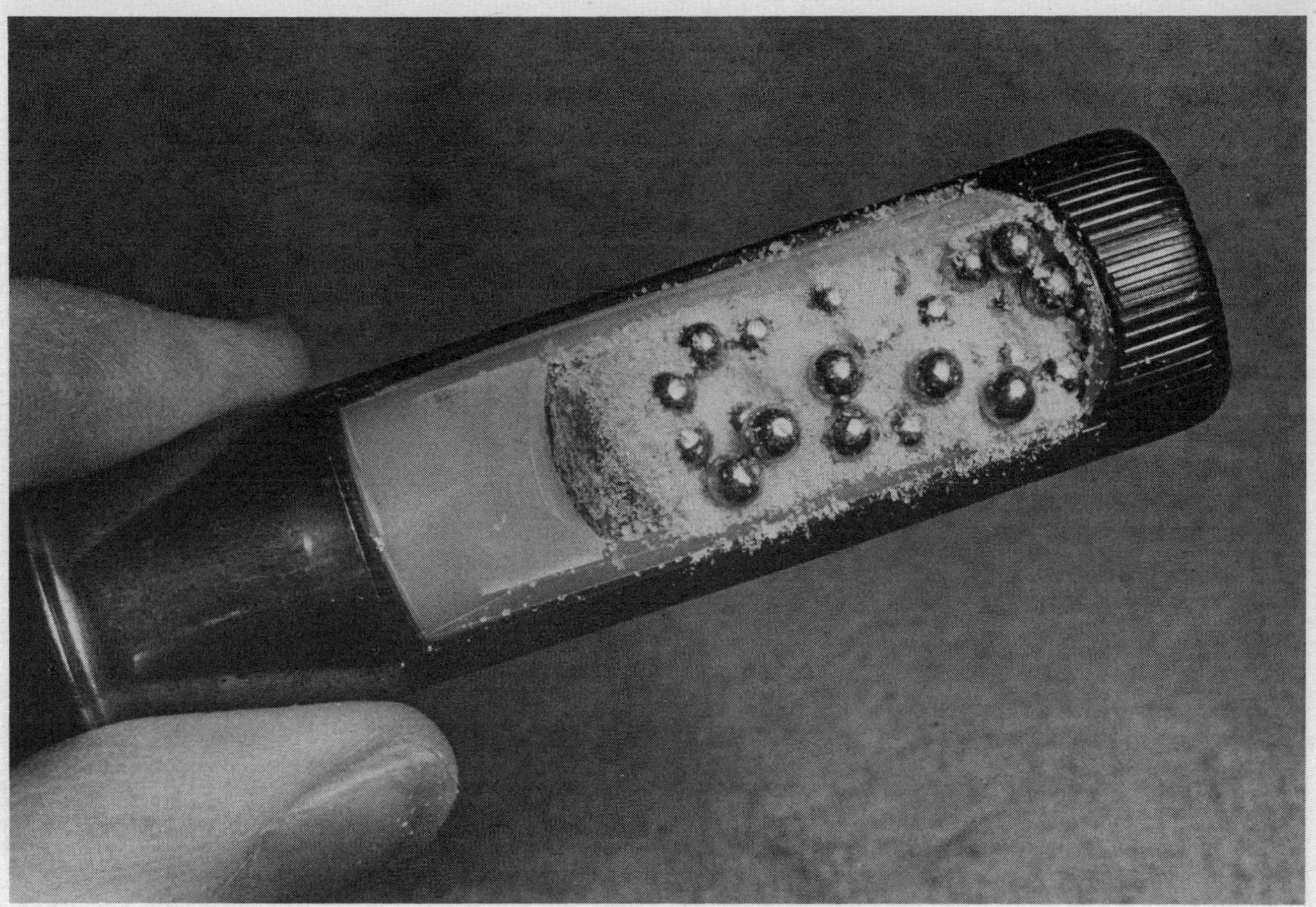

Loads with granulated plastic buffering compound not only cushion the pellets against deformation, but also improve the fluidity of a load of coarse shot. The fine bedding material allows the big pellets to shift about within their mass to squeeze through the forcing cone and choke constriction more smoothly.

Buffered Shot Loads

Looking for improved patterns? Here's how.

by DON ZUTZ

MANY HANDLOADERS think the use of buffered shot charges is something new and different. It isn't. British waterfowlers applied the technique in the 19th century, packing their shot charges in finely ground bone meal. Thus, pellet-bedding practices are a revival of an old art, not a modern innovation. The main difference between us and the British gunners of yore is that modern technology has given us granulated polyethylene as an improved bedding material.

Bedding the shot charge in a soft agent serves two purposes: (A) it cushions the pellets and protects them against deformation; and (B) it helps charges of bulky pellets and buckshot flow more fluidly through the constriction of full-choked shotguns.

Buffered shotshells offer the kind of pattern improvement that makes them a favorite with waterfowlers.

Point A should be easily understood. When pellets are deformed under the set-back pressures of firing and by squeezing down to work through the forcing cone and choke constriction, they pattern poorly and arrive at the target with less energy than still-round members of the same payload. Air resistance works devilishly against flattened or otherwise deformed pellets, slowing them and/or causing them to flare from the main mass. This not only reduces center density, but it also produces a very long in-flight shot string that doesn't get all its pellets on the plane of the target at the point of interception. Thus, if one thinks in terms of optimum pattern density, high retained energy levels and a short shot string, he must also think in terms of protecting pellets against deformation. And that's where buffered shot charges come in—the pellet-bedding material cushions the individual pellets and keeps them from mashing against each other.

Point B is probably less apparent to the average shotgunner, but it is equally as important as Point A, if not more so. Pattern development depends on the way pellets flow through the shotgun barrel's choke constriction. If they move fluidly through, they will generally respond to the choke's dictates and deliver the proper pattern. On the other hand, patterns will suffer if the pellets wedge and jam against each other as they pass into and through the choke constriction. Anyone who has reloaded with coarse shot like 2s or 4s in a modern press should understand this, as such bulky pellets tend to bridge in the press' drop tube and thereby negate the desired payload fluidity.

The wedging and jamming of bulky pellets explains why (1) fine shot, like 7½s and 8s, pattern far better through most full-choked barrels than 4s, 2s and BBs do; and why (2) many heavy charges of coarse duck and goose loads also pattern better from modified chokes (or full-choke barrels that have been "relieved" by a gunsmith). That explanation is improved fluidity. Fine shot, like those 7½s, can move about within their mass when they meet the choke constriction; in this respect, they resemble sand running through an hour glass. And in a barrel with less choke constriction than that of a bona fide full choke, the coarse pellets can also exit with less wedging.

Buffered shot charges, then, are helpful in improving patterns with heavy shot for long-range gunning. In general, there is little advantage, if any whatsoever, in bedding pellets smaller than No. 5. Shot sizes 6 through 9 are small enough to pass smoothly through the choke area without a buffering agent. Moreover, such smaller pellets are hardly long-range missiles, and they normally pattern well enough to give sufficient density inside 45 yards.

Buffering also works well with buckshot reloads. Besides cushioning buckshot against deformation and helping them flow through the choke constriction, a bedding material also tends to reduce or eliminate the spin that buckshot can

compressed, as it is during initial acceleration when it is trapped between the crimp and the wads being rammed forward by mounting gases, it compacts to the point of caking; and this, in turn, produces a slug-like condition that can cause a dangerous rise in chamber pressures. Too, if flour ever becomes moist in a shotshell (as can obviously happen in waterfowl loads), it can harden and again produce a single mass of lead and flour that can cause high chamber pressures because it both exerts a sideways pressure in the hull and doesn't move smoothly from the case into the bore.

Thus, the best bedding material is granulated plastic. It doesn't cake and isn't altered by moisture. However, it does cushion pellets to guard against deformation, and it does serve

Deformed pellets such as these have poor aerodynamic shapes. They are chilled No. 2s fired from a 10-gauge Magnum, and they show how the setback forces of firing destroy pellet shape. They were fired into snow.

(Right) While a "naked" load of buckshot (left) is lucky if it patterns at 50 percent at 40-yards, the bedded load (right) may very well do 90-100 percent at 50 yards.

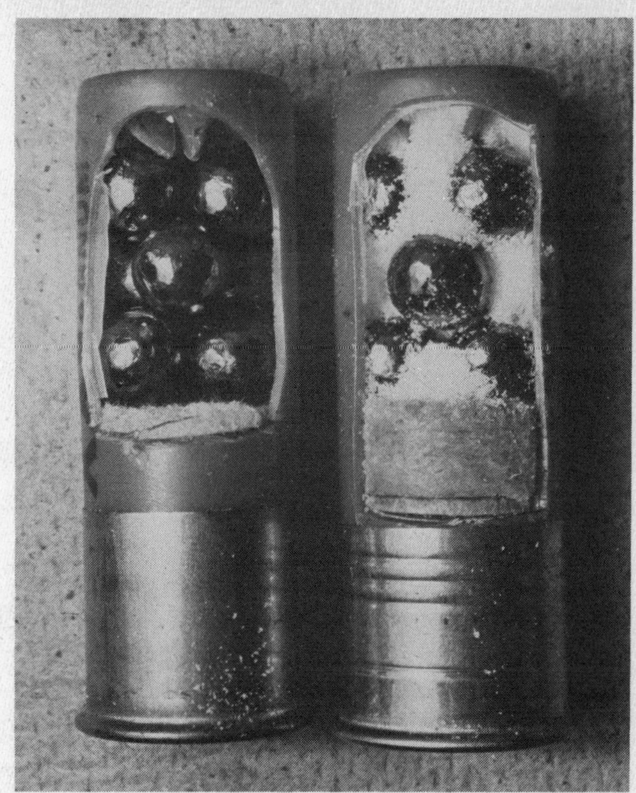

take on as they run through the bore.

Any number of buffering materials have been written up in the past: bone meal, cream of wheat, corn meal, kitchen flour or granulated polyethylene (plastic). The only good one in the list is granulated polyethylene which can be had especially ground for shotshell reloaders, from Ballistic Products, Inc., Box 488, 2105 Shaughnessy Circle, Long Lake, MN 55356. The common kitchen materials that have been used for pellet bedding have their faults; they compress easily and can influence chamber pressures to the high side of exerting a sideways force under acceleration pressures. Kitchen flour, which at one time received wide-spread publicity in the gun press as a bedding agent, is especially dangerous as a buffering agent. For when flour is

Packaged granulated polyethylene made specifically for
the handloader is obtainable from Ballistic Products, Inc.

nicely to move bulky pellets and buckshot through a tight, full-choke barrel.

Besides supplying granulated plastic for payload buffering, Ballistic Products also makes a pair of plastic wads especially suited to buffered loads. These are the Ballistic Pattern Driver 10-gauge unit, otherwise known as the BPD, and the 12-gauge shotcup called the BP-12 "Magnum," which can be used in both 2¾- and 3-inch hulls. The BP-12 shotcup works best with a special overpowder cup, the BPGS, which is shown nearby.

What can one expect with buffered shot charges for long-range shooting? I have had them average 88-92 percent at 40 yards through full-choked guns that did no better than 65-70 percent with the best conventional-type (no pellet bedding agent) long-range reloads. Some hunters have reported patterns close to an amazing 100 percent with specific gun/load combinations! I have also had buffered loads of 2s and BBs do 70-80 percent through 28-inch modified barrels, which turns the intermediate-range modified

tube into a potent duck gun, indeed!

But all is *not* glory when it comes to handloading buffered shot charges! Definitely NOT! It can be an exceedingly dangerous practice when done indiscriminately or haphazardly, because the bedding materials invariably cause higher

(Right) Ballistic Products' wads must be carefully slit by the handloader. If not cut, the wad can "flip" up on exiting the muzzle, and turn into a solid charge.

Specialized wads available from Ballistic Products, Inc. work extremely well with buffered shot charges. At the left is the two-piece 12 gauge unit known as the BPGS overpowder wad and BP-12 "Magnum" shotcup; to the right is the Ballistic Products "Pattern Driver" 10 gauge wad.

chamber pressures due to the way they compress and exert a sideways pressure against the case and bore walls. In other words, buffered shot charges tend to act more as an obstruction to expanding powder gases. Randomly concocted reloads should *never* be given a buffering agent. There is *no* rule of thumb which says that a powder charge can be reduced by, say, 10 percent to produce a safe load with buffered shot charges. None whatsoever! Bedding materials seem to introduce erratic performances, and each load must be tested separately. As a test, I once cut the powder charge of three safe loads by 10 percent, added bedding agent to the payload, and sent them for lab testing. All the reloads had a chamber pressure around 10,000 LUP *without* the bedding material, which is well under the 11,000 LUP maximum working average set for 12-gauge loads. However, when the lab reports came back, every load was well above 13,000 LUP despite the powder reduction! This gets a bit scary when one considers that the modern shotgun is proof tested at 16,000-18,000 LUP! Thus, the pellet bedding concept is nothing to fool around with. The handloader is advised to follow reliable published data and *not* merely sift

A buffered load of nine No. 00 buckshot printed 100 percent at 50 yards through a full-choked Model 96 Winchester over/under. It is far better than what you would get with naked buck in the same barrel. This test load used flour as a bedding agent, a material which the writer no longer recommends.

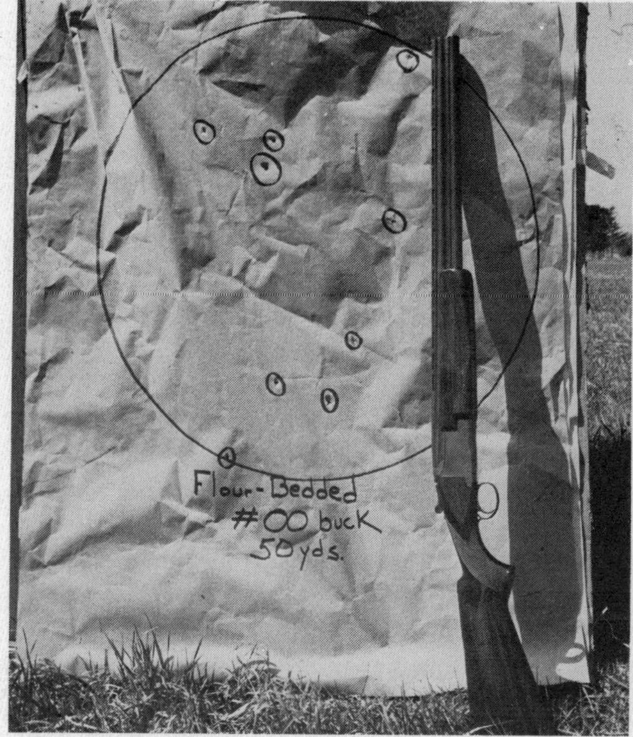

12-Gauge Buffered Reloads

("BPGP" indicates Ballistic
Products Granulated Plastic)

Remington RXP case
- **Primer:** Winchester 209
- **Powder:** 22.0/Unique
- **Wad:** Rem. RP-12
- **Shot:** 1³/₁₆ ounces
- **Buffer:** 20-21 grains of BPGP
- **Pressure:** 11,000 LUP
- **Velocity:** 1200 fps
- **Comment:** Tight-patterning, light recoiling load for featherweight 12s.

Remington 3-inch plastic magnum
- **Primer:** Winchester 209
- **Powder:** 39.0/Hodgdon HS-7
- **Wads:** BPGS + BP-12 with two ¼" 20-gauge fillers
- **Shot:** 1⅜ ounces
- **Buffer:** 20-21 grains of BPGP
- **Pressure:** 10,600 LUP
- **Velocity:** 1290 fps

Winchester 3-inch C/F plastic magnum
- **Primer:** Winchester 209
- **Powder:** 31.5/SR-4756
- **Wads:** BPGS + BP-12
- **Shot:** 1⅝ ounces of shot
- **Buffer:** 20 grains of BPGP
- **Pressure:** 9600 LUP
- **Velocity:** 1200 fps

Peters Blue Magic case
- **Primer:** Winchester 209
- **Powder:** 30.0/SR-4756
- **Wad:** Rem. RP-12
- **Shot:** 1¼ ounces
- **Buffer:** 17-18 grains of BPGP
- **Pressure:** 10,800 LUP
- **Velocity:** 1285 fps
- **Comment:** Good load in the standard 12 with full choke barrel.

Federal 3-inch plastic magnum
- **Primer:** Winchester 209
- **Powder:** 40.0/Hodgdon HS-7
- **Wads:** BPGS + BP-12 with one ¼" 20-gauge filler
- **Shot:** 1⅝ ounces
- **Buffer:** 23-25 grains of BPGP
- **Pressure:** 11,000 LUP
- **Velocity:** 1200 fps

Federal 3-inch plastic magnum
- **Primer:** CCI 209
- **Powder:** 36.5/SR-4756
- **Wads:** BPGS + BP-12
- **Shot:** 1⅝ ounces
- **Buffer:** 22-23 grains of BPGP
- **Pressure:** 11,000 LUP
- **Velocity:** 1280 fps

10-Gauge Buffered Reloads

Remington 2⅞-inch plastic case
- **Primer:** Winchester 209
- **Powder:** 39.0/Hodgdon HS-5
- **Wad:** Remington SP-10
- **Shot:** 1⅝ ounces
- **Buffer:** 21-22 grains of BPGP
- **Pressure:** 10,800 LUP
- **Velocity:** 1329 fps
- **Comment:** These are the lab figures for a test load. It patterns better at 38.0/HS-5 for a slightly lower pressure/velocity performance.

Remington 3½-inch plastic case
- **Primer:** Remington 57★
- **Powder:** 43.0/Blue Dot
- **Wad:** BP Pattern Driver
- **Shot:** 2 ounces
- **Buffer:** 10-12 grains of BPGP
- **Pressure:** 9700 LUP
- **Velocity:** 1225 fps

Remington 3½-inch plastic case

Primer:	Remington 57★
Powder:	41.0/Blue Dot
Wad:	BP Pattern Driver
Shot:	2¼ ounces
Buffer:	10-12 grains of BPGP
Pressure:	10,400 LUP
Velocity:	1175 fps
Comment:	Good reload with BB or No. 2 shot. Heavy recoil. Do not increase the buffering agent.

Remington 3½-inch plastic case

Primer:	Remington 57★
Powder:	43.5/SR-4756
Wad:	BP Pattern Driver
Shot:	1¾ ounces
Buffer:	15-18 grains of BPGP
Pressure:	10,100 LUP
Velocity:	1311 fps

Buffered Buckshot Loads

12 Gauge

Peters Blue Magic

Primer:	Winchester 209
Powder:	33.0/Hodgdon HS-6
Wad:	Remington SP-12
Shot:	9 #00 or 12 #0 buck
Buffer:	22-23 grains of BPGP
Pressure:	10,900 LUP
Velocity:	1365 fps
Comment:	The powder charge can be cut by 1-2 grains for pattern testing without losing effective velocity.

10 Gauge

Remington 3½-inch plastic case

Primer:	CCI 109
Powder:	40.0/HS-7
Wads:	BP Pattern Driver+ one 20-gauge ¼" shotcup
Shot:	52 #4 buck pellets
Buffer:	25-30 grains of BPGP.
Pressure:	10,900 LUP
Velocity:	1200 fps

Buffering materials, especially flour, exert a sideways pressure under acceleration forces. A shotcup is a must in order to keep the bedding material from caking against the shell wall. These test loads were fired using flour and no shotcup. You can easily see how the caked flour offers a dangerous obstruction to wad movement, causing higher-than-normal pressures.

a buffering material into any or all shot loads.

Another bit of cautionary advice is needed. Always use a plastic shotcup or a plastic wrapper with any buffered shot charge. Without them to separate the buffering agent from the shotshell wall, the agent will compact against the roughened case wall and cake there to hinder the forward movement of the payload. Obviously, such caking will cause chamber pressures to rise

Are these geese in range? No! While buffered loads provide an "edge" when it comes to distant ducks or geese, they shouldn't be used to promote sky busting.

accordingly. I once experimented with flour-buffered shot charges without a plastic shotcup, and the flour caked so tightly against the case wall that the forward portion of those Federal plastic field-style hulls actually shot out the barrel with the wads and pellets! The plastic shotcup or wrapper, then, provides better slippage to reduce the "cling" factor.

How does one get the granulated plastic into the load? There are several ways. One is to drop the entire shot charge and then add small helpings of the plastic sawdust, tapping the case gently to settle the buffering agent. This is probably the worst way to do it, however, as the pellets are already resting against each other, and the buffering agent will merely trickle into the voids among the pellets rather than working between the individual members to cushion them. A better way is to drop a small layer of shot and follow it with an amount of bedding agent, again tapping gently to distribute the agent. By tapping gently, the pellets are lifted so that some of the material can sift between them. But perhaps the best way is the "test tube" method: use a test tube or a small, narrow bottle (such as a prescription bottle) to combine the pellets and the buffering agent

before putting them into the shotshell. First drop the shot into the tube or small bottle, followed by a measured amount of buffering agent, and then shake the tube or bottle a couple of times to mix the shot and buffering agent. Pour the mix directly into the hull and crimp snugly.

Seepage is a problem with fine buffering agents, which tend to trickle out of all but the most perfect crimps. To seal the load, simply put a drop of candle wax on the very center of the crimp. It doesn't have to be a big drop, just enough to seal the center. Finally, make certain that the payload is snugly compressed by the crimp so that there is no rattling or jostling of the shot and buffering during handling or carrying. Such looseness allows the buffering agent and the pellets to work about within the case, and they tend to separate as the heavier pellets settle while the lighter buffering agent rises.

All that remains now is to work up a few loads specially developed for buffered shot charges. The preceding list is for 10- and 12-gauge shotguns using *only* granulated plastic as the buffering agent. They were lab tested and are printed here through the courtesy of Hodgdon Powder Co. and Ballistic Products, Inc.

Shotgun Slug Reloading

Sources for data and suggestions for working in the least catered-to field of shotshell reloading.

MANY ASPECTS of reloading in general, and shotshell reloading in particular, have shown encouraging growth and prosperity in recent years. Slug reloading, sad to say, is well to the rear of the pack in that regard.

Smith & Wesson's decision to phase-out their offering of reloading components foretells the day when Air-Wedge and Plastic Gas Seal (PGS) wads will be as scarce and ardently sought as pre-1965 dimes. Both are specified as the pressure-sealing item in a number of slug reloading recipes: one or the other, never both. The shotgun reloading world is going to miss the ever-loving daylights out of the Alcan products, once launched and marketed by Homer Clark, Jr., with their invaluable availability taken for granted, thus not appreciated suitably. You never miss the water until the well goes dry, right? Whether another enterprise moves to fill the breach or not is a good and pertinent question, at this point. A prospect of no more Alcan wads, no more of the splendid Swedish powders,

by DEAN A. GRENNELL

About The Author: A well-known author, Dean Grennell has been writing the Reloading Clinic *column in* Gun World *Magazine for the past 15 years.*

such as AL-5 and AL-7 is bleak, indeed.

The good news about slug reloading is that it conserves cash-flow rather eye-poppingly. Factory slug loads pack a tab of sixty cents or so, per tug of the trigger, and upward from there, and up, and up. That tends to discourage the dedicated zeal with which the slug-shooter conducts applied research for pinning down the probable point of impact at a given distance for a given gun and load. Skimping on the practice and familiarization can and probably will make the difference between venison in the freezer and rueful alibis.

Reloading offers an economically attractive

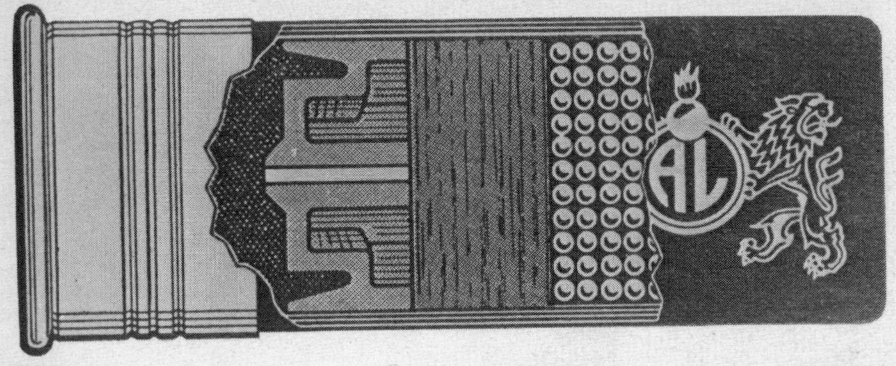

These cross-section diagrams show the Alcan Air-Wedge (left) and the same firm's PGS—Plastic Gas Seal (below). These over-powder wads have long been favored as slug reloading components, however, they will both be off the market soon—get 'em while you can.

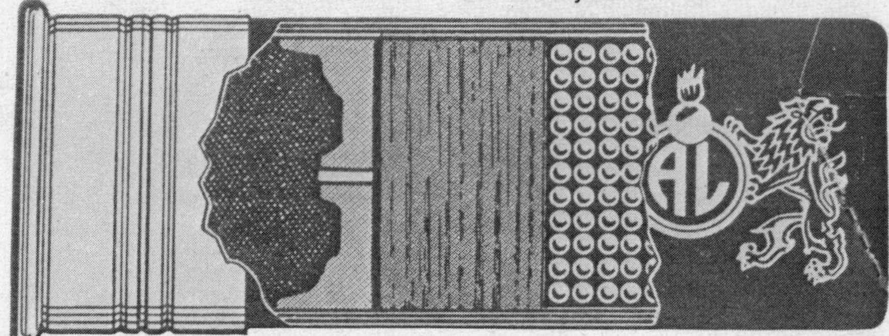

(Below) The Benco-Vitt slug had an Alcan Air-Wedge fastened to its base by means of a screw, with filler wads between A-W and slug.

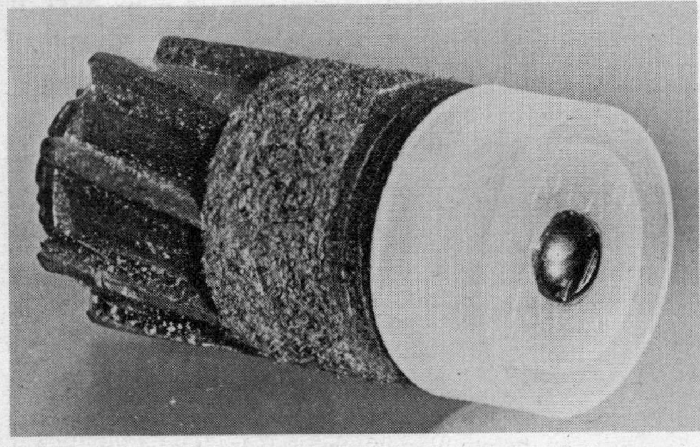

alternative to purchasing slug loads, without undue sacrifice in velocity and energy. As an example of the upper performance levels of factory slug loads, the 30-inch barrels of my Remington Model 3200 over/under drive the Winchester-Western 1-ounce slug load to as much as 1640 fps (feet per second), for 2613 fpe (foot-pounds of energy). As a convenient notation, we'll quote such performance figures as fps/fpe, or 1640/2613, in this instance.

On page 271 of Lyman's second edition of the *Lyman Shotshell Handbook*, they list ten 12-gauge slug loads; seven with 445-grain slugs cast of pure lead in the Lyman 12-gauge mould and three with the 575-grain Vitt-Aerodynamic one-piece slug. The latter is made by Vitt & Boos, 8 Overlook Drive, Westport, CT 06880. Lyman's data specifies use of the Federal Hi-Power plastic case only. It takes the 445-grain Lyman slug up to 1565/2421, and the 575-grain Vitt-Aerodynamic slug to 1535/3009.

Most factory-produced shotgun slugs are termed "rifled," meaning that they carry raised ridges in a spiral pattern around the sides of the lead slug. For practical purposes, they can be considered purely cosmetic, since the ridges impart no significant amount of rotation to the slug, either in passing through the bore of the shotgun or in traveling through the air to the target.

If a shotgun slug flies nose-foremost—and many of them do—it is due to the fact that the center of gravity is well forward of the center of atmospheric resistance. They stabilize for the same reason as does a dart, a badminton bird, an arrow, or a parachute—though usually not as steadily. That's because shotgun slugs cover the greater part of their trajectory at velocities faster than the speed of sound, which is approximately 1086 fps. Stabilizing fins and such things do not perform in the same manner at supersonic velocities as they do at subsonic paces.

When firing slug loads at a paper target, it is not unusual to find a few print holes showing some amount of slug profile, rather than a neat circle. It is hardly surprising that the loads doing so, as a rule, are less accurate than the ones that travel resolutely nose-foremost. The longer slugs, generally speaking, are the ones more severely plagued by keyholing inclinations.

A round lead ball, curiously enough, can be made to deliver accuracy that comes surprisingly close to that of several slugs; presumably because it cannot keyhole, due to its inherent design. When loaded and fired in a plastic wad column having protective plastic sleeves to enclose what would, ordinarily, be the charge of shot pellets, the round lead ball gets out of the bore without picking up any great amount of rotation in any direction.

When selecting a round ball mould for use in such a wad column, it's important to make certain that its diameter is small enough to provide

Recently introduced to replace their ⅞-ounce factory slug load for the 12 gauge, the new 1-ounce offering by Remington has a rudimentary hollow point that may or may not expand on impact! There is, however, no denying that it looks impressive. (Note the "stabilizing" fins.)

The new 12 gauge "ACTIV" cases by Rainel de P.R. accept a roll crimp guide well and should prove suitable for slug reloading.

(Right) When a cast Lyman .672" round ball is used inside Federal's No. ⅞- pellet protector wad column, the excess space can be taken up with granular plastic.

velocity out of a full choke barrel, but the accuracy will be better from a barrel choked modified, Skeet or improved cylinder. My load for the .672-inch round ball from the Lyman mould—at an average weight of 442 grains—in a Federal Champion-II plastic hull with Federal 209 primers, is 30.0 grains of Alcan AL-5 powder, using

clearance to pass through the choke, assuming the bore is choked. The size that seems to work well for most 12-gauge barrels is the .672-inch, which measures .729-inch in diameter when seated in the shot space of a Federal No. 7/8 pellet protector wad column, matching the nominal bore diameter of the 12-gauge barrel. You may not be able to push such an assembly up the bore with ease. In fact, it's pretty difficult to push the wad column past a full choke, without the ball in place. The important thing is to assure that solid projectiles will pass up the bore and through the choke without encountering severe resistance that would boost the peak pressures to dangerous levels.

Usually, a given load will develop a bit more

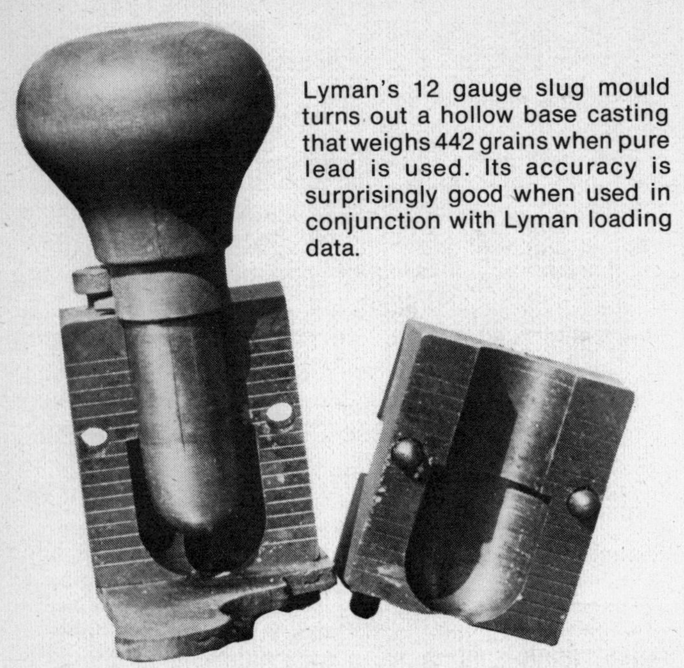

Lyman's 12 gauge slug mould turns out a hollow base casting that weighs 442 grains when pure lead is used. Its accuracy is surprisingly good when used in conjunction with Lyman loading data.

with slugs, it is mandatory to follow the load data listings in the books exactly, using only the precise components that they specify, with no substitutions. That can pose problems, since some of the specified components may not be on hand or readily available.

Apart from the *Lyman Shotshell Handbook*, other sources of load data for slugs include the No. 23 *Hodgdon's Data Manual*, the *Reloaders' Guide for Hercules Smokeless Powders*, and the *Du Pont Handloader's Guide for Smokeless Powders*.

The Hodgdon book, on page 247, lists one load for a 16-gauge slug, the ¾-ounce Meyer Brothers, at 328 grains. As far as I know, that slug is not currently available. The only 16-gauge slug presently offered, to the best of my knowledge, is the Brenneke, weighing about 417 grains

(Left) On the left are two cast Lyman slugs next to a cast Lyman round ball that measures .672", Both average 442 grains, slightly over 1 ounce.

(Below) Hodgdon's HS5 and Trap 100 powders were also popular with slug shooters who preferred the now-discontinued Meyer Brothers slugs.

the Federal No. 7/8 pellet protector wad column and enough granular polyethylene plastic filler to take up the surplus space in front of the shot sleeve. I give this load a folded crimp, rather than the rolled crimp usually prescribed for slug loads, and find that it works quite well. From the 26-inch Skeet barrel on my Remington Model 870 pump, it delivers 1331/1739, grouping in the area of 6 to 8 inches at 50 yards.

Admittedly, there are other slug loads that cluster considerably tighter than that, as well as many that deliver hotter ballistics. The reason I'm fond of that punkin'-ball load is that it's easy, simple and inexpensive to make up, and considerably below the maximum peak pressures permissible for use in shotguns. If you feel that you must get up into the topmost performance ranges

Here's a close look at the Brenneke slug, complete with screwed-in felt base wad. From left to right: 20, 16 and 12 gauge.

(Below) Hercules Unique and Herco are two respected favorites. They enjoy superb reputations with shotgunners worldwide.

and thus not suited for use with Hodgdon's data for the 328-grain Meyer Brothers slug. I've been unable to find any recommendation of data for use with the 16-gauge Brenneke.

Apart from that, Hodgdon lists data for the ⅞-ounce Meyer slug (383-grain) on page 244, using their Trap 100 powder, and a load for the ⅝-ounce (273-grain) Meyer slug on page 253, specifying their HS-5 powder for that one.

The Brenneke slugs are distributed in this country by Dynamit Nobel of America, Inc., 105 Stonehurst Court, Northvale, NJ 07647, in three gauges with weights as noted:

Gauge	Weight
20-gauge	371 grains
16-gauge	417 grains
12-gauge	478 grains

The same firm offers the Brenneke slugs in a factory load by Rottweil, in all three gauges. They provide a chart showing remaining energy and time of flight for each of the three gauges of Rottweil loads to one hundred meters (110 yards). A copy of that chart has been supplied here for your edification.

Ballistic Data
ROTTWEIL Shotgun Cartridges
with BRENNEKE Slug

Distance yds.	Velocity ft./sec.	Energy ft. lbs.			Time of flight milliseconds
	12/16/20 ga.	12 ga.	16 ga.	20 ga.	
muzzle	1410	2110	1840	1640	0
27	1215	1550	1370	1240	63
55	1085	1220	1080	980	134
85	985	1010	905	820	214
110	900	860	770	700	302

The box in which the Brenneke slugs are packed carries a rather intriguing notice on each side, in both French and English, to the effect that it is " . . . most suitable for deer, big game, pachyderms, etc. . . . On battue particularly preferred for wild boars." The wording is the same, on all three gauges, although I'll confess I'd feel pretty trepid about gunning for elephant—if that's what they mean by pachyderms—with a slug-loaded shotgun, even with Brenneke slugs and especially in 20-gauge. (Battue refers to driven game.)

The current printing of the Hercules data book—marked as revised 10-80, at the lower left corner of the back page—carries a block of data for 12-gauge slug loads on page 27; three for the ⅞-ounce slug (383-grain), using both Unique and Herco powders, and two using only Herco for the 12-gauge Brenneke slug, which they list as weighing 1 ounce, although it's more like 1¹/₁₂ ounces in actual weight. All eight loads are rated at 1570 fps, which would give you 2097 fpe with the ⅞-ounce and 2395 fpe with a true 1-ounce

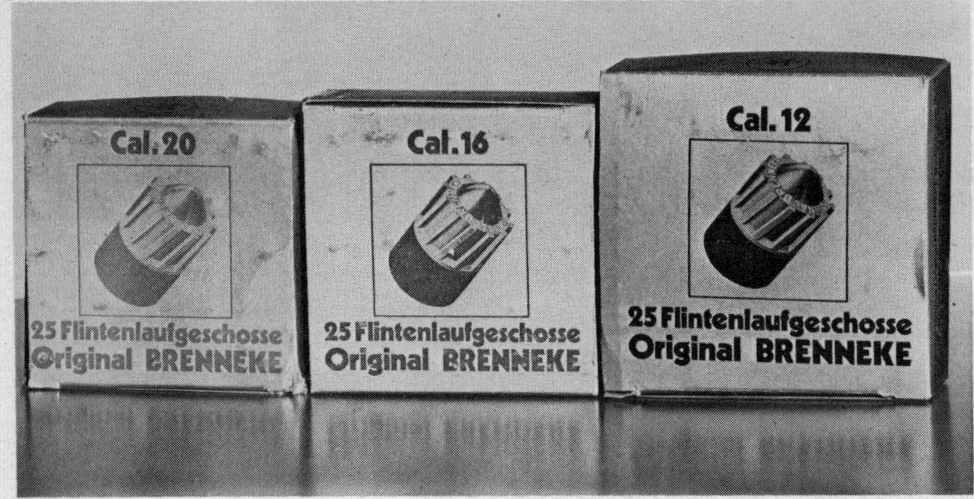

Brenneke slugs for reloaders are available 25 to the pack in 12, 16 and 20 gauge. (Dynamit Nobel is the importer.)

(Right) Dupont lists their PB, SR-4756, SR-7625 propellants (as well as 700X) for use with the 12 and 20 gauge Brenneke slugs.

(437.5-grain) slug, or 2617 fpe with the 12-gauge Brenneke's actual weight of 478 grains.

The Du Pont Guide provides 12-gauge slug data on page 25, and 20-gauge data on page 30, specifying charges of their 700-X, PB, SR 7625 and SR 4756 for the 12-gauge, and PB and SR 7625 for the 20-gauge. Both listings are for the respective Brenneke slugs in those gauges. The SR 4756 load for the 12-gauge is the highest velocity in that size, at a maximum of 1440/2201. The hotter of the two 20-gauge loads, with the SR 7625 charge, is rated at 1270/1329.

The BRI slugs and slug loads, available in the past from Ballistics Research, Incorporated, are off the market again at date of writing. That was a remarkably effective and accurate slug of about .500-inch diameter for the 12-gauge, using a pair of plastic sabots to carry the slug up through the bore, shedding as they left the muzzle.

There's no way to say for certain the exact number of firms and individuals currently engaged in development of new shotgun slug systems, although I know of at least one. That's KTS (710 Cooper-Foster Park Road West, Lorain, OH 44053), whose president, Dr. Paul J. Kopsch, M.D., reports that their slug has reached a pleasantly capable level of development, and they hope to market it fairly soon.

The KTW slug load carries a caliber .30— .308-inch—slug that weighs 220 grains, packed in the center of a 12-gauge collar that's of one-piece construction, rather than the two-piece sabots of the BRI load. Atmospheric resistance strips the one-piece collar or sabot free from the base of the slug as it leaves the muzzle.

Tests conducted for KTW at the H.P. White laboratories indicate that their load develops 2500/3054, at a peak pressure of 12,000 LUP (lead units of pressure). Dr. Kopsch rates the present accuracy of the KTW slug load as good, and he hopes to improve it further, with a goal of 2-inch groups at 100 yards. If they achieve that, it would represent truly remarkable performance from a 12-gauge shotgun.

Naturally, it would tax a Natty Bumppo to fire 2-inch groups at 100 yards with the single front bead sight commonly employed on shotguns. KTW is conducting their test firing with a shotgun that has been fitted with a scope sight. The KTW .30 caliber slug has off-center vanes at the rear for purposes of stabilizing it to fly nose-foremost and to build up some amount of rotation in flight. Its design is said by Dr. Kopsch to be similar to modern aircraft bombs, as to fin design.

Since many hunters reside and/or hunt in areas where *only* the shotgun slug is sanctioned for hunting deer, it makes a lot of good sense to expend some time and attention toward obtaining the best possible performance from shotgun slug loads. It is probable that the point of impact, for a given slug load, will differ somewhat from the center of the pattern when using conventional shotshells. With that fact in mind, manufacturers such as Brenneke urge the user to fire at least five shots by way of establishing the relationship between the point of impact and the line of sight.

Weaver offers a remarkably convenient and efficient mount for use of either their Qwik-Point or low-magnification scopes on either the Model 870 or 1100 Remington shotguns. The mount goes on or comes off, quickly and easily, requiring no drilling, tapping or other modifications to the shotgun. For owners of the two Remington models, it's an approach well worth considering, since the use of shotgun slugs puts a high premium upon any advantage that you can gain. ●

Ballistics Research, Inc. (BRI) once made a remarkably effective and accurate 440-grain saboted 12-gauge slug. While not currently on the market, it's possible a dedicated slug shooter might find a "stash" of this gem if he searches hard enough.

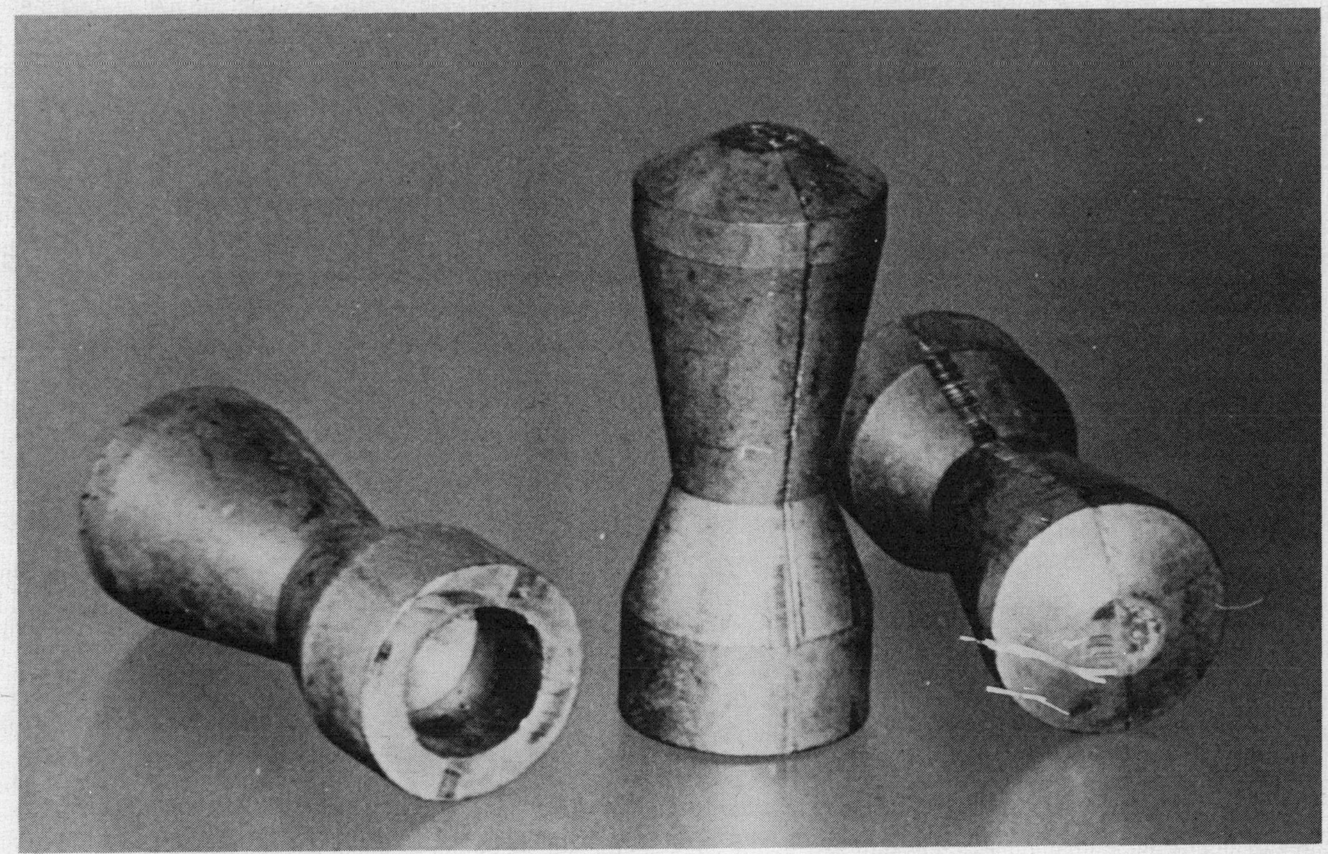

Questions & Answers

by EDWARD A. MATUNAS

Ed Matunas was Winchester-Western's powder and components man for over a decade. Here are Ed's answers to shotshell reloading's 15 most frequently asked questions.

SHOTSHELL LOADING, like any similar undertaking has its own peculiarities. This unique area of reloading inevitably leads to questions—and then more questions. Whether you are an old pro or a newcomer to shotshell reloading, you have, or will come up with, some of your own.

As a result of my many contacts with shotshell shooters/reloaders during the past 24 years, certain questions seem to arise again and again. In order to help you avoid the need to ask, and to help build your store of shotshell reloading knowledge, we will go through the fifteen most often asked. How often are they asked? I *guarantee* that I have answered each of these questions a *minimum* of 1,000 times—in some cases, 10,000 times! Somewhere along the way, even I asked each of these questions myself. Hopefully, many of the answers will help you with problems you have already encountered or are yet to encounter.

Mixing Components

Question 1: *I note that the various reloading data sources list very specific components. I have selected a load that I wish to use. However, I cannot purchase the specific primer called for (a Federal 209) in the data. My dealer has Winchester 209 primers in stock. He has advised me that I can use the Winchester primers interchangeably with Federal or Remington or CCI primers. He says that there are only two basic shotshell primer sizes: the so-called Winchester 209 size and the Remington 57 size. I bought 1000 but hesitate to use them. Was my dealer simply trying to make a sale or can I use the primers?*

Answer: Physical size or similar appearance has little to do with ballistic performance. Look-alike components seldom perform at the same ballistic level. A change in primers can easily cause a pressure change of 2000 LUP's up or down, depending upon the exact load. The switching of a specific primer can easily result in a load with extremely poor ballistic uniformity or make a given load dangerous to use.

Unfortunately, a specific graph cannot be offered to indicate the performance of one primer vs. another. However, the substitution of primers might mean a change in primer performance; and, the specifics of each load (case used, weight of shot and pressure level) would also affect the

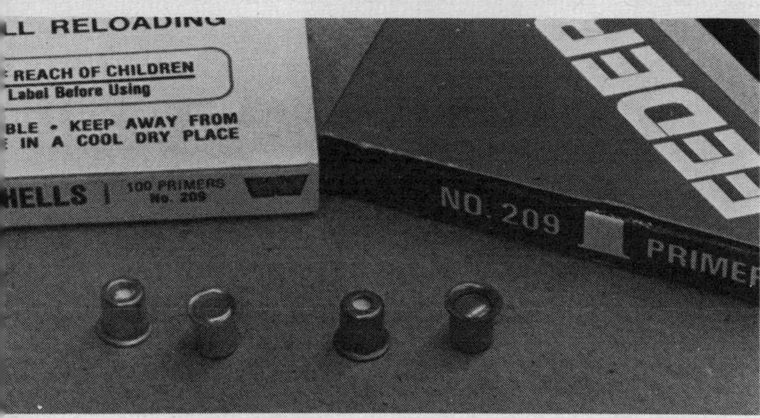

The Winchester and Federal primers pictured have a similar appearance and almost identical dimensions; but regardless of such similarities, shotshell components cannot be interchanged. You must use the exact component specified in your data source or run the risk of a change in ballistics and safety.

outcome. A substitution that may give 1200 LUP **less** in one load may produce 1600 LUP **more** in another load. Or, in some cases, the two components may perform in a somewhat similar fashion.

I just recently completed a test on a specific case wherein one primer (in a specific load) afforded an extreme velocity variation of 23 fps with an extreme pressure variation of 700 LUP. The primer used was a Federal product. The Winchester primer gave an extreme velocity variation of 47 fps and an extreme pressure variation of 1300 LUP. This is double the variations obtained with the Federal primer. The average pressure was 1000 LUP higher with the Winchester primer while velocity was only 5 fps faster. And the differences reversed themselves when the shot weight, powder, and wad combination was changed.

Such variations can and do occur with all components. **No component in a loading recommendation should ever be substituted whether it be the case, primer, powder, or wad.** To do so is to invite poor results and run the risk of assembling a dangerous load. Sometimes components can be changed without a significant change in results. However, this information cannot be interpolated. You must have the data to support your desire. If you cannot find a load in the data tables of this book or in the powder manufacturers' data for the primer you have (in conjunction with your other components) then you should *not* use that primer.

With respect to your dealer's intentions: he may just have wanted to make the sale. But if you damaged your gun or if a personal injury resulted from his advice he could find himself involved in a costly lawsuit. Based on the results his actions could have brought about, I suspect that he simply did not know any better. It pays to shop for reloading components with a "savvy" dealer. But the final burden will always remain yours. Do not substitute components!

Waterfowl Loads

Question 2: *Late season ducks are very hard to kill due to the extra fat and down they carry at that time of year. My friends have suggested larger size shot, smaller size shot, different primers, different chokes, etc. In fact it seems that almost everyone has a pet theory on how to kill ducks more efficiently in cold weather. What's your advice?*

Answer: Late season (very cold weather) birds are not really any more difficult to harvest than birds of earlier season. Sure, they have extra fat and down on them but this increase in insulation has no practical effect on pellet penetration. The shot-to-shot velocity difference in ammunition has a greater effect on penetration than a sixteenth of an inch of down and fat. The real problem in killing late season birds is the drastic fall-off in velocity due to cold temperature ignition of the shotshell. A shell that turns in 1330 fps at 70° F may turn in only 1250 fps at the muzzle in 0° F temperatures. A load that produces 1200 fps at 70° F may only turn in 1100 fps at 0° F. Additionally, many of the one-piece wads used in reloading (and factory shells) tend to fracture to some degree in the cold weather. These fractures can cause sub-normal velocities and very large extreme variation in pressure and velocity. All this can add up to a sub-standard performance of the shotshell with respect to bagging game. The uninformed shooter, not realizing the fall-off in shotshell performance, naturally assumes the birds are harder to kill.

The reloader can combat this problem by selecting safe loads with as high a muzzle velocity as practical. The use of the 1⅜-ounce, 1½-ounce, and 1⅝-ounce 12-gauge loads will also ensure better results than the usual 1¼-ounce loads. Beyond high muzzle velocity, you should also select loads which are proven performers in cold temperatures. Certain components seem to perform better than others in this respect. For instance, it is my experience that Winchester wads tend to fracture less at cold temperatures. The load data section of this book makes reference to specific loads which perform well at cold temperatures. Select a load from amongst these and use it only in once or twice fired cases. Hulls which have been loaded frequently do not afford as firm a crimp as newer cases—and a firm crimp is a must for cold weather performance.

Finally you should realize that even with everything as right as possible some reduction in performance is inevitable in cold weather. Therefore, use good decoys in order to reduce the range you must shoot at birds. Whatever range you find to be maximum for your gun/load combination at 50°F should be reduced by at least 5 yards (and ideally 10 yards) for 0°F shooting. Also keep in mind that 4's are the ideal shot size for ducks under almost all conditions.

Hulls for Hunting

Question 3: *Cases are hard to come by and are getting more expensive. I find that I am frequently unable to pick up cases when hunting. Therefore I use my newer cases for reloading my Skeet and trap loads. Then, when I feel the cases are just about worn out, I load them with heavy hunting loads. My target loads function and perform flawlessly. However my hunting loads are dirty burning and the noise level varies considerably. My friends tell me that this is due to the slow burning powders used for heavy hunting loads. But I wonder if the number of times a shell has been reloaded affects the ballistics. Can you help?*

Answer: Yes, if you are willing to accept that your approach has been somewhat backwards. As stated in Question and Answer #2, cold temperatures require a firm crimp to insure that the intended velocity and uniformity are obtained. Cases with worn out mouths simply cannot accommodate a firm crimp! The cases shown nearby were picked up from the floor of a duck blind in a public hunting area. I doubt if it is coincidental that there were no duck feathers on the floor of the blind. Such shells are, of course, representative of the extreme condition of worn out crimps. However, these shells were loaded (only to prove a point) with a Skeet load using a very fast burning powder. They appeared to perform flawlessly. This is due to the fact that fast burning powders are quite forgiving. However, velocities and uniformity will fall off even with fast burning powders when used with such cases. When slow burning powders are used, the need for strong crimps is, I assure you, accentuated.

Therefore load your hunting loads only in newer cases. Preferably only once or twice fired. The few cases lost in hunting is a cheap trade off for the birds bagged by properly performing ammunition.

Worn-out case mouths can cause all sorts of ammunition performance problems ranging from erratic pressure and velocity to potentially dangerous bloopers.

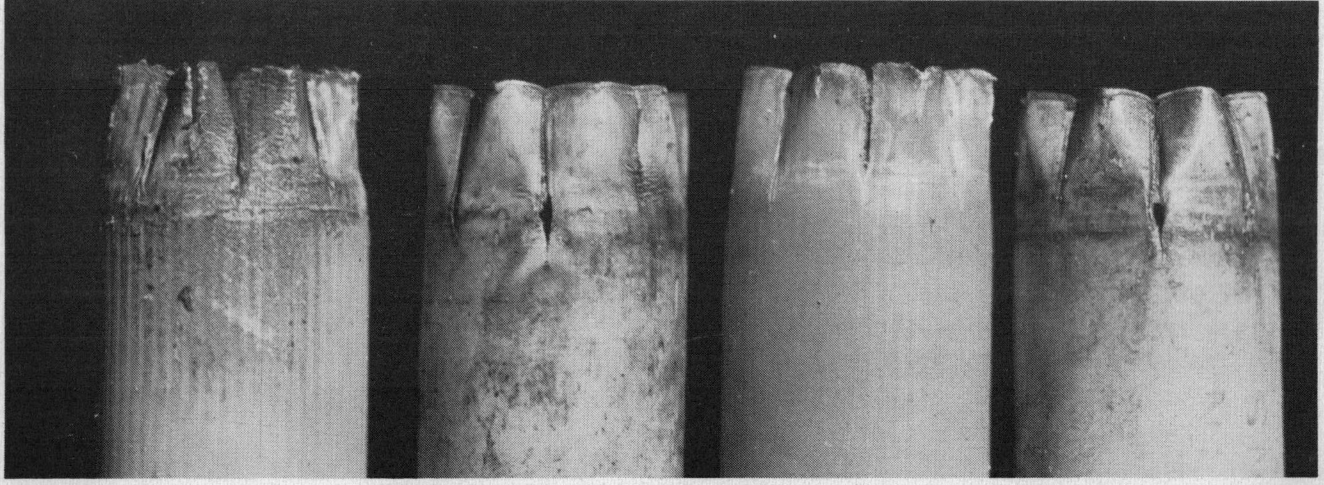

Dirty Burning

Question 4: *My loads are exactly according to the powder manufacturer's data. I use only the specified components and load my shells only three times. Yet I still get dirty burning of powder. This is not a problem in my doubles or my pump gun. However, my semiautomatic shotgun gets all kinds of residue in the action. By the time I have fired 50 shells the gun begins to malfunction from all the crud that has built up. Is there anything I can do besides giving up on my semiauto?*

Answer: Yes, you have two options. The first is to try switching components. Some primers and powders leave behind more residue than others. In target loads, for instance, my experience has shown DuPont "Hi-Skor" 700X to be very clean burning while both Winchester 452 AA and Hercules Red Dot will leave some small amount of residue.

The heavy bevel on the crimp (left) can sometimes help clean up a dirty-burning powder problem that may be incurred with a normal crimp (right). Not every loading tool will be able to form this heavy bevel. The various MEC tools will perform this task admirably.

Based on your description of a malfunctioning shotgun I suspect, however, that the use of a faster burning powder would help you considerably. But, when shooting magnum-type loads, a faster burning powder cannot always be used. In this case, option two is all that is left.

Option two is to put a heavy bevel on the end of the case mouth. Such a bevel will strengthen the crimp's resistance to the initial push of the primer thus affording better ignition of the powder. This improved ignition will often result in cleaner burning of the powder, especially when slow burning powders are used.

Crimp Problems

Question 5: *My shotshell tool makes a beautiful looking shell whenever I turn out target loads. However, the crimps on my hunting loads vary from fair to horrible. Some cases have a spiral crimp, some have a hole in the center, some have dished centers, etc., depending on the load I use. What gives?*

Answer: Shotshell loading tools are adjusted by the manufacturer for target loads. In the case of the 12 gauge, this is a 1⅛-ounce load using a popular wad and a relatively light charge of fast burning powder. When you switch to a heavier shot charge and/or a different wad (and finally a heavier powder charge), your loading requirements have changed. With such conditions it is reasonable to expect that some adjustment may have to be accomplished on your loading dies.

Once in a great while you may have to lower the crimp starter. On most tools this can be accomplished with the use of spacers. More often than not the crimp plunger may need adjustment;

To lower the crimp starter on most shotshell loading tools you will have to use washers to increase the space between the die holder head and the crimp starter body.

or, the crimp plunger cam may need adjustment. Not all loading tools have all these adjustments. If you can not make such adjustments then your tool may not be up to your requirements.

All die adjustments should be made in very small increments. And make only one kind of adjustment at a time. It might be handy to try to remember or record the settings for future requirements.

Help!

Question 6: *I am unable to put together a heavy field load exactly as indicated in my data source due to the fact that one or more of the components cannot be purchased in my area. What can I do?*

Answer: Write the powder manufacturer. I have found DuPont to be especially helpful in this area. Simply tell them what kind of a load you would like using their powder. Then advise them of the various cases, primers and wads available to you. If they can, they will supply a workable combination. In the past, I have found the people at Hercules to be helpful as well.

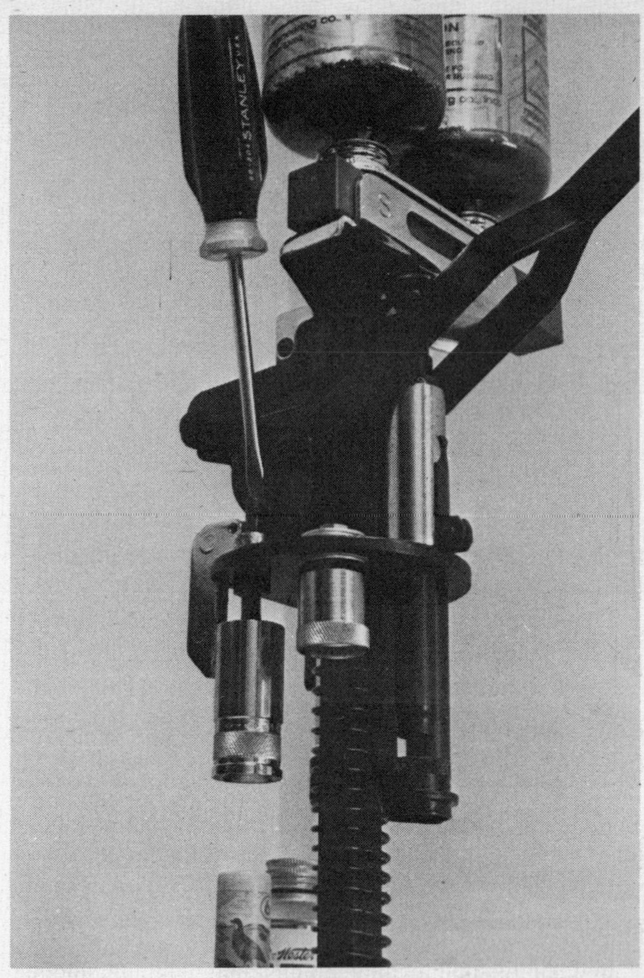

To adjust the depth of crimp, the plunger screw in the crimping die can be raised or lowered. This photo shows a screw driver inserted at the correct point to accomplish this adjustment.

(Below) Need a load not listed in the usual data sources? Sometimes the powder manufacturers are willing to help.

Crimp"Pop"

Question 7: *After adjusting my crimp starter and final crimp die I am still having problems with my crimps. After a short period of time the crimps start to pop open. If I am loading with fine shot, the shot will spill from the crimp when it "pops" slightly. What's wrong?*

Answer: If your crimping die has been properly adjusted and you have tried a heavy bevel on the case mouth, one of two problems is likely: 1.) the load selected simply does not fit the case well; 2.) you have forgotten one important die adjustment—wad pressure.

Wad pressure is very important when reloading shotshells. The usual approach is to have sufficient wad pressure to insure that the wad is seated firmly on the powder with no air space. This can mean anywhere from 10 to 40 pounds of pressure depending upon the exact components used. Most reloaders properly select the 40-

The case on the left was loaded with 60 pounds of wad pressure. The case on the right with 25 pounds of wad pressure. To avoid problems with crimps "popping" sufficient wad pressure must be used.

pound setting to avoid problems. However there are circumstances where wad pressures of up to 100 pounds are required to make a load fit the case properly and to avoid crimp "pops." The nearby photo shows two cases loaded under identical conditions except wad pressure. The photo was taken approximately 6 hours after loading the shells. The case on the left, with a perfectly acceptable crimp, was loaded with 60 pounds of wad pressure and the case on the right was loaded with 25 pounds of wad pressure. The differences are obvious. The crimp on the right (with insufficient wad pressure) is opening up. Two days after the photo was taken the crimp on the left case was normal and the crimp on the right case had opened enough for the shot to spill out when the case was inverted. This condition can also occur from improper crimping die adjustment. So check both areas carefully.

You say that you cannot adjust the wad pressure on your loading tool. The answer is that your reloading press is not capable of turning out all the possible combinations that a tool with adjustable wad pressure can handle.

Drop Tube Swap

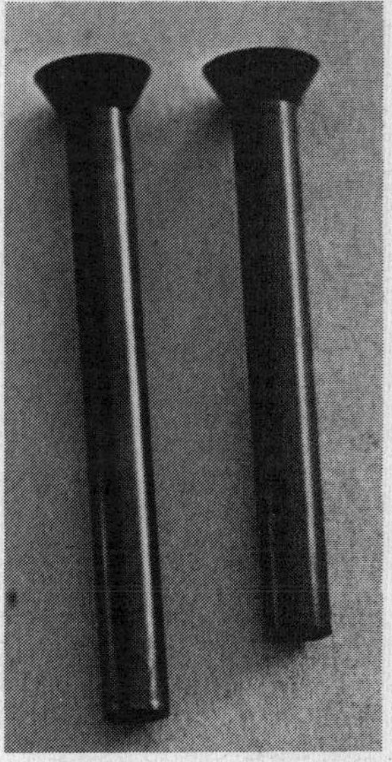

Drop tubes on some 12 gauge and 20 gauge MEC tools are of different lengths—the 12 gauge tube is longer. For 20 gauge loads requiring very heavy wad pressure you will need to replace your short drop tube with the longer 12 gauge version.

Question 8: *My MEC presses have adjustable wad pressure. I have no problems with my 12-gauge unit being able to adjust for a full 100 pounds of wad pressure on the rare occasion that it is needed. However I cannot get my 20-gauge MEC to adjust for more than 65 pounds without having trouble with the drop tube coming out of position. What can I do?*

Answer: This one is a snap. Simply replace the drop tube on your 20 gauge press with a drop tube from a 12 gauge press. The 12 gauge tube is longer and will correct the problem. With some combinations of loads you will have to switch back to the shorter tube. However, the longer tube will load almost all data combinations without a hitch. It takes just a few seconds to accomplish the switch.

Die Adjustment?

Question 9: *I have had a very savvy reloader adjust my shotshell press to give perfect crimps. Suddenly the crimps look horrible. Are my dies wearing out? Nothing has moved as all die adjustments are still locked up tight.*

Answer: The accompanying photo probably shows some of the crimps you are now getting. Something indeed is worn out. But it is not your loading dies. It is your cases. All of the cases shown in our photo (except the center case) were worn out two or three reloadings before the loading that produced the crimps shown. Case life is an iffy thing. However it is seldom as long as the manufacturer of the case might like you to think. My experience has shown the following approximate case lives. Naturally, the exact components used and the loading conditions can drastically affect such averages.

From left to right we have: a spiralled crimp with an excessive opening in center; a spiralled but closed crimp; a perfect crimp; a horrible example of a crimp; and finally a case with splits on crimp lines and an excessive opening.

Case	Reloads
AA (Winchester) type	6 to 10
RXP (Remington) type	6 to 8
Blue Magic (Peters)	6 to 10
Polyformed (Reifenhauser) type	1 to 3
SP (Remington) type	3 to 6
Reiwelin (Rainel/ACTIV) type	6 to 11

Bridging Problems

Question 10: *I have almost no problems with my shotshell reloader when using shot sizes between No. 11 and No. 5. But No. 4 shot and especially No. 2 shot give me nothing but trouble. The larger size shot frequently sticks in the drop tube leaving few if any pellets in the case. Also, when I raise the press handle (suddenly) often the shot that is stuck in the tube will dump through leaving spilled shot rolling all over the bench. This is not only annoying but very expensive with shot at $18.50 per bag. Please help. I load approximately 1500 rounds of duck loads each winter. I need to be able to accomplish the task without all this grief.*

Answer: The "bridging" of large shot in drop tubes is common. When the larger size shot try to escape from a relatively large shot bar opening, the constriction in the drop tube can cause the shot to impact against one another and thoroughly jam the drop tube. (This problem can even happen with powder. One powder, Winchester 230, was removed from the market because of its tendency to bridge in the drop tubes of automatic loading machines.) You can help to lessen the problem to some degree (but not completely eliminate it) in a number of ways.

First be sure that the inside of the drop tube is free from burrs or grit, then use a little more "bang" when metering the shot bar. One point that often goes unnoticed by the reloader is that certain brands of shot are rounder than others. The roundest shot will bridge far less often than rough shot so try changing brands of shot. These suggestions will keep bridging down to a minimum when loading No. 4 shot. As you raise the drop tube, also try pausing and lightly tapping the drop tube with the wood handle of a screw driver. Be careful to avoid damaging (read that, "denting") the drop tube which will only make matters worse.

If you are a machinist, and if your drop tube will allow it, you can try machining an irregular radius in the drop tube. Properly done this can work wonders.

A product that's not on the market, but one

A shot pallet (normally used for counting exact numbers of pellets for very exacting loading requirements) can help speed up the loading of large size shot.

that will also solve the problem, is something called a "shot pallet." This pallet, when used in conjunction with a roller-brush paint tray, affords a highly accurate and very fast means of obtaining a quick shot charge. In use, the pallet is dropped into a paint trough (which is full of shot) and removed. A slight jiggle of the pallet will allow excess pellets to fall from the pallet. Then with the use of a large aluminum or plastic funnel (available at most hardware stores) a very precise shot charge can be quickly dumped into the shell.

Shot pallets such as the one pictured are under production consideration by PROmat Enterprises (P.O. Box 286, Clinton, CT 04313). If enough interest is expressed, perhaps they can be persuaded to get the shot-pallet into the marketplace.

Powder Reservoir Static

Question 11: *I am having difficulty with a static charge in my powders (I use Winchester Ball powders exclusively). The powder not only sticks to the sides of the powder hopper but also to the inside of the drop tube of my loading tool causing erratic charges. Can this problem be avoided?*

Answer: A static charge in powder is not uncommon or limited only to Ball powders. It may be incurred when the powder has insufficient graphite coating or when environmental conditions are conducive to the build-up of a static charge. As you have indicated a severe condition can cause a variation in powder charge.

This problem can be easily overcome with the help of a piece of ordinary household fabric softener normally used in home clothes dryers. In my case I use "Bounce" because it's what my wife uses in her dryer. A strip placed into the powder hopper will completely eliminate the problem. **Caution:** Never simply stuff the strip of softener completely into the powder hopper. It will quickly work its way to the bottom of the hopper (if free to do so) and plug up the bushing opening which will result in squib loads and all the associated dangers. It is best to insert the fabric softener strip into an empty hopper. Push it straight down until it is about 1½ inches from the bottom of the powder hopper. Then bend it over and using a very small strip of tape attach it to the outside of the hopper. Pour in the powder and then insert the hopper plug. The plug will add additional security in holding the softener in place. The tape will also insure that the softener does not slip further into the hopper when it is filled with powder. When signs of "powder-stick" eventually reappear, simply replace the worn out fabric softener. My wife's "Bounce" seems to last a very long time and I can usually run about 5 pounds of powder through the machine before it needs replacing.

Case Problems?

Question 12: *I have noted that my reloads have suddenly developed a funny sound and that the case mouths are looking unusual in that the crimps do not iron out nearly as much as they used to. I have tried new cases, thinking perhaps that my old cases were worn out, but still the problem persists. What am I doing wrong?*

Answer: (Author's note: This question invariably comes up in cold weather.) Based on the date of your letter and the return address, I'll

Low chamber pressures can cause problems. Evidence of low pressure loads can be detected by the condition of the case mouth after firing. The shells shown were fired at low chamber pressures and, as could be expected, the crimps show little evidence of ironing-out. Cold weather can contribute to low pressure problems.

wager that your problems started with the arrival of the cold weather. I'll also guess that the problem is that the load selected has a pressure of less than 8500 LUP in the data source. Such low pressure loads frequently get very erratic at low temperatures. I can remember one "ballistic phenomenon" a companion and I experienced about 15 years or so ago. We were trying out a low-pressure load of PB powder. It was cold and damp. We were shooting Skeet "under the lights." Almost every round fired would result in a very tiny fireball dancing around the circumference of the front end of the barrel. On several occasions when the breech was opened a little fireball appeared to emanate from the breech, jump out of the action and dance about on the receiver. Granted such unusual occurrences are very rare, but bloopers and sub-ballistics are somewhat common with very low pressure loads in cold weather. At this point I should also say that "bloopers" are potentially dangerous. Select a load with a pressure range between 8500 LUP and 10,500 LUP (or very slightly higher, depending upon gauge and load) and your problems should disappear. The ammunition factories try to keep the average pressures of all shotshell loads at 9000 LUP's or more with good reason. It is prudent for the reloader to do the

same. The accompanying photo shows examples of crimps failing to iron out properly due to low chamber pressures.

Is a Powder Scale Necessary?

Question 13: *I have read numerous times that a powder and shot scale is a necessity when loading shotshells. My press has interchangeable shot bars, and, about 50 powder bushings are available for it. The tool came with a very elaborate chart indicating the powder charge thrown using all the various powders with each bushing. Obviously the tool is "self-contained" and I do not need a powder/shot scale. Right?*

Answer: WRONG! Shotshell reloading tool powder bushings do not throw the exact charge specification in many cases. The reasons are many and some include:

1. Variations in gravimetric density of powders from lot to lot. The tolerance is plus or minus .025 grams per cubic centimeter. This tolerance applies to most canister powders.
2. Usually, a bushing chart lists the nominal weight of a powder charge based on normal packing as a result of free flow and gravimetric

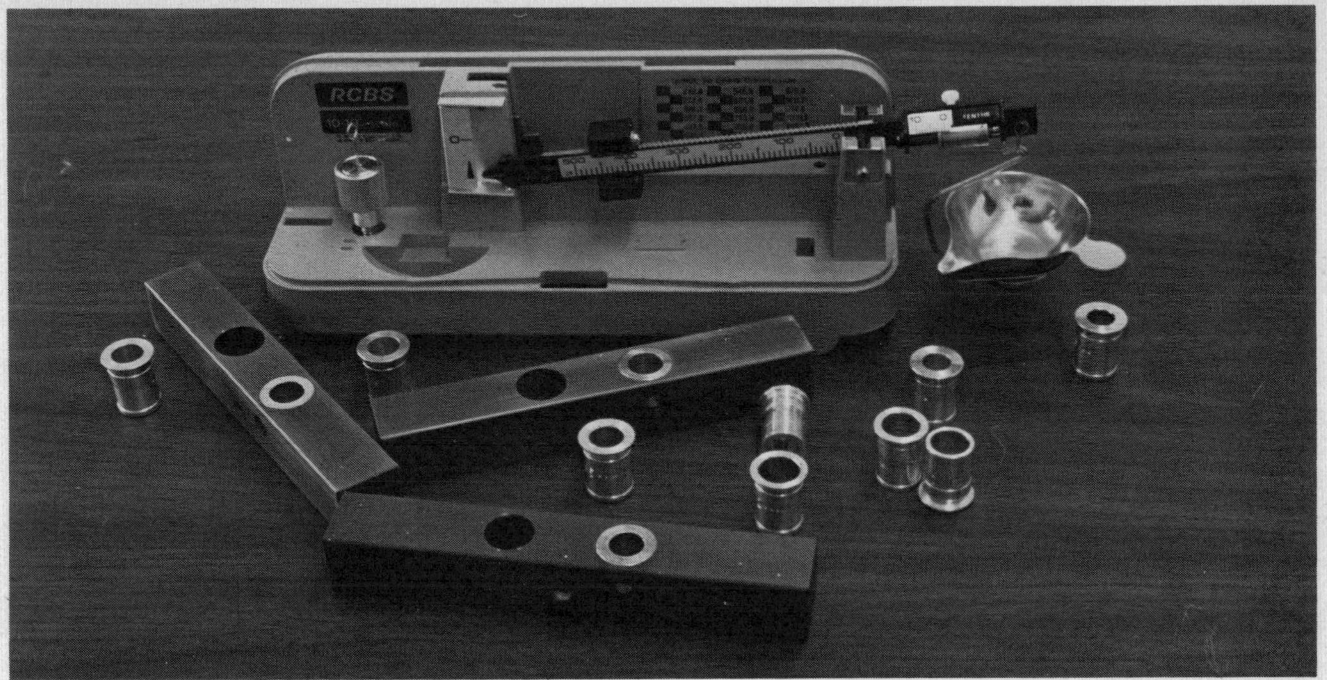

Powder bushings and shot bars are not always exactly what we expect for a variety of reasons. A powder scale is a *must* for every shotshell reloader when it comes to verifying bushing charge weights.

density of a powder **or** on bushing volume and the **nominal** gravimetric powder density at 100 percent packing.

3. Various operators of a tool will get various powder weights from an identical tool and bushings. This is due to the change in force of operation and the amount of vibration transmitted to the tool with resultant amount of packing of powder.
4. The amount of sizing force required on cases being loaded can cause a change in powder drop due to the change in tool vibration.
5. Bushing manufacturing tolerances.
6. Tool manufacturing tolerances.
7. Mismarked bushings.

As you can see, a bushing listing chart cannot be interpreted as an **absolute.** They simply can represent what the manufacturer believes to be the nominal charge thrown with the listed bushing and powder.

A **reloading scale is an absolute must** and charges thrown must be carefully checked and changes in bushing sizes made where required.

Do not try to determine the powder charge thrown by simply metering the powder bar back and forth and weighing charges.

To accurately check the weight of the charge being thrown by your bushing, the press must be run through the complete loading cycle to insure the same amount of vibration and powder packing as will take place in a normal loading cycle. Powder charges measured under these two conditions—on a scale and through a bushing— could vary as much as several grains.

The same identical reasoning applies to shot bars. **A tolerance of plus 3 grains and minus 10 grains on a shot bar will prove satisfactory. A tolerance of plus nothing and minus 3 percent will prove satisfactory in most cases for powder bushings.**

Remember that you **must** check your shot and powder charges and they **must** be checked as I have outlined.

Needs a Die Set

Question 14: *All the manufacturers of shotshell tools offer interchangeable die sets for their presses to enable the reloader to convert a tool from one gauge to another. I have tried all the dealers within a 50-mile radius of my home and not a single one stocks die sets. Why?*

Answer: Yes, tool manufacturers do generally offer die sets for their presses. However, these

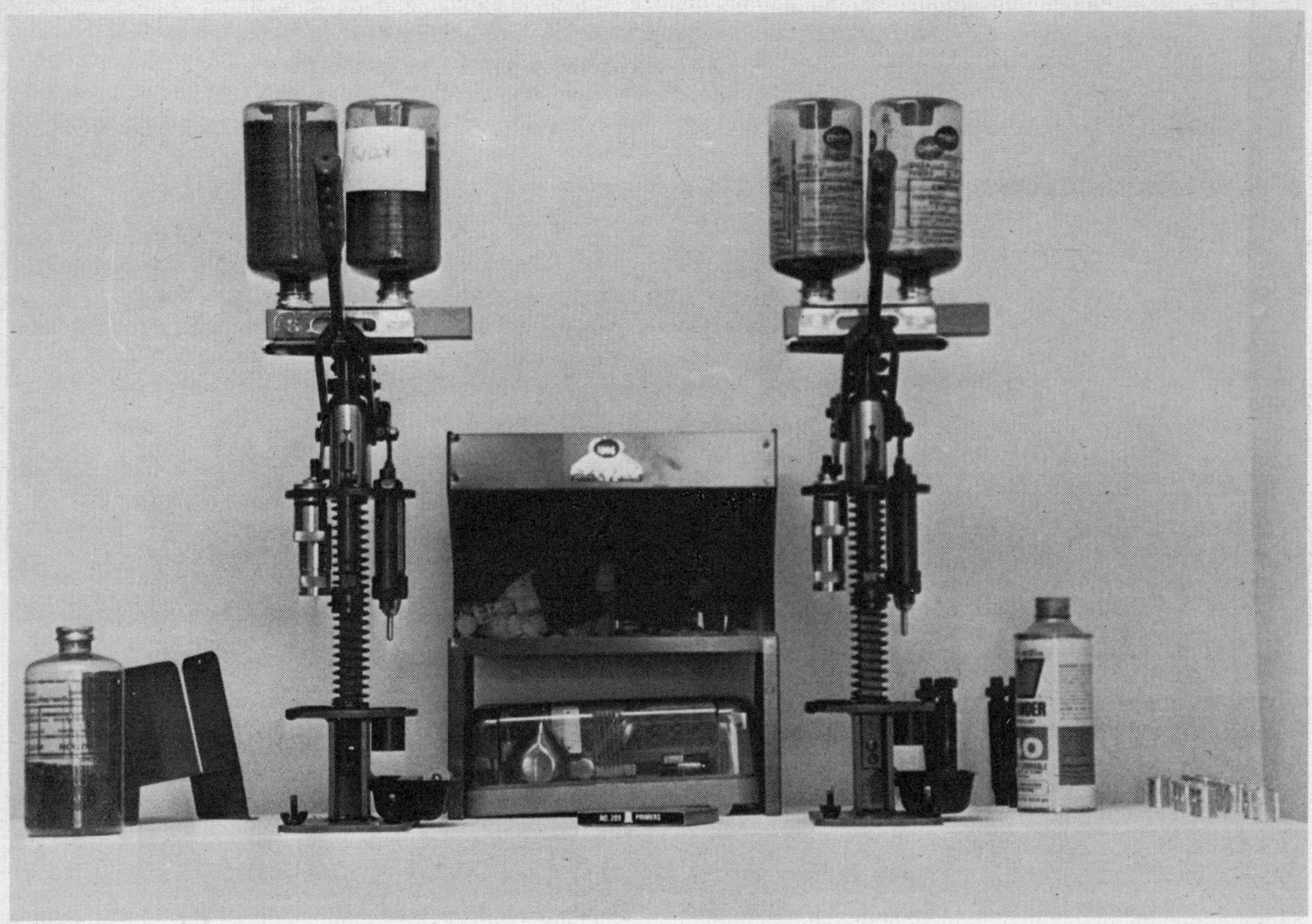

Most shotshell reloaders purchase separate machines to load each gauge. It is not really practical to interchange die sets on the shotshell presses. Pictured is the author's 12-gauge bench. Due to the high usage of field loads the author finds it practical to use two 12-gauge reloading presses.

die sets are comparatively expensive. Additionally the time required to make a change over from one gauge can be as long as 30 minutes by the time dies are properly adjusted. In addition, die parts can be damaged during change-over if care is not exercised. For these reasons most reloaders find it far more convenient to simply purchase another press for each gauge. I strongly endorse this approach. Your shopping experience is typical. It's proof of the fact that only a very few reloaders will bother with extra die sets. This is one area that differs sharply from the practice of metallic cartridge reloading wherein it's normal to change dies. But metallic dies are inexpensive and easily changed.

Steel Shot

Question 15: *I feel that the ammunition manufacturers are really sticking it to the public on steel shot. Unless you are part of the conspiracy, how about letting me have a good recipe for a steel shot load?*

Answer: The reloading of steel shot sounds quite simple on the surface, however, there are some dangerous pitfalls. In my opinion, the best answer to ever appear in print, just happens to be in this same book. The article is entitled "Steel Shot—The Question of Reloadability." Read it.

SHOTSHELL RELOADING TABLES

by EDWARD A. MATUNAS

20 Gauge

Heavy Waterfowl & Upland Game Loads 3″ Shell
Winchester-Western Compression-Formed Cases
1¼-oz. loads 173
1³/₁₆-oz. loads 173
1⅛-oz. loads 174

Remington SP Plastic Cases
1¼-oz. loads 174
1³/₁₆-oz. loads 175
1⅛-oz. loads 175

All Upland Game Loads 2¾″ Shell
Winchester-Western Compression-Formed Cases
1⅛-oz. loads 176
1-oz. loads 177

Remington-Peters RXP Plastic Cases
1⅛-oz. loads 178
1-oz. loads 178

Remington-Peters SP Plastic Cases
1⅛-oz. loads 179
1-oz. loads 180

Light Loads for Skeet & Upland Game 2¾″ Shell
Winchester-Western Compression-Formed Cases
⅞-oz. loads 181

Remington-Peters RXP Plastic Cases
⅞-oz. loads 182

28 Gauge

Light Loads for Skeet & Upland Game 2¾″ Shell
Winchester-Western Compression-Formed Cases
¾-oz. loads 183

Remington-Peters Plastic Target Cases
¾-oz. loads 184

.410 Bore

Light Upland Game Loads 3″ Shell
Winchester-Western Compression-Formed Cases
¹¹/₁₆-oz. loads 185

Remington-Peters SP Plastic Cases
¹¹/₁₆-oz. loads 185

Skeet Loads 2½″ Shell
Winchester-Western Compression-Formed Cases
½-oz. loads 186

Remington-Peters *New* SP Plastic Cases
½-oz. loads 186

CAUTION

Loads recommended and suggested herein have been carefully listed, but are intended solely as a guide to the reader. In that neither the publisher nor the author can control the use of this data, the components selected, the manner in which they are assembled or the firearm in which the loads may be used, neither the publisher nor the author can accept responsibility for the use of this data.

Gauge/Game Application Chart

	10 GA. 3½″	12 GA. 3″	12 GA. 2¾″	16 Ga. 2¾″	20 GA. 3″	20 GA. 2¾″	28 GA. 2¾″	.410 3″	.410 2½″
Geese	•	•	•	•	•	TL	TL	TL	TL
Ducks	•	•	•	•	•	TL	TL	TL	TL
Pheasant	TH	•	•	•	•	•	•	TL*	TL
Partridge	TH	TH	•	•	•	•	TL*	TL*	TL
Grouse	TH	TH	•	•	•	•	TL*	TL*	TL
Crows	TH	TH	•	•	•	•	•	•	TL
Pigeons	TH	TH	•	•	•	•	•	•	TL
Dove	TH	TH	•	•	•	•	TL*	TL*	TL
Quail	TH	TH	•	•	•	•	TL*	TL*	TL
Woodcock	TH	TH	•	•	•	•	TL*	TL*	TL
Snipe	TH	TH	•	•	•	•	TL*	TL*	TL
Rail	TH	TH	•	•	•	•	TL*	TL*	TL
Rabbits	TH	TH	•	•	•	•	•	•	TL
Squirrel	TH	TH	•	•	•	•	•	•	TL
Fox/Turkey	•	•	•	TL	TL	TL	TL	TL	TL
Trap	N/A	N/A	•	N/A	N/A	N/A	N/A	N/A	N/A
Skeet	N/A	N/A	•	•	N/A	•	•	N/A	•

TH: Too Heavy **TL:** Too Light **N/A:** Not allowed by rules governing this shotshell game.
*In the hands of *experienced* shooters, this gauge may be used to take the indicated game animal under proper field conditions.

AS A RELOADER you are probably aware of the many sources of reliable shotshell data. All four powder suppliers (Du Pont, Hercules, Hodgdon and Winchester) have free publications which list a great many loads. Also, Lyman and Hodgdon both offer a reasonably priced handbook. The total number of different loads available from all of these sources runs well over 5,000.

However, in none of these listings are there any suggestions as to which load or loads from each category the user should select. Obviously few reloaders are capable of determining which load is the most uniform ballistically. Two loads with identical average velocity and pressure may have performed drastically different in terms of shot-to-shot uniformity. For example, look at the following velocity pressure level variations of two different loads.

standard deviation of 20 fps or less is a very good load.

Pressure variations were equally different. The extreme variation on load No. 1 was a rather poor 3,200 LUP (std. deviation 917 LUP) while load No. 2 had an acceptable variation of 1,900 LUP (std. deviation 568 LUP). Obviously load No. 2 is the preferred load. But the data publishers do not list extreme variations and/or standard deviations. Such figures would perhaps show much data as being less than desirable. Whatever their reasons for not listing this vital information, the net result is that the handloader is deprived of a very useful tool in selecting his loads.

However, even knowing which loads are the most uniform (from a ballistic standpoint) may not be enough. What charge weight of shot should

12 Gauge 2¾″ Shell
1½ Ounces of Shot

	LOAD NO. 1		LOAD NO. 2	
	Velocity fps	Pressure LUP	Velocity fps	Pressure LUP
1.	1301	10,300	1259	9,500
2.	1258	9,200	1254 (low)	9,400
3.	1276	10,200	1294 (high)	10,700 (high)
4.	1302 (high)	11,800 (high)	1276	10,100
5.	1276	9,700	1254 (low)	8,800 (low)
6.	1250	9,000	1257	9,400
7.	1269	9,800	1271	10,400
8.	1297	10,700	1282	10,100
9.	1289	10,100	1276	9,800
10.	1229 (low)	8,600 (low)	1273	9,400
Avg.	1275	9,900	1270	9,800
Ext. Var.	73	3,200	40	1,900
Std. Dev.	24	917	13	568

The average velocity difference of these two loads was only 5 fps and the average pressure difference was only 100 LUP. These differences are so small that repeated testing could easily show the average pressure and velocity of both loads to be identical. However, let's look at the individual shot-by-shot differences. Load No. 1 had an extreme velocity variation (high to low) of full 73 fps while load No. 2 showed only 40 fps extreme variation. The standard deviation for load No. 1 works out to 24 fps and for load No. 2 it is only 13 fps. From a ballistic standpoint, a

you use, what size shot, or is one wad preferred over another for a specific purpose? And so on. For these and all the many other reasons you can think of we will list our data for this handbook by application. Covered will be turkey, geese, ducks, pheasant, upland game (partridge, squirrel, rabbit, etc.) and small birds such as woodcock, quail and rail. Skeet and trap loads will also be covered.

The tables, as you will see, work on a descending power scale. The mighty 10-gauge is first, followed by the 12, 16, 20, 28 and finally the .410 bore.

Within each gauge listing, the tables, again, work on a descending power scale—from 3½-inch shells (where applicable) and their weighty shot charges, on down to 2¾-inch (or smaller) hulls and their smaller shot charges. Within each gauge, this descending power scale is individually applied to Remington, Winchester, Federal and other popular brands of shotshell hulls.

Nothing can replace your actual experience in load selection. However, by starting with the loads shown in the following data you will insure good, uniform ballistics and performance. Then you can try just a few loads for patterning and field potential. You will be choosing from loads that have already proven their worth. Thus, instead of trying for a lucky guess, you will be selecting your loads from proven winners. All you need to do is to put the required care into the assembly of your loads.

Be sure to examine the shot size selection chart and the shot weight charts which follow. You will need to make a decision on shot size and charge weight *before* selecting data.

In that we cannot control the actual practice of reloading, variations in components or the firearms used, neither the author nor the publisher accepts any responsibility for the use of this data. If you have any questions on a load, contact the manufacturer of the powder listed. And remember, you *cannot* substitute one component for another without altering the ballistic performance of the load. Always load with the exact *specified* components — *no variations of any kind should be attempted except where specifically noted in the comments.*

The loads shown in these data listings were selected based on the author's extensive experience which includes the loading and firing of almost 750,000 rounds of shotshells, both in the lab and in the field. Good shooting!

Shot Size Selection Chart

Intended Purpose[1]	Shot Size	Shot Dia.
Large geese*, fox*, and turkey	BB	.18″
Large geese over decoys, turkey, small geese* at all ranges, large ducks such as blacks, mallards, and white-winged scoter	2	.15″
Ducks (all species)*, small geese*, pheasant*, turkey, squirrel and rabbit	4	.13″
Ducks over decoys (all species), small ducks (bluebill, buffle head, wood duck, teal, old squaw) at all ranges, pheasant, rabbit, squirrel and large grouse	5	.12″
Short range pheasant, grouse, dove, pigeon, partridge, rabbit*, crow* and squirrel*	6	.11″
Grouse, dove, pigeon, partridge, rabbit, crow and squirrel	7	.10″
Grouse*, dove*, pigeon*, partridge*, rabbit, crow, squirrel, quail, woodcock, snipe, large rail (clapper) and trap shooting*	7½	.095″
Woodcock, snipe, quail, large rail and trap shooting	8	.09″
Woodcock*, snipe*, quail* all rail and Skeet shooting*	9	.08″
Small rail (sora)*	11	.06″

1. Please note that ranges, cover, choke, and personal preference can alter shot selection up or down a full size. However, deviation of more than one size would produce less than optimum performance.
*Game indicated by an asterisk * in a particular group reflects the generally accepted ideal shot size. For example, for ducks of all species, the ideal shot selection is No. 4. Also usable are No. 2 and No. 5 shot sizes.

Shot Weight Chart

When selecting a shot size there is a minimum weight of charge that should be used with each shot size in order to insure sufficient pattern density. For instance, if you select No. 4 shot for ducks then the minimum shot charge you should use is 1¼ ounces. This means that a 2¾-inch 20 gauge gun (or smaller) is unsuitable for the application as the heaviest charge you can load in current 20 gauge 2¾-inch shells is 1⅛ ounces of shot.

Minimum Shot Weight	Shot Size	Application
1½ ounces	BB	For all suggested intended purposes for this shot size.
1⅜ ounces	2	For all suggested intended purposes for this shot size.
1¼ ounces	4 & 5	For all suggested intended purposes for this shot size except rabbit where 1⅛ ounces is acceptable.
1⅛ ounces	6	For all suggested intended purposes for this shot size.
1 ounce	7 & 7½	For all suggested intended purposes for this shot size except crow where a minimum shot weight of 1⅛ ounces is suggested
⅞-ounce	8	For all suggested intended purposes for this shot size.
¾-ounce	9 & 11	For all suggested intended purposes for this shot size.

Note: The foregoing leaves the .410 bore gun as an exception. In this gun, when chambered for 3-inch shells, No. 9 and No. 7½ shot sizes are recommended with either ¾- or ¹¹/₁₆-ounce charges. Use should be restricted to grouse, partridge, woodcock, snipe, rail, rabbit and squirrel with *maximum* range *never* exceeding 25 yards. The 2½-inch shell should be restricted to Skeet shooting with ½-ounce of No. 9s. The .410 bore is a ballistic midget and must, in the interest of sportsmanship, be restricted in its application.

The following data does not include every possible case, primer, powder, wad, and shot combination. But it does include the very best loads using the most popular components in the most frequently loaded cases.

Be absolutely *certain* that you have properly identified the shotshell case(s) you wish to reload for, *before* you start reloading. When in doubt, contact the manufacturer of the shotshell case in question.

10 GAUGE 3½″

GAME: geese, turkey, fox, and duck

SHOT SIZE: Unless noted otherwise, BBs, 2s, 4s, or 5s.

3½″ Winchester Western Polyformed Plastic Cases

2¼ Ounces Shot

LOAD 1
PRIMER: Winchester WW209
POWDER: 47.0 grains of Winchester 571
WAD: Remington SP10
VELOCITY: 1210 fps
PRESSURE: 9,900 LUP
COMMENTS: Works the Ithaca auto well leaving a minimum of residue. Patterns well in most guns. The preferred cold weather load.

LOAD 2
PRIMER: Winchester WW209
POWDER: 48.0 grains of Winchester 571
WAD: Pacific plastic
VELOCITY: 1210 fps
PRESSURE: 10,000 LUP
COMMENTS: Patterns satisfactorily

2 Ounces Shot

LOAD 1
PRIMER: Winchester WW209
POWDER: 44.0 grains of Winchester 540
WAD: Remington SP10 with 16 ga. ¼" Federal fiber filler
VELOCITY: 1210 fps
PRESSURE: 8,700 LUP
COMMENTS: Clean burning load

3½"
Remington Plastic Cases

2 Ounces Shot

LOAD 1
PRIMER: Remington 57★
POWDER: 34.0 grains of Hercules Herco
WAD: Remington SP10 with 16 ga. ¼" Federal fiber filler
VELOCITY: 1210 fps
PRESSURE: 10,200 LUP

1⅞ Ounces Shot

LOAD 1

PRIMER: Remington 57★
POWDER: 37.0 grains of Hercules Herco
WAD: Remington SP10 with 16 ga. ¼" Federal fiber filler
VELOCITY: 1280 fps
PRESSURE: 10,500 LUP
COMMENTS: A good patterning load which keeps the cost of reloading down due to the 1⅞ ounce charge of shot. This load has proven to be extremely effective on all sorts of waterfowl and it is the author's favorite 10-gauge loading.

3½"
Federal Plastic Cases

2 Ounces Shot

LOAD 1

PRIMER: Federal 209
POWDER: 43.5 grains of Hercules Blue Dot
WAD: Remington SP10
VELOCITY: 1210 fps
PRESSURE: 10,200 LUP
COMMENTS: Good ballistic uniformity

12 GAUGE 3″

GAME: Geese, turkey, fox and duck

SHOT SIZE: Unless noted otherwise, BBs, 2s, 4s or 5s

3″
Winchester Western Compression-Formed Cases

1⅞ Ounces Shot

LOAD 1
PRIMER: Winchester WW209
POWDER: 38.5 grains of Hercules Blue Dot
WAD: Remington RP12
VELOCITY: 1250 fps
PRESSURE: 10,800 LUP
COMMENTS: This is perhaps the very best 1⅞ ounce load for the Winchester compression-formed case. Velocity is excellent for this shot weight and the load patterns well from most guns. This load will leave a fair amount of powder residue in the actions of semi-automatic shotguns. This residue should be removed after each day afield to insure maximum shotgun reliability.

1⅝ Ounces Shot

LOAD 1

PRIMER: Winchester WW209
POWDER: 35.0 grains of Dupont SR4756
WAD: Winchester WAA12R
VELOCITY: 1250 fps
PRESSURE: 10,100 LUP
COMMENTS: Clean burning, very effective cold weather load.

LOAD 2

PRIMER: Winchester WW209
POWDER: 36.0 grains of Winchester 571
WAD: Winchester WAA12
VELOCITY: 1205 fps
PRESSURE: 10,500 LUP
COMMENTS: A good, uniform load.

LOAD 3

PRIMER: Winchester WW209
POWDER: 41.0 grains of Hercules Blue Dot
WAD: Remington SP12
VELOCITY: 1300 fps
PRESSURE: 10,800 LUP
COMMENTS: This is about as fast as you can push 1⅝ ounces of shot. A bit of dirty burning is normal with this load. Clean shotguns after each use.

1⅜ Ounces Shot

LOAD 1
PRIMER: Winchester WW209
POWDER: 31.0 grains of Dupont SR7625
WAD: Winchester WAA12
VELOCITY: 1285 fps
PRESSURE: 9,700 LUP
COMMENTS: A relatively moderate but effective load that employs easy-to-obtain components. Good pheasant load using Nos. 4, 5 or 6 shot.

LOAD 2
PRIMER: Winchester WW209
POWDER: 27.0 grains of Hercules Unique
WAD: Winchester WAA12
VELOCITY: 1300 fps
PRESSURE: 10,900 LUP
COMMENTS: A clean burning load that employs easy-to-obtain components.

3″
Remington-Peters
SP Plastic Cases

1⅞ Ounces Shot

LOAD 1
PRIMER: Remington 57★
POWDER: 38.5 grains of Hercules Blue Dot
WAD: Remington RP12
VELOCITY: 1250 fps
PRESSURE: 9,400 LUP
COMMENTS: Good velocity but guns should be cleaned after each use due to powder residue accumulation.

1⅝ Ounces Shot

LOAD 1

PRIMER: C.C.I. 157
POWDER: 34.5 grains of Dupont SR4756
WAD: Winchester WAA12R
VELOCITY: 1235 fps
PRESSURE: 10,400 LUP
COMMENTS: This load performs very well, but doesn't provide maximum velocity.

LOAD 2

PRIMER: Remington 57*
POWDER: 41.0 grains of Hercules Blue Dot
WAD: Remington SP12
VELOCITY: 1300 fps
PRESSURE: 9,100 LUP
COMMENTS: About as fast as you can go.

1⅜ Ounces Shot

LOAD 1

PRIMER: C.C.I. 157
POWDER: 36.0 grains of Winchester 540
WAD: Winchester WAA12
VELOCITY: 1295 fps
PRESSURE: 9,800 LUP

LOAD 2

PRIMER: Remington 57*
POWDER: 27.5 grains of Hercules Unique
WAD: Winchester WAA12 or Remington RXP12
VELOCITY: 1295 fps
PRESSURE: 10,300 LUP
COMMENTS: Easy to find components. Also good on pheasant when using Nos. 4, 5 or 6 shot.

1⅞ Ounces Shot

LOAD 1
PRIMER: Federal 209
POWDER: 39.5 grains of Hercules Blue Dot
WAD: Remington RP12
VELOCITY: 1250 fps
PRESSURE: 10,500 LUP
COMMENTS: The very best 12 ga., 3″, 1⅞-ounce load for this case.

1⅝ Ounces Shot

LOAD 1
PRIMER: Federal 209
POWDER: 39.0 grains of Hercules Blue Dot
WAD: Winchester WAA12F114
VELOCITY: 1300 fps
PRESSURE: 9,900 LUP
COMMENTS: An especially good cold weather load for this case.

1³⁄₈ Ounces Shot

LOAD 1

PRIMER: Federal 209
POWDER: 30.0 grains of Hercules Unique
WAD: Remington RXP12
VELOCITY: 1300 fps
PRESSURE: 10,800 LUP
COMMENTS: A clean burning load. Also great on pheasant when using Nos. 4, 5 or 6 shot.

LOAD 2

PRIMER: Federal 209
POWDER: 32.0 grains of Hercules Herco
WAD: Winchester WAA12
VELOCITY: 1300 fps
PRESSURE: 10,300 LUP
COMMENTS: A good cold weather load. Good on pheasant.

12 GAUGE 2¾"

GAME: geese, turkey, fox, duck, pheasant and crow

SHOT SIZES: Unless noted otherwise, BBs, 2s, 4s, 5s, 6s and 7½s

2¾"
Winchester Western Compression-Formed Cases

1½ Ounces Shot

LOAD 1

PRIMER: Winchester WW209
POWDER: 36.5 grains of Winchester 571
WAD: Winchester WAA12R
VELOCITY: 1260 fps
PRESSURE: 10,300 LUP
COMMENTS: This load duplicates the nominal velocity of the factory 2¾" Magnum shells. This particular load is my favorite 1½ ounce load for this case. A Remington RP12 wad can be substituted with a drop of 500 LUP in pressure. However, the Remington wad does not seem to perform as well at low temperatures. A number of these wads have fractured at low temperature testing.

LOAD 2
PRIMER: C.C.I. 109
POWDER: 35.5 grains of Winchester 571
WAD: Winchester WAA12R
VELOCITY: 1260 fps
PRESSURE: 10,500 LUP
COMMENTS: This load also duplicates the factory nominal velocity for a 2¾" Magnum load.

LOAD 3
PRIMER: Winchester WW209
POWDER: 36.5 grains of Hercules Blue Dot
WAD: Winchester WAA12R
VELOCITY: 1275 fps
PRESSURE: 9,600 LUP
COMMENTS: Some dirty burning is normal.

1³⁄₈ Ounces Shot

LOAD 1
PRIMER: Winchester WW209
POWDER: 32.5 grains of Dupont SR4756
WAD: Winchester WAA12R
VELOCITY: 1295 fps
PRESSURE: 10,600 LUP
COMMENTS: A good performing load; a fine pheasant load.

LOAD 2

PRIMER: Winchester WW209
POWDER: 39.5 grains of Winchester 571
WAD: Winchester WAA12R
VELOCITY: 1330 fps
PRESSURE: 9,800 LUP
COMMENTS: Author's favorite 1⅜-ounce load. This is a superb duck load. Due to the high muzzle velocity, this load will usually outperform the 1½ ounce, 12 ga., Magnum loads (1260 fps). If temperature will not fall below 40° F a Remington RP12 wad can be used if you are unable to find the WAA12R wads. A terrific pheasant load. Very devastating on crows.

LOAD 3

PRIMER: Winchester WW209
POWDER: 37.0 grains of Hercules Blue Dot
WAD: Winchester WAA12R
VELOCITY: 1300 fps
PRESSURE: 9,300 LUP
COMMENTS: Due to dirty burning this load is not recommended for automatics.

1¼ Ounces Shot

LOAD 1

PRIMER: Winchester WW209
POWDER: 33.0 grains of Winchester 540
WAD: Winchester WAA12F114
VELOCITY: 1330 fps
PRESSURE: 10,400 LUP
COMMENTS: This load duplicates the nominal velocity of the factory 1¼ ounce Super-X load. A Winchester WAA12 wad can be used if you cannot find the WAA12F114 at your dealers. You would then have to increase the powder charge to 34.5 grains of Winchester 540 to maintain the velocity and pressure levels. This is a fine crow and pheasant load. However, it is on the light side for geese, turkey, fox or ducks.

LOAD 2

PRIMER: Winchester WW209
POWDER: 33.5 grains of Dupont SR4756
WAD: Winchester WAA12R
VELOCITY: 1335 fps
PRESSURE: 9,200 LUP
COMMENTS: A fine crow and pheasant load. It is on the light side for geese, turkey, fox or ducks.

LOAD 3

PRIMER: Winchester WW209
POWDER: 28.5 grains of Dupont SR7625
WAD: Winchester WAA12R
VELOCITY: 1330 fps
PRESSURE: 9,800 LUP
COMMENTS: This load duplicates the velocity of the factory Super-X load. It is an extremely clean burning load and very much favored by the author for 1¼ ounce high velocity applications.

LOAD 4

PRIMER: Winchester WW209
POWDER: 28.5 grains of Hercules Herco
WAD: Winchester WAA12F114
VELOCITY: 1330 fps
PRESSURE: 9,700 LUP
COMMENTS: A Remington SP12 wad may be used with an increase of 600 LUP in pressure.

2¾"
Remington-Peters
SP Plastic Cases

1½ Ounces Shot

LOAD 1

PRIMER: C.C.I. 157
POWDER: 35.0 grains of Winchester 540
WAD: Winchester WAA12R or Remington RP12
VELOCITY: 1260 fps
PRESSURE: 10,300 LUP
COMMENTS: Duplicates the nominal factory velocity for 2¾" Magnum shells. The author prefers the Winchester WAA12R wad for cold weather shooting.

1⅜ Ounces Shot

LOAD 1

PRIMER: C.C.I. 157
POWDER: 35.5 grains of Winchester 540
WAD: Remington RP12
VELOCITY: 1295 fps
PRESSURE: 9,300 LUP
COMMENTS: As good a 1⅜-ounce load as can be made using this case.

LOAD 1

PRIMER: Remington 57★
POWDER: 26.0 grains of Hercules Unique
WAD: Remington SP12 or Winchester WAA12R
VELOCITY: 1330 fps
PRESSURE: 10,700 LUP
COMMENTS: Duplicates the factory nominal velocity for the 1¼ ounce high-velocity loading in this case. The Winchester WAA12R wad is preferred by the author for temperatures below 40° F. A bit light for waterfowl, turkey or fox.

LOAD 2

PRIMER: C.C.I. 157
POWDER: 36.0 grains of Winchester 540
WAD: Pacific Blue Verelite
VELOCITY: 1330 fps
PRESSURE: 9,200 LUP
COMMENTS: This is an old wad and may be hard to locate.

2¾″ Remington-Peters RXP Plastic Cases

1½ Ounces Shot

LOAD 1

PRIMER: Winchester WW209
POWDER: 36.5 grains of Winchester 571
WAD: Remington RP12
VELOCITY: 1240 fps
PRESSURE: 10,400 LUP
COMMENTS: This is the very best 1½-ounce load for this case.

1⅜ Ounces Shot

LOAD 1

PRIMER: Winchester WW209
POWDER: 30.0 grains of Dupont SR4756
WAD: Winchester WAA12R
VELOCITY: 1245 fps
PRESSURE: 10,800 LUP
COMMENTS: A good load that performs very well in cold weather.

LOAD 2

PRIMER: Remington 97*
POWDER: 35.5 grains of Hercules Blue Dot
WAD: Remington RP12
VELOCITY: 1300 fps
PRESSURE: 9,700 LUP
COMMENTS: Patterns well.

LOAD 3

PRIMER: Winchester WW209
POWDER: 37.5 grains of Winchester 571
WAD: Winchester WAA12R
VELOCITY: 1295 fps
PRESSURE: 10,100 LUP
COMMENTS: This is the best heavy load for this case. It will outperform all other 1½-ounce and 1⅜-ounce loads with respect to filling the game bag. If temperatures will remain above 40° F, a Remington RP12 wad can be used. This is the author's favorite heavy load in this case.

1¼ Ounces Shot

LOAD 1

PRIMER: Winchester WW209
POWDER: 32.0 grains of Dupont SR4756
WAD: Winchester WAA12R
VELOCITY: 1330 fps
PRESSURE: 10,000 LUP
COMMENTS: A good crow and pheasant load.

LOAD 2

PRIMER: Winchester WW209
POWDER: 33.5 grains of Winchester 540
WAD: Winchester WAA12
VELOCITY: 1330 fps
PRESSURE: 10,300 LUP
COMMENTS: Duplicates the nominal velocity of a 1¼ ounce high-velocity load. (This case is loaded only with 1⅛ ounces at the factory.)

2¾"
Federal Hi-Power
Plastic Cases

1½ Ounces Shot

LOAD 1

PRIMER: Winchester WW209
POWDER: 34.5 grains of Winchester 540
WAD: Winchester WAA12R
VELOCITY: 1260 fps
PRESSURE: 10,400 LUP
COMMENTS: Velocity duplicates the factory loaded 2¾" Magnum shell. If temperatures won't be below 40° F, a Remington RP12 wad may be used. Burns clean.

LOAD 2

PRIMER: Federal 209
POWDER: 36.0 grains of Hercules Blue Dot
WAD: Remington RP12
VELOCITY: 1275 fps
PRESSURE: 9,500 LUP
COMMENTS: A very fast load considering the weight of shot.

1⅜ Ounces Shot

LOAD 1
PRIMER: Federal 209
POWDER: 33.5 grains of Dupont SR4756
WAD: Winchester WAA12R
VELOCITY: 1280 fps
PRESSURE: 9,800 LUP
COMMENTS: Good on pheasant and crows.

LOAD 2
PRIMER: Federal 209
POWDER: 37.5 grains of Hercules Blue Dot
WAD: Winchester WAA12F114
VELOCITY: 1300 fps
PRESSURE: 9,100 LUP

1¼ Ounces Shot

LOAD 1
PRIMER: Federal 209
POWDER: 25.5 grains of Hercules Unique
WAD: Remington SP12
VELOCITY: 1330 fps
PRESSURE: 10,200 LUP
COMMENTS: Clean burning.

LOAD 2
PRIMER: Federal 209
POWDER: 29.0 grains of Hercules Herco
WAD: Winchester WAA12R
VELOCITY: 1330 fps
PRESSURE: 10,500 LUP
COMMENTS: A fine cold weather load that duplicates the nominal velocity of the factory 1¼ ounce high velocity loads.

2¾″
Rainel Activ
All-Plastic Cases

Note: This data is for cases having an overall length of 2.6 inches.

1⁵⁄₈ Ounces Shot

LOAD 1

PRIMER: Winchester 209
POWDER: 29.5 grains of Dupont SR4756
WAD: Winchester WAA12R
VELOCITY: 1250 fps
PRESSURE: 11,100 LUP
COMMENTS: This is the heaviest shot charge that can be handled from a 2¾″ chamber at Magnum velocities. This load will, in effect, make any 2¾″ gun perform on an equal basis with 3″ guns. A fine, uniform cold weather load. A Federal 209 primer may also be used with this load, as can a Remington 97★. However, the Winchester primer is the preferred choice. The author's most favored waterfowl and turkey load.

1½ Ounces Shot

LOAD 1
PRIMER: Federal 209
POWDER: 31.0 grains of Dupont SR4756
WAD: Winchester WAA12R
VELOCITY: 1270 fps
PRESSURE: 9,800 LUP
COMMENTS: The Winchester 209 primer can be used as a second choice with this load. The Federal primer provides very uniform ballistics with this load.

1⅜ Ounces Shot

LOAD 1
PRIMER: Winchester 209
POWDER: 37.0 grains of Winchester 540
WAD: Remington R12L
VELOCITY: 1335 fps
PRESSURE: 9,700 LUP
COMMENTS: A fine, clean burning load.

1¼ Ounces Shot

LOAD 1
PRIMER: Federal 209
POWDER: 29.0 grains of Winchester 473AA
WAD: Remington RXP12
VELOCITY: 1315 fps
PRESSURE: 10,700 LUP
COMMENTS: A very uniform load that burns very clean.

LOAD 2
PRIMER: Federal 209
POWDER: 29.0 grains of Dupont SR7625
WAD: Remington RXP12
VELOCITY: 1350 fps
PRESSURE: 9,500 LUP
COMMENTS: A fast load with very uniform ballistics.

GAME: heavy upland game loads for rabbit, pheasant, squirrel, grouse, partridge, dove, pigeon, etc.

SHOT SIZE: Unless noted otherwise, 4s, 5s, 6s and 7½s.

2¾″
Winchester
Compression-Formed Cases

1¼ Ounces Shot

LOAD 1
PRIMER: Winchester WW209
POWDER: 31.0 grains of Winchester 540
WAD: Winchester WAA12F114
VELOCITY: 1255 fps
PRESSURE: 9,100 LUP
COMMENTS: A dense patterning long-range upland load. A good cold weather load.

LOAD 2
PRIMER: Federal 209
POWDER: 24.5 grains of Dupont SR7625
WAD: Remington SP12
VELOCITY: 1220 fps
PRESSURE: 9,300 LUP

LOAD 3
PRIMER: Winchester WW209
POWDER: 21.5 grains of Hercules Green Dot
WAD: Winchester WAA12R
VELOCITY: 1220 fps
PRESSURE: 10,400 LUP
COMMENTS: A Remington SP12 wad may be used as a second choice. This will increase pressures in this load by about 400 LUP. The Winchester wad is preferred when the temperatures will be low.

LOAD 4
PRIMER: Winchester WW209
POWDER: 23.5 grains of Hercules Unique
WAD: Winchester WAA12F114
VELOCITY: 1220 fps
PRESSURE: 9,900 LUP
COMMENTS: Usually patterns quite densely.

LOAD 5
PRIMER: Winchester WW209
POWDER: 25.0 grains of Winchester 473AA
WAD: Winchester WAA12
VELOCITY: 1220 fps
PRESSURE: 10,300 LUP
COMMENTS: Pattern density can be increased with the use of the Winchester WAA12F114 wad. Also, the Remington RXP12 wad can be used for temperatures above 40° F.

LOAD 6
PRIMER: Federal 209
POWDER: 25.0 grains of Winchester 473AA
WAD: Winchester WAA12
VELOCITY: 1220 fps
PRESSURE: 10,500 LUP
COMMENTS: A very uniform load.

LOAD 7
PRIMER: C.C.I. 109
POWDER: 24.5 grains of Winchester 473AA
WAD: Winchester WAA12
VELOCITY: 1220 fps
PRESSURE: 9,800 LUP

LOAD 8
PRIMER: Winchester WW209
POWDER: 23.5 grains of Winchester 473AA
WAD: Winchester WAA12
VELOCITY: 1150 fps
PRESSURE: 9,400 LUP
COMMENTS: A mild recoiling 1¼-ounce load. Ideal for ranges that will not exceed 30 yards. The Winchester WAA12F114 wad may be substituted for slightly denser patterns if required (squirrel shooting).

2¾"
Remington-Peters
SP Plastic Cases

1¼ Ounces Shot

LOAD 1
PRIMER: Remington 57★
POWDER: 21.0 grains of Hercules Green Dot
WAD: Winchester WAA12R
VELOCITY: 1220 fps
PRESSURE: 10,100 LUP
COMMENTS: A clean burning uniform load. A Remington RP12 may be used if not shooting at less than 40° F.

LOAD 2
PRIMER: Remington 57★
POWDER: 22.5 grains of Hercules Green Dot.
WAD: Winchester WAA12F114
VELOCITY: 1220 fps
PRESSURE: 10,900 LUP
COMMENTS: Patterns on the dense side.

LOAD 3
PRIMER: Remington 57★
POWDER: 24.0 grains of Hercules Unique
WAD: Winchester WAA12F114
VELOCITY: 1220 fps
PRESSURE: 9,500 LUP
COMMENTS: A good, uniform load.

LOAD 4
PRIMER: Remington 57★
POWDER: 20.0 grains of Hercules Red Dot
WAD: Remington RP12
VELOCITY: 1220 fps
PRESSURE: 10,600 LUP
COMMENTS: Burns clean.

2¾"
Remington-Peters
RXP Plastic Cases

1¼ Ounces Shot

LOAD 1
PRIMER: Federal 209
POWDER: 23.5 grains of Dupont SR7625
WAD: Winchester WAA12R
VELOCITY: 1225 fps
PRESSURE: 9,400 LUP
COMMENTS: A fine, all-weather load.

LOAD 2

PRIMER: Remington 97★
POWDER: 22.0 grains of Hercules Green Dot
WAD: Winchester WAA12F114
VELOCITY: 1220 fps
PRESSURE: 10,900 LUP
COMMENTS: A Winchester WAA12R wad may also be used.

LOAD 3

PRIMER: Remington 97★
POWDER: 22.5 grains of Hercules Unique
WAD: Winchester WAA12R
VELOCITY: 1220 fps
PRESSURE: 9,400 LUP

LOAD 4

PRIMER: Winchester WW209
POWDER: 30.0 grains of Winchester 540
WAD: Winchester WAA12F114
VELOCITY: 1255 fps
PRESSURE: 9,600 LUP
COMMENTS: A fine long-range upland load. Patterns tight. An excellent choice for squirrels.

LOAD 5

PRIMER: Winchester WW209
POWDER: 25.0 grains of Winchester 473AA
WAD: Winchester WAA12
VELOCITY: 1220 fps
PRESSURE: 10,300 LUP
COMMENTS: Author's favorite heavy upland game load in this case.

2¾"
Peters Blue Magic
Plastic Cases

1¼ Ounces Shot

LOAD 1
PRIMER: Federal 209
POWDER: 24.5 grains of Dupont SR7625
WAD: Winchester WAA12F114
VELOCITY: 1225 fps
PRESSURE: 10,600 LUP
COMMENTS: A fine ballistic balance. Good for all temperature conditions.

LOAD 2
PRIMER: Remington 97*
POWDER: 23.0 grains of Hercules Unique
WAD: Winchester WAA12F114
VELOCITY: 1220 fps
PRESSURE: 10,700 LUP

LOAD 3
PRIMER: Winchester WW209
POWDER: 25.5 grains of Winchester 473AA
WAD: Winchester WAA12
VELOCITY: 1220 fps
PRESSURE: 10,500 LUP
COMMENTS: A very fine load using easy-to-find components.

2¾″
Federal Plastic
Hi-Power Cases

1¼ Ounces Shot

LOAD 1

PRIMER: Federal 209
POWDER: 23.0 grains of Hercules Unique
WAD: Winchester WAA12F114
VELOCITY: 1220 fps
PRESSURE: 9,400 LUP
COMMENTS: A Winchester WAA12 wad may also be used where slightly more open patterns are desired.

2¾″
Federal Champion II
Plastic Cases

1¼ Ounces Shot

LOAD 1

PRIMER: Winchester WW209
POWDER: 24.5 grains of Winchester 473AA
WAD: Remington RXP12
VELOCITY: 1220 fps
PRESSURE: 10,500 LUP
COMMENTS: Burns clean.

2¾"
Rainel Activ
All-Plastic Cases

Note: This data is for cases having an overall length of 2.6 inches.

1¼ Ounces Shot

LOAD 1
PRIMER: Winchester WW209
POWDER: 28.0 grains of Winchester 473AA
WAD: Winchester WAA12
VELOCITY: 1275 fps
PRESSURE: 9,800 LUP
COMMENTS: A fast upland game load with very uniform ballistics.

LOAD 2
PRIMER: Federal 209
POWDER: 23.5 grains of Hercules Green Dot
WAD: Remington R12L
VELOCITY: 1225 fps
PRESSURE: 9,600 LUP
COMMENTS: An extremely uniform load.

12 GAUGE 2¾"

GAME: light upland game loads for rabbit, grouse, partridge, dove, pigeon, quail and rail

SHOT SIZE: Unless noted otherwise, 4s, 5s, 6s, 7½s and 8s.

(Note: The loads listed for Skeet and trap may also be used for these purposes with the appropriate shot sizes.)

2¾" Winchester Western Compression-Formed Cases

1⅛ Ounces Shot

LOAD 1
PRIMER: Federal 209
POWDER: 24.5 grains of Winchester 473AA
WAD: Winchester WAA12
VELOCITY: 1255 fps
PRESSURE: 9,900 LUP
COMMENTS: A C.C.I. 109 primer may be used (pressure on this load would then be 9,400 LUP).

LOAD 2
PRIMER: Winchester WW209
POWDER: 20.0 grains of Dupont "Hi-Skor" 700-X
WAD: Winchester WAA12
VELOCITY: 1245 fps
PRESSURE: 10,500 LUP
COMMENTS: Very clean burning and uniform. Good for all temperatures.

2¾"
Remington-Peters
SP Plastic Cases

1⅛ Ounces Shot

LOAD 1
PRIMER: Remington 57★
POWDER: 20.0 grains of Hercules Red Dot
WAD: Winchester WAA12
VELOCITY: 1255 fps
PRESSURE: 10,900 LUP

LOAD 2
PRIMER: Remington 57★
POWDER: 20.5 grains of Dupont "Hi-Skor" 700-X
WAD: Remington R12H
VELOCITY: 1260 fps
PRESSURE: 10,300 LUP
COMMENTS: Clean burning and very uniform.

2¾"
Remington-Peters
RXP Plastic Cases

1⅛ Ounces Shot

LOAD 1
PRIMER: Remington 97★
POWDER: 19.5 grains of Dupont "Hi-Skor" 700-X
WAD: Winchester WAA12
VELOCITY: 1255 fps
PRESSURE: 10,400 LUP
COMMENTS: Burns clean.

LOAD 2
PRIMER: Winchester WW209
POWDER: 25.0 grains of Winchester 473AA
WAD: Winchester WAA12
VELOCITY: 1255 fps
PRESSURE: 9,600 LUP

2¾"
Peters Blue Magic
Plastic Cases

1⅛ Ounces Shot

LOAD 1
PRIMER: Winchester WW209
POWDER: 19.5 grains of Dupont "Hi-Skor" 700-X
WAD: Winchester WAA12
VELOCITY: 1240 fps
PRESSURE: 10,900 LUP
COMMENTS: A fine uniform load; very good at all temperatures.

LOAD 2
PRIMER: Winchester WW209
POWDER: 25.0 grains of Winchester 473AA
WAD: Winchester WAA12
VELOCITY: 1255 fps
PRESSURE: 9,400 LUP

1⅛ Ounces Shot

LOAD 1
PRIMER: Winchester WW209
POWDER: 25.0 grains of Winchester 473AA
WAD: Winchester WAA12
VELOCITY: 1255 fps
PRESSURE: 10,200 LUP
COMMENTS: A Federal 12S1 wad may be used.

LOAD 2
PRIMER: Federal 209
POWDER: 24.5 grains of Winchester 473AA
WAD: Winchester WAA12
VELOCITY: 1255 fps
PRESSURE: 10,500 LUP
COMMENTS: A Federal 12S1 wad may be used.

12 GAUGE 2¾″

GAME: Skeet and trap loads.

SHOT SIZES: Skeet — 9s; trap — 7½s or 8s.

Loads at 1200 fps are considered "heavy" (3 dram equivalent) loads and loads at 1145 fps are considered "light" (2¾ dram equivalent loads). **Note: All** of these loads may be used for light upland game with an appropriate shot size. However, they are not recommended for pheasant or squirrels.

2¾″ Winchester Western Compression-Formed Cases

1⅛ Ounces Shot

LOAD 1

PRIMER: Winchester WW209
POWDER: 19.0 grains of Dupont "Hi-Skor" 700-X
WAD: Winchester WAA12
VELOCITY: 1200 fps
PRESSURE: 9,200 LUP
COMMENTS: A very fine load. One of the best for this velocity level.

LOAD 2

PRIMER: Federal 209
POWDER: 17.0 grains of Dupont "Hi-Skor" 700-X
WAD: Winchester WAA12
VELOCITY: 1145 fps
PRESSURE: 9,500 LUP
COMMENTS: One of the best "light" target loads.

LOAD 3
PRIMER: Federal 209
POWDER: 18.0 grains of Dupont "Hi-Skor" 700-X
WAD: Winchester WAA12
VELOCITY: 1190 fps
PRESSURE: 10,400 LUP

LOAD 4
PRIMER: C.C.I. 209
POWDER: 19.0 grains of Dupont "Hi-Skor" 700-X
WAD: Winchester WAA12
VELOCITY: 1215 fps
PRESSURE: 10,200 LUP

LOAD 5
PRIMER: Winchester WW209
POWDER: 18.0 grains of Hercules Red Dot
WAD: Winchester WAA12
VELOCITY: 1200 fps
PRESSURE: 10,400 LUP
COMMENTS: A favorite load of a great many serious shooters. A C.C.I. 109 primer can also be used.

LOAD 6
PRIMER: Winchester WW209
POWDER: 17.0 grains of Hercules Red Dot
WAD: Winchester WAA12
VELOCITY: 1145 fps
PRESSURE: 10,000 LUP

LOAD 7
PRIMER: Winchester WW209
POWDER: 20.5 grains of Winchester 452AA
WAD: Winchester WAA12
VELOCITY: 1200 fps
PRESSURE: 10,100 LUP
COMMENTS: Duplicates the factory "heavy" target load in this case.

LOAD 8

PRIMER: C.C.I. 109
POWDER: 20.5 grains of Winchester 452AA
WAD: Winchester WAA12
VELOCITY: 1200 fps
PRESSURE: 10,500 LUP
COMMENTS: A Federal 209 primer may be used. Pressure will drop approximately 500 LUP when the Federal primer is used with this load.

LOAD 9

PRIMER: Winchester WW209
POWDER: 19.5 grains of Winchester 452AA
WAD: Winchester WAA12
VELOCITY: 1145 fps
PRESSURE: 9,400 LUP
COMMENTS: Duplicates the factory "light" target load in this case.

LOAD 10

PRIMER: C.C.I. 109
POWDER: 19.0 grains of Winchester 452AA
WAD: Winchester WAA12
VELOCITY: 1145 fps
PRESSURE: 9,600 LUP

LOAD 11

PRIMER: Federal 209
POWDER: 23.5 grains of Winchester 473AA
WAD: Winchester WAA12
VELOCITY: 1200 fps
PRESSURE: 9,200 LUP
COMMENTS: If temperatures will not go below 40° F, a C.C.I. 109 primer may be used.

2¾″ Remington-Peters RXP Cases

1⅛ Ounces Shot

LOAD 1
PRIMER: Federal 209
PRIMER: 16.5 grains of Dupont "Hi-Skor" 700-X
WAD: Remington RXP12
VELOCITY: 1140 fps
PRESSURE: 9,600 LUP
COMMENTS: A fine "light" target load.

LOAD 2
PRIMER: Federal 209
POWDER: 16.5 grains of Dupont "Hi-Skor" 700-X
WAD: Winchester WAA12
VELOCITY: 1160 fps
PRESSURE: 10,400 LUP
COMMENTS: Works well in cold weather.

LOAD 3
PRIMER: Federal 209
POWDER: 18.0 grains of Dupont "Hi-Skor" 700-X
WAD: Remington RXP12
VELOCITY: 1195 fps
PRESSURE: 10,300 LUP

LOAD 4
PRIMER: Winchester WW209
POWDER: 16.5 grains of Dupont "Hi-Skor" 700-X
WAD: Winchester WAA12
VELOCITY: 1150 fps
PRESSURE: 9,400 LUP
COMMENTS: Author's favorite target load for the RXP case.

LOAD 5

PRIMER: Winchester WW209
POWDER: 17.5 grains of Dupont "Hi-Skor" 700-X
WAD: Winchester WAA12
VELOCITY: 1195 fps
PRESSURE: 10,100 LUP
COMMENTS: Author's favorite load is the RXP case for extremely cold weather.

LOAD 6

PRIMER: Winchester WW209
POWDER: 21.0 grains of Winchester 452AA
WAD: Winchester WAA12
VELOCITY: 1200 fps
PRESSURE: 10,500 LUP

LOAD 7

PRIMER: Winchester WW209
POWDER: 19.5 grains of Winchester 452AA
WAD: Winchester WAA12
VELOCITY: 1145 fps
PRESSURE: 9,700 LUP

LOAD 8

PRIMER: C.C.I. 109
POWDER: 18.0 grains of Hercules Red Dot
WAD: Winchester WAA12
VELOCITY: 1200 fps
PRESSURE: 9,500 LUP
COMMENTS: A Federal 12C2 wad may also be used.

LOAD 9

PRIMER: C.C.I. 109
POWDER: 17.0 grains of Hercules Red Dot
WAD: Winchester WAA12
VELOCITY: 1145 fps
PRESSURE: 9,300 LUP
COMMENTS: A Remington 97★ primer may be used.

1⅛ Ounces Shot

LOAD 1
PRIMER: Federal 209
POWDER: 17.0 grains of Dupont "Hi-Skor" 700-X
WAD: Winchester WAA12
VELOCITY: 1150 fps
PRESSURE: 9,600 LUP

LOAD 2
PRIMER: C.C.I. 209
POWDER: 18.5 grains of Dupont "Hi-Skor" 700-X
WAD: Remington RXP12
VELOCITY: 1195 fps
PRESSURE: 9,700 LUP

LOAD 3
PRIMER: C.C.I. 209
POWDER: 18.5 grains of Dupont "Hi-Skor" 700-X
WAD: Winchester WAA12
VELOCITY: 1200 fps
PRESSURE: 10,100 LUP

LOAD 4
PRIMER: Winchester WW209
POWDER: 17.0 grains of Dupont "Hi-Skor" 700-X
WAD: Winchester WAA12
VELOCITY: 1140 fps
PRESSURE: 9,100 LUP

LOAD 5

PRIMER: Winchester WW209
POWDER: 18.5 grains of Dupont "Hi-Skor" 700-X
WAD: Winchester WAA12
VELOCITY: 1205 fps
PRESSURE: 10,200 LUP
COMMENTS: A fine all-around target load. Excellent performance at all temperatures.

LOAD 6

PRIMER: C.C.I. 109
POWDER: 18.5 grains of Hercules Red Dot
WAD: Winchester WAA12
VELOCITY: 1200 fps
PRESSURE: 9,900 LUP
COMMENTS: A Federal 12C1 wad may be used.

LOAD 7

PRIMER: C.C.I. 109
POWDER: 17.5 grains of Hercules Red Dot
WAD: Winchester WAA12
VELOCITY: 1145 fps
PRESSURE: 9,100 LUP

LOAD 8

PRIMER: C.C.I. 209
POWDER: 20.0 grains of Winchester 452AA
WAD: Winchester WAA12
VELOCITY: 1200 fps
PRESSURE: 10,400 LUP

LOAD 9

PRIMER: C.C.I. 209
POWDER: 20.5 grains of Winchester 452AA
WAD: Remington RXP12
VELOCITY: 1200 fps
PRESSURE: 9,800 LUP

LOAD 10
PRIMER: C.C.I. 209
POWDER: 18.5 grains of Winchester 452AA
WAD: Winchester WAA12
VELOCITY: 1145 fps
PRESSURE: 9,500 LUP
COMMENTS: A fine, uniform load.

LOAD 11
PRIMER: Winchester WW209
POWDER: 19.5 grains of Winchester 452AA
WAD: Winchester WAA12
VELOCITY: 1145 fps
PRESSURE: 10,100 LUP
COMMENTS: A fine, uniform load.

2¾″
Federal Champion II
Plastic Cases

1⅛ Ounces Shot

LOAD 1
PRIMER: Federal 209
POWDER: 16.5 grains of Dupont "Hi-Skor" 700-X
WAD: Winchester WAA12
VELOCITY: 1155 fps
PRESSURE: 9,600 LUP
COMMENTS: A very uniform load.

LOAD 2

PRIMER: Winchester WW209
POWDER: 18.5 grains of Dupont "Hi-Skor" 700-X
WAD: Winchester WAA12
VELOCITY: 1205 fps
PRESSURE: 10,400 LUP
COMMENTS: A very uniform load.

LOAD 3

PRIMER: Federal 209
POWDER: 17.5 grains of Hercules Red Dot
WAD: Remington RXP12
VELOCITY: 1200 fps
PRESSURE: 10,500 LUP

LOAD 4

PRIMER: Federal 209
POWDER: 19.5 grains of Winchester 452AA
WAD: Winchester WAA12
VELOCITY: 1145 fps
PRESSURE: 10,100 LUP

LOAD 5

PRIMER: Winchester WW209
POWDER: 19.5 grains of Winchester 452AA
WAD: Federal 12C2
VELOCITY: 1145 fps
PRESSURE: 10,000 LUP

LOAD 6

PRIMER: Federal 209
POWDER: 21.0 grains of Winchester 452AA
WAD: Federal 12C2
VELOCITY: 1200 fps
PRESSURE: 10,500 LUP

1⅛ Ounces Shot

LOAD 1
PRIMER: Federal 209
POWDER: 20.0 grains of Hercules Red Dot
WADS: Remington R12L plus one Federal .200″ 20 gauge card wad inserted into shot cup as a filler.
VELOCITY: 1210 fps
PRESSURE: 8,800 LUP
COMMENTS: A very uniform load.

GAME: special light target and light upland game

SHOT SIZE: Trap — 7½s or 8s; Skeet — 9s; Upland game — 6s, 7½s, 8s and 9s.

2¾″ Winchester Western Compression-Formed Cases

1 Ounce Shot

LOAD 1

PRIMER: Winchester WW209
POWDER: 22.0 grains of Winchester 452AA
WAD: Remington R12L
VELOCITY: 1290 fps
PRESSURE: 9,900 LUP

LOAD 2

PRIMER: Federal 209
POWDER: 22.0 grains of Winchester 452AA
WAD: Winchester WAA12
VELOCITY: 1290 fps
PRESSURE: 10,100 LUP

LOAD 3

PRIMER: Winchester WW209
POWDER: 19.0 grains of Hercules Red Dot
WAD: Winchester WAA12
VELOCITY: 1290 fps
PRESSURE: 10,500 LUP

2¾″
Remington-Peters
RXP Plastic Cases

1 Ounce Shot

LOAD 1

PRIMER: Winchester WW209
POWDER: 22.5 grains of Winchester 452AA
WAD: Winchester WAA12
VELOCITY: 1290 fps
PRESSURE: 10,300 LUP
COMMENTS: A Remington R12L or Federal 12S1 wad may be used.

2¾″
Peters Blue Magic
Plastic Cases

1 Ounce Shot

LOAD 1

PRIMER: Federal 209
POWDER: 19.5 grains of Dupont "Hi-Skor" 700-X
WAD: Remington RXP12
VELOCITY: 1285 fps
PRESSURE: 10,000 LUP

16 GAUGE 2¾"

GAME: field loads for all upland game

SHOT SIZE: 4s, 5s, 6s, 7½s or 8s.

2¾"
Winchester Western Compression-Formed Cases

1¼ Ounces Shot

LOAD 1

PRIMER: Winchester WW209
POWDER: 30.5 grains of Winchester 571
WAD: Remington SP16
VELOCITY: 1230 fps
PRESSURE: 10,500 LUP
COMMENTS: Also for waterfowl at short ranges using 4, 5, 6 or 7½ shot. Some dirty burning.

1⅛ Ounces Shot

LOAD 1

PRIMER: Winchester WW209
POWDER: 28.5 grains of Winchester 540
WAD: Remington R16
VELOCITY: 1290 fps
PRESSURE: 10,300 LUP

LOAD 2
PRIMER: Winchester WW209
POWDER: 27.5 grains of Winchester 540
WAD: Remington R16
VELOCITY: 1240 fps
PRESSURE: 9,400 LUP

LOAD 3
PRIMER: Winchester WW209
POWDER: 27.0 grains of Dupont SR4756
WAD: Remington SP16
VELOCITY: 1285 fps
PRESSURE: 9,400 LUP

LOAD 4
PRIMER: Winchester WW209
POWDER: 28.0 grains of Hercules Blue Dot
WAD: Remington SP16
VELOCITY: 1260 fps
PRESSURE: 9,600 LUP
COMMENTS: Some dirty burning.

LOAD 5
PRIMER: Winchester WW209
POWDER: 21.5 grains of Hercules Herco
WAD: Remington SP16 or R16
VELOCITY: 1240 fps
PRESSURE: 11,000 LUP

2¾"
Remington-Peters
SP Plastic Cases

1⅛ Ounces Shot

LOAD 1
PRIMER: Remington 57★
POWDER: 22.5 grains of Hercules Herco
WAD: Remington SP16
VELOCITY: 1260 fps
PRESSURE: 9,900 LUP

LOAD 2
PRIMER: Remington 57★
POWDER: 19.0 grains of Hercules Unique
WAD: Remington SP16 or R16
VELOCITY: 1240 fps
PRESSURE: 10,400 LUP
COMMENTS: Burns reasonably clean.

16 GAUGE 2¾"

GAME: trap, Skeet and light upland game

SHOT SIZE: Trap — 7½ or 8s; Skeet — 9s; game — 6s, 7½s or 8s.

2¾" Winchester Western Compression-Formed Cases

1⅛ Ounces Shot

LOAD 1
PRIMER: Winchester WW209
POWDER: 18.5 grains of Hercules Unique
WAD: Remington SP16 or R16
VELOCITY: 1185 fps
PRESSURE: 9,600 LUP

LOAD 2
PRIMER: Federal 209
POWDER: 20.0 grains of Dupont SR7625
WAD: Remington SP16
VELOCITY: 1180 fps
PRESSURE: 9,900 LUP
COMMENTS: A fine target load.

1 Ounce Shot

LOAD 1
PRIMER: Winchester WW209
POWDER: 17.5 grains of Winchester 452AA
WAD: Remington R16
VELOCITY: 1165 fps
PRESSURE: 10,300 LUP

LOAD 2
PRIMER: Winchester WW209
POWDER: 15.5 grains of Dupont "Hi-Skor" 700-X
WAD: Remington R16
VELOCITY: 1160 fps
PRESSURE: 9,600 LUP
COMMENTS: Burns clean.

LOAD 3
PRIMER: Winchester WW209
POWDER: 15.0 grains of Hercules Red Dot
WAD: Remington R16
VELOCITY: 1165 fps
PRESSURE: 10,400 LUP

2¾"
Remington-Peters
SP Plastic Cases

1⅛ Ounces Shot

LOAD 1
PRIMER: Remington 57★
POWDER: 18.0 grains of Hercules Unique
WAD: Remington R16
VELOCITY: 1185 fps
PRESSURE: 10,300 LUP

LOAD 2
PRIMER: C.C.I. 157
POWDER: 21.0 grains of Dupont SR7625
WAD: Remington SP16
VELOCITY: 1190 fps
PRESSURE: 9,100 LUP

LOAD 1
PRIMER: Remington 57★
POWDER: 15.5 grains of Hercules Red Dot
WAD: Remington R16
VELOCITY: 1165 fps
PRESSURE: 10,000 LUP

LOAD 2
PRIMER: Remington 57★
POWDER: 15.5 grains of Dupont "Hi-Skor" 700-X
WAD: Remington R16
VELOCITY: 1160 fps
PRESSURE: 10,000 LUP
COMMENTS: Burns very clean.

GAME: heavy upland including pheasant and waterfowl at short ranges

SHOT SIZE: Waterfowl — 2s, 4s and 5s; upland game — 4s, 5s, 6s and 7½s.

3″
Winchester Western
Compression-Formed Cases

1¼ Ounces Shot

LOAD 1

PRIMER: Winchester WW209
POWDER: 25.0 grains of Hercules Blue Dot
WAD: Remington SP20
VELOCITY: 1185 fps
PRESSURE: 10,500 LUP
COMMENTS: This is the only worthwhile handload for this case with this shot weight. Velocities run too low with all other loads.

1³/₁₆ -Ounces Shot

LOAD 1

PRIMER: Winchester WW209
POWDER: 27.5 grains of Hercules Blue Dot
WAD: Remington SP20
VELOCITY: 1295 fps
PRESSURE: 11,500 LUP
COMMENTS: The best load you can put together for this case.

20 GAUGE 3″

LOAD 1

PRIMER: Winchester WW209
POWDER: 27.5 grains of Hercules Blue Dot
WAD: Remington SP20
VELOCITY: 1285 fps
PRESSURE: 11,200 LUP
COMMENTS: Not for waterfowl.

LOAD 2

PRIMER: Winchester WW209
POWDER: 27.0 grains of Winchester 571
WAD: Winchester WAA20
VELOCITY: 1220 fps
PRESSURE: 11,000 LUP
COMMENTS: Not for waterfowl.

LOAD 3

PRIMER: Winchester WW209
POWDER: 23.5 grains of Dupont SR4756
WAD: Remington SP20
VELOCITY: 1200 fps
PRESSURE: 10,900 LUP
COMMENTS: Not for waterfowl.

3″
Remington SP Plastic Cases

1¼ Ounces Shot

LOAD 1

PRIMER: Remington 57★
POWDER: 25.0 grains of Hercules Blue Dot
WAD: Remington SP20
VELOCITY: 1185 fps
PRESSURE: 10,700 LUP

LOAD 2

PRIMER: C.C.I. 157
POWDER: 28.5 grains of Winchester 571
WAD: Remington SP20
VELOCITY: 1220 fps
PRESSURE: 10,000 LUP
COMMENTS: Duplicates the nominal velocity of the factory 1¼ ounce 3″, 20-gauge loading. Best load for 1¼ ounces of shot in this case.

1 3/16-Ounces Shot

LOAD 1

PRIMER: Remington 57★
POWDER: 27.5 grains of Hercules Blue Dot
WAD: Remington SP20
VELOCITY: 1295 fps
PRESSURE: 11,300 LUP
COMMENTS: The best load you can put together for this case.

1⅛ Ounces Shot

LOAD 1

PRIMER: Remington 57★
POWDER: 27.5 grains of Hercules Blue Dot
WAD: Remington SP20
VELOCITY: 1285 fps
PRESSURE: 10,900 LUP

GAME: all upland game

SHOT SIZE: 4s, 5s, 6s, 7½s, 8s and 9s.

2¾"
Winchester Western Compression-Formed Cases

1⅛ Ounces Shot

LOAD 1
PRIMER: Winchester WW209
POWDER: 24.0 grains of Winchester 571
WAD: Winchester WAA20F1
VELOCITY: 1150 fps
PRESSURE: 10,700 LUP
COMMENTS: This load is a favorite of the author. However, the actual loading is critical. You must use 80 to 100 pounds wad pressure and crimping dies must be adjusted exactly.

LOAD 2
PRIMER: Winchester WW209
POWDER: 24.5 grains of Winchester 571
WAD: Remington RP20
VELOCITY: 1175 fps
PRESSURE: 10,200 LUP
COMMENTS: A C.C.I. 109 primer can also be used.

LOAD 3
PRIMER: Federal 209
POWDER: 24.0 grains of Winchester 571
WAD: Remington RP20
VELOCITY: 1175 fps
PRESSURE: 11,000 LUP
COMMENTS: A very uniform load.

1 Ounce Shot

LOAD 1
PRIMER: Winchester WW209
POWDER: 25.5 grains of Winchester 571
WAD: Winchester WAA20F1
VELOCITY: 1250 fps
PRESSURE: 10,800 LUP

LOAD 2
PRIMER: Winchester WW209
POWDER: 22.5 grains of Winchester 540
WAD: Winchester WAA20F1
VELOCITY: 1220 fps
PRESSURE: 10,900 LUP
COMMENTS: Duplicates the nominal velocity of the factory 1-ounce, high-velocity loading.

LOAD 3
PRIMER: Winchester WW209
POWDER: 20.5 grains of Dupont SR4756
WAD: Remington RP20
VELOCITY: 1165 fps
PRESSURE: 9,400 LUP
COMMENTS: Not for pheasant.

LOAD 4
PRIMER: Winchester WW209
POWDER: 16.0 grains of Hercules Unique
WAD: Remington SP20
VELOCITY: 1165 fps
PRESSURE: 11,500 LUP
COMMENTS: Not for pheasant.

2¾″ Remington-Peters RXP Plastic Cases

1⅛ Ounces Shot

LOAD 1
PRIMER: Winchester WW209
POWDER: 23.5 grains of Winchester 571
WAD: Winchester WAA20F1
VELOCITY: 1150 fps
PRESSURE: 11,100 LUP

1 Ounce Shot

LOAD 1
PRIMER: Winchester WW209
POWDER: 22.0 grains of Winchester 540
WAD: Winchester WAA20F1
VELOCITY: 1220 fps
PRESSURE: 10,700 LUP
COMMENTS: Burns clean.

LOAD 2
PRIMER: Remington 97 *
POWDER: 18.0 grains of Hercules Herco
WAD: Remington RXP20
VELOCITY: 1220 fps
PRESSURE: 11,000 LUP

LOAD 3
PRIMER: Remington 97 *
POWDER: 15.5 grains of Hercules Unique
WAD: Winchester WAA20
VELOCITY: 1165 fps
PRESSURE: 11,200 LUP
COMMENTS: Not for pheasant.

2¾"
Remington-Peters
SP Plastic Cases

1⅛ Ounces Shot

LOAD 1
PRIMER: C.C.I. 157
POWDER: 25.0 grains of Winchester 571
WAD: Remington RP20
VELOCITY: 1175 fps
PRESSURE: 10,200 LUP

1 Ounce Shot

LOAD 1
PRIMER: C.C.I. 157
POWDER: 23.5 grains of Winchester 540
WAD: Winchester WAA20F1
VELOCITY: 1250 fps
PRESSURE: 9,700 LUP
COMMENTS: Good for cold weather.

LOAD 2
PRIMER: C.C.I. 157
POWDER: 19.0 grains of Dupont SR7625
WAD: Remington SP20
VELOCITY: 1210 fps
PRESSURE: 10,200 LUP
COMMENTS: Burns clean.

LOAD 3
PRIMER: Remington 57*
POWDER: 17.0 grains of Hercules Unique
WAD: Remington RP20
VELOCITY: 1220 fps
PRESSURE: 10,100 LUP

20 GAUGE 2¾"

GAME: Skeet and very light upland game

SHOT SIZE: Skeet—9s; upland game—4s, 5s, 6s, 7½s, 8s and 9s.

2¾"
Winchester Western Compression-Formed Cases

⅞-Ounce Shot

LOAD 1
PRIMER: Winchester WW209
POWDER: 18.0 grains of Winchester 473AA
WAD: Winchester WAA20
VELOCITY: 1200 fps
PRESSURE: 10,900 LUP
COMMENTS: Author's favorite 20 gauge Skeet load.

LOAD 2
PRIMER: C.C.I. 109
POWDER: 17.5 grains of Winchester 473AA
WAD: Winchester WAA20
VELOCITY: 1200 fps
PRESSURE: 10,900 LUP

LOAD 3
PRIMER: Winchester WW209
POWDER: 16.0 grains of Hercules Unique
WAD: Winchester WAA20
VELOCITY: 1200 fps
PRESSURE: 10,500 LUP

2¾″
Remington-Peters
RXP Plastic Cases

⁷⁄₈-Ounce Shot

LOAD 1
PRIMER: Winchester WW209
POWDER: 17.5 grains of Winchester 473AA
WAD: Remington RXP20
VELOCITY: 1200 fps
PRESSURE: 10,800 LUP

LOAD 2
PRIMER: C.C.I. 109
POWDER: 16.0 grains of Hercules Unique
WAD: Winchester WAA20
VELOCITY: 1200 fps
PRESSURE: 10,800 LUP

LOAD 3
PRIMER: C.C.I. 109
POWDER: 14.5 grains of Hercules Green Dot
WAD: Remington RXP20
VELOCITY: 1200 fps
PRESSURE: 10,900 LUP

28 GAUGE 2¾"

GAME: Skeet and very light upland game

SHOT SIZE: Skeet—9s; upland game—4s, 5s, 6s, 7½s, 8s and 9s.

2¾"
Winchester Western Compression-Formed Cases

¾-Ounce Shot

LOAD 1

PRIMER: Federal 209
POWDER: 17.5 grains of Winchester 540
WAD: Winchester WAA28
VELOCITY: 1200 fps
PRESSURE: 10,200 LUP
COMMENTS: A C.C.I. 109 primer or a Winchester WW209 primer may be used as second and third choices (respectively).

LOAD 2

PRIMER: Winchester WW209
POWDER: 20.5 grains of Winchester 571
WAD: Winchester WAA28
VELOCITY: 1260 fps
PRESSURE: 11,000 LUP
COMMENTS: A C.C.I. 109 primer may be used. Not for Skeet.

LOAD 3
PRIMER: Winchester WW209
POWDER: 14.5 grains of Dupont SR7625
WAD: Winchester WAA28
VELOCITY: 1210 fps
PRESSURE: 11,400 LUP

2¾"
Remington-Peters
Plastic Target Cases

¾-Ounce Shot

LOAD 1
PRIMER: C.C.I. 109
POWDER: 12.0 grains of Hercules Green Dot
WAD: Winchester WAA28 or Remington SP28
VELOCITY: 1200 fps
PRESSURE: 10,400 LUP

.410 BORE 3"

GAME: Extremely light and short-range upland game

SHOT SIZE: 6s, 7½s, 8s and 9s.

3"
Winchester Western
Compression-Formed Cases

¹¹/₁₆-Ounce Shot

LOAD 1

PRIMER: Winchester WW209
POWDER: 13.5 grains of Winchester 296
WAD: Winchester WAA41
VELOCITY: 1135 fps
PRESSURE: 10,800 LUP
COMMENTS: This duplicates the nominal velocity of the factory 3" shell.

3"
Remington-Peters
SP Plastic Cases

¹¹/₁₆-Ounce Shot

LOAD 1

PRIMER: Remington 97★
POWDER: 14.0 grains of Hercules 2400
WAD: Remington SP4103
VELOCITY: 1135 fps
PRESSURE: 12,500 LUP

.410 3"

.410 BORE 2½"

GAME: Skeet   **SHOT SIZE:** 9s

2½"
Winchester Western
Compression-Formed Cases

½-Ounce Shot

LOAD 1
PRIMER: Winchester WW209
POWDER: 14.0 grains of Winchester 296
WAD: Federal 410SC
VELOCITY: 1200 fps
PRESSURE: 10,300 LUP
COMMENTS: Best possible Skeet load for this case.

2½"
Remington-Peters
New SP Plastic Cases

½-Ounce Shot

LOAD 1
PRIMER: C.C.I. 109
POWDER: 14.5 grains of Hercules 2400
WAD: Remington SP410
VELOCITY: 1200 fps
PRESSURE: 11,600 LUP

Powder Storage Guide and Bushing Charts

Ball Powder

Powder Storage

The following information has been extracted from a pamphlet entitled "Properties and Storage of Smokeless Powder" issued by the Sporting Arms and Ammunition Manufacturers Institute at 420 Lexington Avenue, New York, New York 10017. For a free copy of the complete pamphlet send a self-addressed, stamped envelope to the above address and request the pamphlet by title.

Considerations for Storage of Smokeless Powder

Smokeless powder is intended to function by burning, so it must be protected against accidental exposure to flame, sparks or high temperatures.

For these reasons, it is desirable that storage enclosures be made of insulating materials to protect the powder from external heat sources.

Once smokeless powder begins to burn, it will normally continue to burn (and generate gas pressure) until it is consumed.

D.O.T. approved containers are constructed to open up at low internal pressures to avoid the effects normally produced by the rupture or bursting of a strong container.

Storage enclosures for smokeless powder should be constructed in a similar manner:

1. *Of fire-resistant and heat insulating materials to protect contents from external heat.*

2. *Sufficiently large to satisfactorily vent the gaseous products of combustion which would result if the quantity of smokeless powder within the enclosure accidentally ignited.*

If a small, tightly enclosed storage enclosure is loaded to capacity with containers of smokeless powder, the walls of the enclosure will expand or move outwards to release the gas pressure—if the powder in storage is accidentally ignited.

Under such conditions, the effects of the release of gas pressure are similar or identical to the effects produced by an explosion.

Hence only the smallest practical quantities of smokeless powder should be kept in storage, and then in strict compliance with all applicable regulations and recommendations of the National Fire Protection Association (reprinted at end of leaflet).

Recommendations for Storage of Smokeless Powder

STORE IN A COOL, DRY PLACE. Be sure the storage area selected is free from any possible sources of excess heat and is isolated from open flame, furnaces, hot water heaters, etc. Do not store smokeless powder where it will be exposed to the sun's rays. Avoid storage in areas where mechanical or electrical equipment is in operation. Restrict from the storage areas heat or sparks which may result from improper, defective or overloaded electrical circuits.

DO NOT STORE SMOKELESS POWDER IN THE SAME AREA WITH SOLVENTS, FLAMMABLE GASES OR HIGHLY COMBUSTIBLE MATERIALS.

STORE ONLY IN DEPARTMENT OF TRANSPORTATION APPROVED CONTAINERS. Do not transfer the powder from an approved container into one which is not approved.

DO NOT SMOKE IN AREAS WHERE POWDER IS STORED OR USED. Place appropriate "No Smoking" signs in these areas.

DO NOT SUBJECT THE STORAGE CABINETS TO CLOSE CONFINEMENT.

STORAGE CABINETS SHOULD BE CONSTRUCTED OF INSULATING MATERIALS AND WITH A WEAK WALL, SEAMS OR JOINTS TO PROVIDE AN EASY MEANS OF SELF-VENTING.

DO NOT KEEP OLD OR SALVAGED POWDERS. Check old powders for deterioration regularly. Destroy deteriorated powders immediately.

OBEY ALL REGULATIONS REGARDING QUANTITY AND METHODS OF STORING. Do not store all your powders in one place. If you can, maintain separate storage locations. Many small containers are safer than one or more large containers.

KEEP YOUR STORAGE AND USE AREA CLEAN. Clean up spilled powder promptly. Make sure the surrounding area is free of trash or other readily combustible materials.

Pressure

When gases expand in a confined space they exert pressure. When smokeless powder burns it forms gases which occupy many times the volume of the solid propellant. And the heat of burning expands these gases even more.

When a cartridge is fired in a rifle or shotgun the gas pressure is exerted equally in all directions. The area where this pressure most easily results in expansion of the gas volume is on the base of the bullet or wad column. The bullet or shot is free to move and the expanding gases rapidly push it down the barrel and out the muzzle.

If pressure is too low, non-uniform ignition will result, and with it non-uniform velocities and poor accuracy. In extreme cases, there will not be enough gas pressure to push the bullet or shot out the barrel. An obstruction will be left that will result in damage to the barrel on the next shot. Shot shell pressures should be maintained at a minimum average of 7500 LUP.

If pressure is too high, gas pressure builds up so fast that damage to the firearm may result before the bullet or shot can move down the barrel and personal injury can result.

Follow the loading data given and avoid trouble.

Pressures are designated by "CUPS" and "LUPS," meaning "Copper Units of Pressure" and "Lead Units of Pressure." The actual numbers are identical with those designated in the past as P.S.I. (pounds per square inch).

Source of Empty Cases

Winchester Western does not sell empty shotshell cases as a component. All Winchester cases used in shotshell loading are obtained as a result of the first firing of factory loaded ammunition. The demands on our manufacturing equipment for factory ammunition eliminates the possibility of making runs of these cases to be sold as components.

In a great many instances, once-fired Double A cases and other Winchester shotshells can be purchased from local skeet and trap ranges, gun clubs, and dealers catering to the shotshell reloaders. In case this service is not available, the only means of obtaining these cases would be as the result of firing factory ammunition.

Powder Bushings and Scales

Shotshell reloading tool powder bushings do not throw the exact charge specification in many cases. The reasons are many and some include:

1. Variations in gravimetric density of powders from lot to lot. The tolerance is plus or minus .025 grams per cubic centimeter. This tolerance applies to most canister powders.

2. Usually a bushing chart lists the nominal weight of a powder charge based on normal packing as a result of free flow and gravimetric density of a powder or on bushing volume and the *nominal* gravimetric powder density at 100% packing.

3. Various operators of a tool will get various powder weights from an identical tool and bushing. This is due to the change in force of operation and the amount of vibration transmitted to the tool with resultant amount of packing of powder.

4. The amount of sizing force required on cases being loaded can cause a change in powder drop due to the change in tool vibration.

5. Bushing manufacturing tolerances.

6. Tool manufacturing tolerances.

7. Mismarked bushings.

As you see, a bushing listing chart cannot be interpreted as an absolute. They simply can represent what the manufacturer believes to be the nominal charge thrown with the listed bushing and powder.

A reloading scale is an absolute must and charges thrown must be carefully checked and changes in bushing sizes made where required.

Do not try to determine the powder charge thrown by simply metering the powder bar back and forth and weighing charges.

The tool must be cycled through the complete loading cycle to insure the same amount of vibration and powder packing as will take place in a normal loading cycle. Powder charges measured under these two conditions could vary as much as several grains.

For your reference a bushing chart follows:

NOTE—IMPORTANT CAUTION: These tables are not loading recommendations. Read "Powder Bushings/Scales" before using these tables. This information has been supplied by the tool manufacturers and is not a result of Winchester Western testing.

MEC Bushing Chart

Bushing #	452AA	473AA	540	571	296
10					13.6
11					14.4
12					15.4
A12			15.5		16.4
13			16.1	16.6	17.0
14			17.9	18.4	
15			18.8	19.3	
16			19.8	20.4	
17			20.7	21.3	
18			21.6	22.3	
19		15.8	22.6	23.2	
20		16.6	23.7	24.4	
21		17.3	24.7	25.4	
22		18.1	25.8	26.6	
23		18.7	26.8	27.7	
24	16.1	19.5	27.9	28.8	
25	16.7	20.3	28.9	29.9	
26	17.5	21.2	30.3	31.2	
27	18.1	21.9	31.2	32.3	
28	18.8	22.8	32.6	33.6	
29	19.4	23.5	33.6	34.7	
30	20.3	24.5	35.0	36.2	
31	20.9	25.3	36.2	37.4	
32	21.7	26.5	37.8	38.9	
33	22.4	27.3	39.0	40.1	
34	23.3	28.3	40.4		
35	23.7	29.8	41.1		
36	24.9	30.1			

Bair Bushing Chart

Bushing #	452AA	473AA	540	571	296
269					13.5
300			17.5		
312				19.0	
327			21.0		
345			23.0		
354			24.0	24.0	
360				25.0	
366		18.0	26.0		
375				27.0	
384		20.0	28.5		
399		17.5			
405			32.0		
411				33.0	
414	19.0	23.5			
417			34.0	34.0	
420		24.0			
423			35.0		
429	20.0				
432		25.0	36.0		
435				36.5	
438		26.0			
441	21.0				
444		27.0			
450	22.0				
459	23.0				
465	23.5				

Ponsness Warren Bushing Chart

Bushing #	452AA	473AA	540	571	296
1A					13.7
2A					14.8
3A			15.3		15.6
A			16.8	17.1	17.5
B			17.6	18.2	
C			18.5	18.8	
C1			19.6	20.1	
D			20.4	21.0	
D1		15.5	21.3	22.4	
E		16.8	23.5	24.2	
E1		17.1	24.0	24.7	
E2		18.0	26.1	26.5	
F	15.6	19.6	27.5	28.5	
F1	16.4	20.1	28.3	29.3	
G	18.3	22.7	31.2	32.3	
G1	19.0	23.0	32.7	33.4	
H	19.9	24.1	34.0	34.8	
I	20.3	24.7	34.4	36.5	
J	21.5	25.4	35.5	37.1	
J1	22.3	26.8	36.9	38.8	
K	22.5	27.0	37.1	39.0	
L	23.4		39.5		
M	24.0				

Pacific Bushing Chart for Models "DL-155, DL-105 and DL-155APF"

| | Bushing Numbers | | | | |
Grains	452AA	473AA	540	571	296
13					250
14					259
15					
16					
17	393	351			
18	396	363	303		
19	402	372		312	
20	414	381		318	
21	423	393	327	327	
22	432	399	333		
23	444	405	342	345	
24	453	417	348	351	
25	462	426		357	
26		435	363	366	
27		444	372	375	
28		453	378	381	
29			384		
30				393	
31			399	399	
32			405		
33			411	411	
34			417	417	
35			423	423	
36			429	429	
37			435	435	
38			441		

Pacific Bushing Chart for Model "DL-266"

| | Bushing Numbers | | | | |
Grains	452AA	473AA	540	571	296
13					256
14					266
15					
16					
17	384	357	300		
18	396	366	309		
19	408	378	315	318	
20	420	387	321	327	
21	432	396	333	333	
22	441	402	339	339	
23	450	411	348	351	
24	459	423	354	357	
25	474	432	360	363	
26		438	369	369	
27		450	375	378	
28		456	384	387	
29			390	393	
30			396	399	
31			402	405	
32			408	411	
33			414	417	
34			420	423	
35			429	429	
36			435	435	
37			441	441	
38			447		

Pacific Bushing Chart for Model "DL-366"

| | Bushing Numbers | | | | |
Grains	452AA	473AA	540	571	296
13					256
14					266
15					
16					
17	390	357	300		
18	402	369	309		
19	411	381	318	318	
20	420	390	327	330	
21	432	399	336	339	
22	441	408	345	348	
23	450	414	351	357	
24	462	426	360	363	
25	474	435	366	369	
26		444	375	378	
27		450	381	384	
28		462	387	390	
29			393	396	
30			402	405	
31			408	411	
32			414	417	
33			423	423	
34			429	429	
35			435	438	
36			441	444	
37			444	450	
38			450		

Texan Bushing Chart Models GT, FW, LT, A, AP, D and DP

Bushing #	452AA	473AA	540	571	296
101					13.5
102					14.1
103					14.6
104					15.3
105					16.0
106					
107			16.9		
108			17.7		
109			18.3	18.6	
110			19.4	19.7	
111			20.2	20.6	
112			21.0	21.4	
113			21.9	22.3	
114			22.7	23.2	
115		17.2	23.6	24.2	
116		18.0	24.8	25.3	
117		18.6	25.6	26.2	
118		19.4	26.7	27.4	
119	16.9	19.9	27.5	28.1	
120	17.7	20.8	28.8	29.5	
121	18.0	21.4	29.4	30.2	
122	18.7	22.2	30.5	31.4	
123	19.3	22.9	31.6	32.4	
124	19.8	23.5	32.4	33.3	
125	20.3	24.2	33.5	34.5	
126	21.0	25.1	34.6	35.6	
127	21.6	25.9	35.6	36.6	
128	22.2	26.6	36.6	37.6	
129	22.8	27.3	37.5	38.6	
130	23.5	28.1	38.6	39.9	
131	24.1	29.0	39.9	41.1	
132	24.7		40.9	42.1	
133	25.3			43.2	
134				44.4	

Texan Bushing Chart Model "M" Only

Bushing #	452AA	473AA	540	571	296
101					13.1
102					13.6
103					14.1
104					14.7
105					15.3
106					16.1
107					
108					
109			17.4		
110			18.3	18.9	
111			19.2	20.6	
112			19.9	19.6	
113			20.8	20.4	
114			21.6	21.3	
115			22.5	23.4	
116		17.0	23.6	24.3	
117		17.6	24.4	25.2	
118		18.4	25.5	26.3	
119		18.9	26.2	27.0	
120		19.9	27.4	28.3	
121	17.1	20.3	28.1	29.0	
122	17.7	21.0	29.1	30.1	
123	18.3	21.7	30.2	31.2	
124	18.8	22.3	30.9	32.0	
125	19.5	22.9	31.7	33.0	
126	20.1	23.8	33.0	34.3	
127	20.7	24.5	34.0	35.3	
128	21.2	25.2	34.9	36.3	
129	21.8	25.9	35.9	37.3	
130	22.4	26.6	36.9	38.5	
131	23.0	27.5	38.1	39.6	
132	23.6	28.2	39.0	40.7	
133	24.3	29.0	40.1	41.8	
134	24.9			42.9	
135	25.3			43.8	
136				45.2	

Lyman Bushing Chart

Bushing #	452AA	473AA	540	571	296
H1			16.5	16.5	17.0
H2			17.5	17.5	
H3			18.5	19.0	
H4		14.0	20.0	20.5	
H5	13.0	16.0	23.0	23.5	
H6	15.5	18.5	26.5	27.5	
H7	17.5	21.0	30.5	31.0	
H8	19.0	23.0	33.0	33.5	
H9	19.5	23.5	34.0	34.5	
H10	20.0	24.0	34.5	35.5	
H11	21.0	26.0	37.0	38.0	
H11A	22.5	27.5	39.0	40.0	
H12	23.0	28.0	40.5	41.5	
H13	25.0	30.0			
H14	25.5				

Redding Bushing Chart

Bushing #	452AA	473AA	540	571	296
1			16.5	16.5	17.0
2			18.0	18.0	
3			19.0	19.0	
4			20.5	20.5	
5			21.5	21.5	
6		16.5	23.5	23.5	
7		17.0	24.5	24.5	
8		18.5	26.0	26.0	
9	16.2	19.0	27.5	27.5	
10	17.0	20.0	29.0	28.5	
11	18.1	21.5	31.5	31.0	
12	19.5	23.5	33.5	34.0	
13	20.4	25.0	34.0	36.0	
14	21.8	27.0	39.0	39.0	
15	24.8	29.0	41.5	41.5	
16	25.8	31.0			
23					12.0

Catalog of Shotshell Reloading Equipment and Components

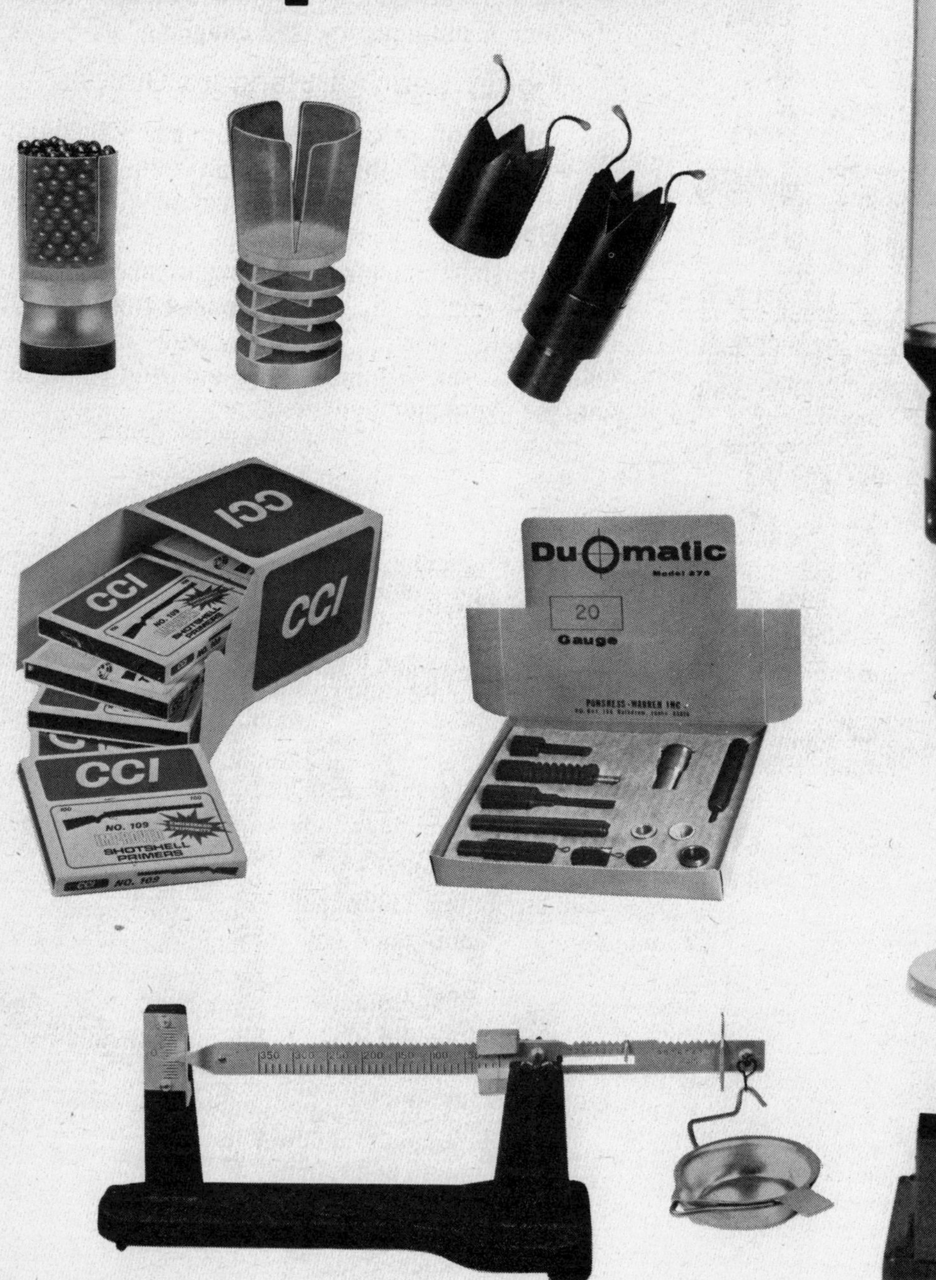

Reloading Presses

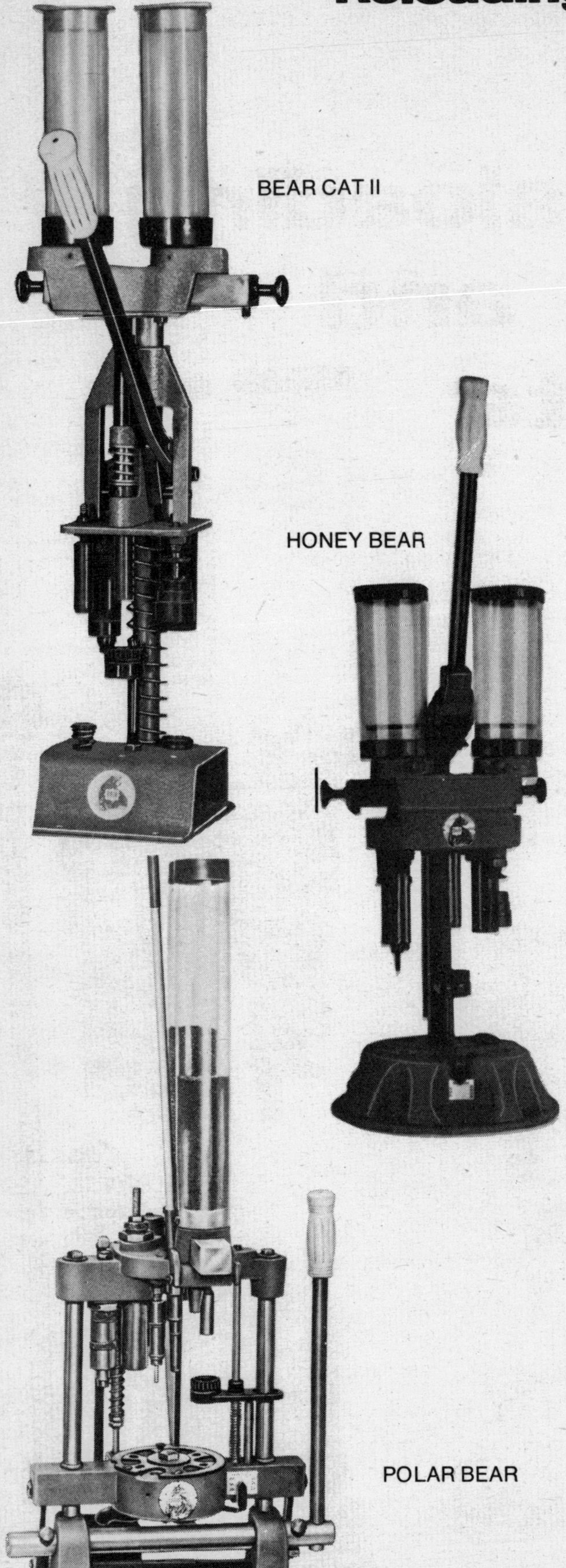

BEAR CAT II

HONEY BEAR

POLAR BEAR

HOLLYWOOD

Glacier Bear All Standard Gauges

The experienced reloader can produce more than 250 rounds per hour with this tool. Reloads paper or plastic shells without changing dies. Visible wad pressure gauge eliminates guesswork. All operations end on complete stop. Positive charge bar—pull out for powder, push in for shot—cannot be reversed.

Bear Cat II All Standard Gauges

This is a low-cost single stage press for loading all standard gauges. High and low brass cases of all kinds are efficiently handled with a minimum of effort. Complete for one gauge.

Honey Bear All Standard Gauges

Capable of reloading 225 paper or plastic rounds per hour, this lightweight compact press yet offers sufficient leverage for easy operation. Positive rod ejection drives case from the nylon-bushed size die. Easily removable hoppers rotate ¼-turn to stop powder/shot flow and tapered sides permit stacking. Fully adjustable wad pressure, with indicator, and built-in primer catcher are other features.

Polar Bear All Standard Gauges

A semi-automatic tool which can produce up to 600 completed rounds per hour, either plastic or paper cases without changing dies. "Tilt-Top" feature allows charge bar bushings to be changed at any time. Wad pressure is fully adjustable and visible indicator helps operator produce consistent ammunition. Automatic primer feed (included) holds 100 primers. Complete for one gauge.

Hollywood Senior Turret

Loads 200 shotshells or more per hour, and is rugged enough for metallic case full-length resizing and bullet swaging in any caliber. Turret head has 8 stations, tapped for 1½″ die sets or in combination of 1½″ and ⅞″ for both metallic and shot-shell dies. Shotshell dies, powder and shot measures, shell holder, etc.

Lee Load-All Junior

A complete reloading press for 12 gauge shotgun shells. Loads all types of shells including plastic 6 or 8 segment crimp, high or low brass, trap, field or Magnum loads. Full length sizes, adjustable shot measure, nylon dies, load data and complete instructions. Easily adjusted to load 2¾″ or 3″ shells. Everything you need to start loading including the screws for mounting.

Lee Load-All

This is a low cost but durable shotshell press that will load plastic or paper shells in 6 or 8 segment crimps, with trap, field and magnum load 2¾″ or 3″ lengths. Dies are made of nylon. Built-in shot and powder baffles. Each step of the loading process ends at a positive stop. No wad pressure adjustments. Full length sizes the entire head and rim. Press comes with a new charge bar with 24 replaceable shot and powder bushings (may be bought separately to update older models). Complete with load data, 12, 16 and 20 gauge.

Lyman 100 SL Shotshell Press

One of the fastest single-station presses, it offers full length sizing of high or low brass without adjustments, an automatic primer feed with optional 100 primer reservoir, floating wad guide, clear view wad pressure indicator, floating crimp starter. The crimping die applies a uniformly tight crimp to each shell. Quick-dump reservoirs are emptied by activating a dump valve. Consistent and accurate powder and shot charging is foolproof—12 or 20 gauge only.

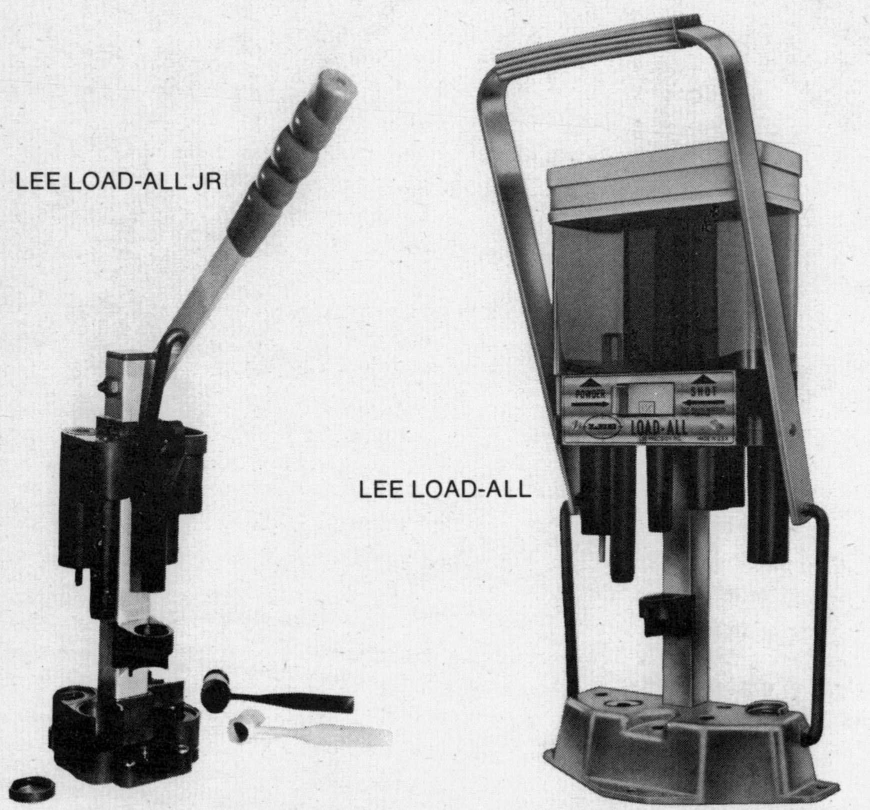

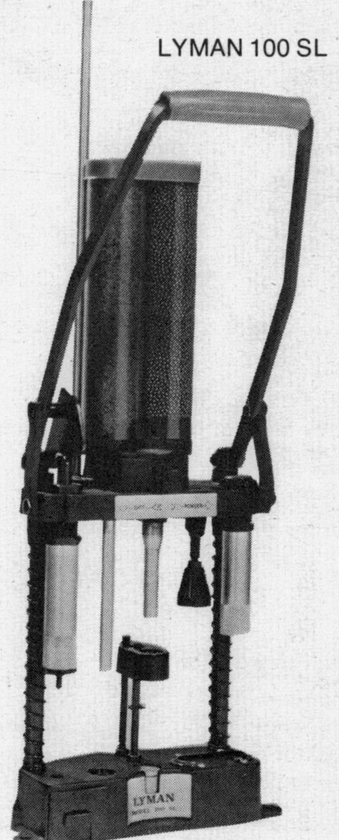

MEC 600 JR All Standard Gauges

The 600 Jr. is a single stage tool that has a cam-actuated crimper. Produces loads at the rate of approximately 200 to 250 shells per hour. Press comes completely fitted with Spindex Crimp Head. Available in 10, 12, 16, 20, 28 or .410.

MEC Hustler 76

The "Hustler 76" utilizes all of the features of the Grabber 76 and adds the benefits of hydraulic power. It features a toe-touch control that allows continuous action or stops anywhere in the cycle, as desired by the operator. The hydraulic 110 volt unit attaches with a single hose. Comes in 12 gauge only. Press is available minus the hydraulic system at a greatly reduced price.

MEC Sizemaster

Available in 10, 12, 16, 20, 28 and .410 gauges, the Sizemaster handles both brass or steel heads, high or low base. Auto primer feed and charge bar window are standard equipment. The Spindex Crimper changes heads in seconds from six to eight-point or smooth cone. A primer feed is included with this press.

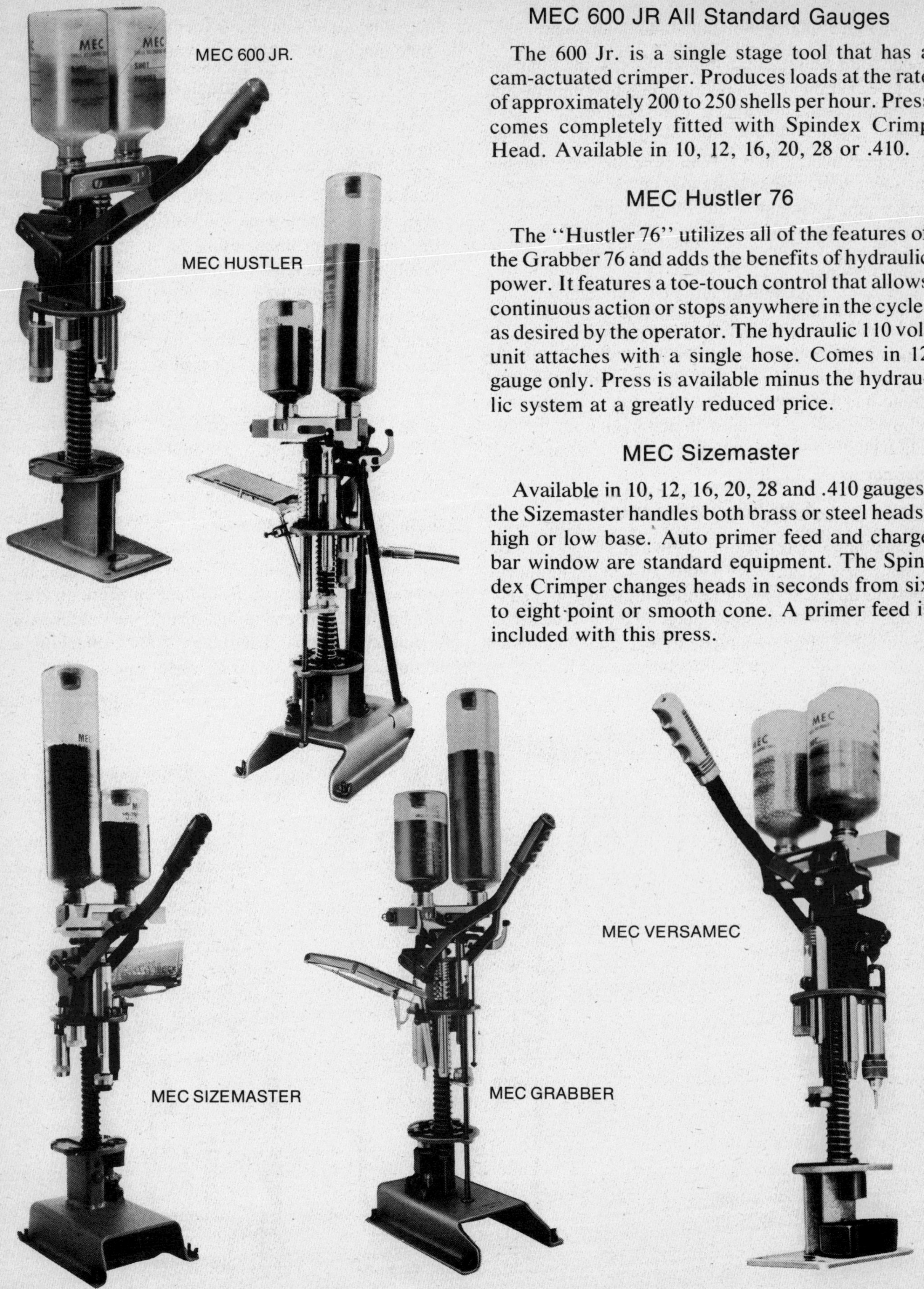

MEC Grabber

MEC's new "Grabber" combines the operations of six stations with every pull of the handle—a finished shell is produced with each stroke. Resizing, primer feed and cycle charge bar are all automatic. Crimping is cam actuated for uniformity and the Spindex Crimper Head changes inserts in seconds. All units include a powder and shot measure, large powder container and Magnum shot container. Press comes complete for 12 gauge only.

MEC Versamec 700

Has same features as MEC 600 Jr. plus the Platform Cam which provides a longer ejection stroke at the resize station, and the Pro-Check which programs the charge bar and wad guide. No adjustments or part changes are required for different brass length. Quickly changes from 6 or 8 point plastic crimp spinner to the smooth cone for fired paper shells. Available in 10, 12, 16, 20, 28 gauge.

Pacific Model 105

In using the Pacific Model 105, all operations are the same as more expensive loaders, but this model is designed and constructed to lower costs for the beginner. Not available with auto primer feed. Comes in 12, 16 or 20 gauge only. Well made, economic press.

Pacific 155/155APF Loader 12/12 Mag., 16, 20, 20 Mag., 28 and .410 gauge

This loader sizes head and rim of cases before loading and the rest of the case after. Loads over 200 shells per hour and turns out a shell that functions in all types of actions. Model 155APF comes with automatic primer feed.

Pacific Model 266 Loader

Over 250 uniform rounds can be reloaded per hour. All operations end on a complete stop. Charge bar is of the positive action type. Available in 12, 12 Mag., 20, 20 Mag.

Pacific 366 Auto Loader

A new progressive tool that has an automatic turntable and swingout wad guide in addition to other high-production features. Eight shells move around the turntable and eight different operations are performed automatically with each stroke of the operating lever. After loading,

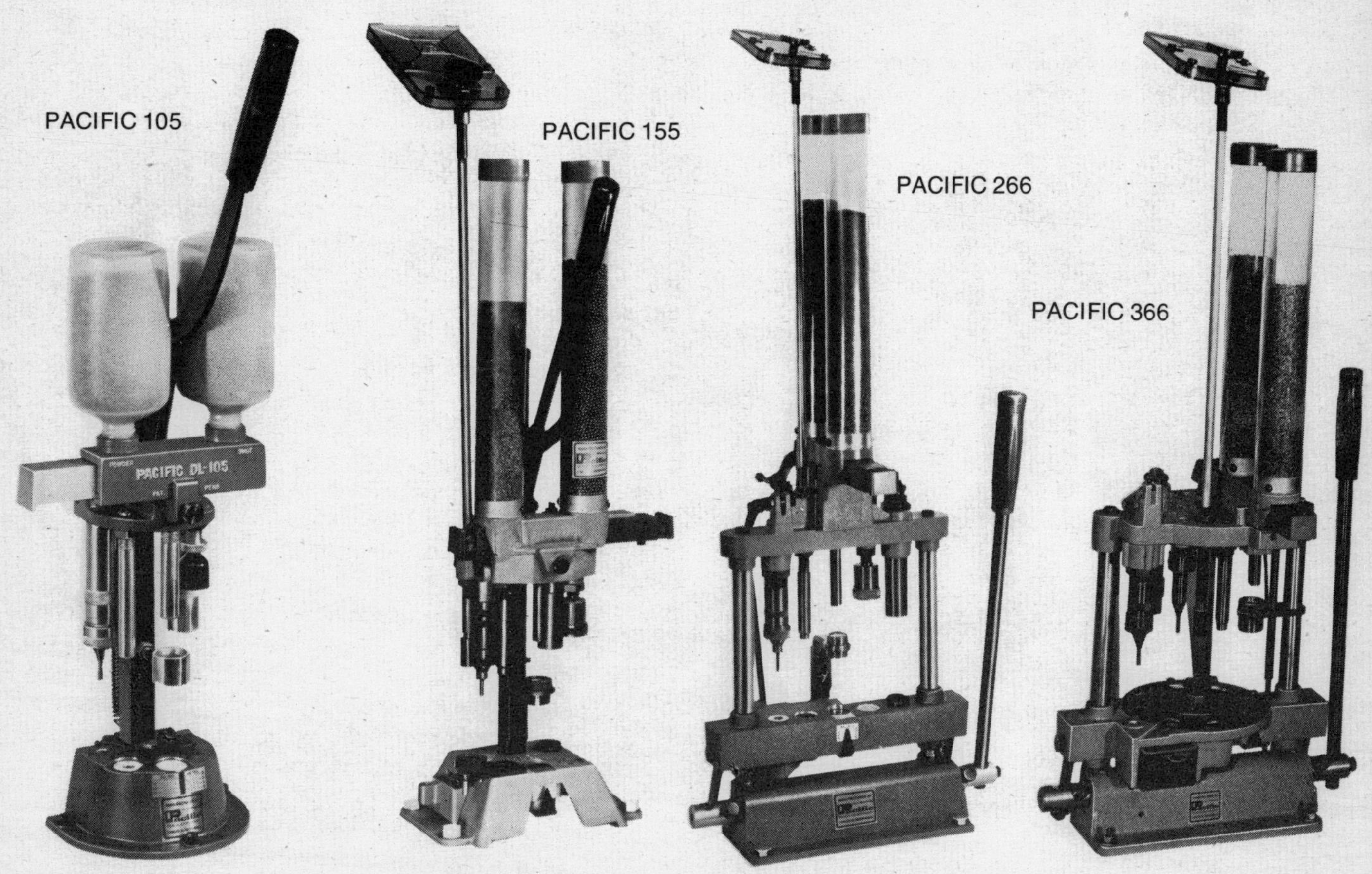

the finished shell is ejected. Operator simply sets an empty hull on the shell plate and inserts a wad in the machine. The new tool also has a shot and powder shutoff. Available in 12, 16, 20 or 28 gauge. The older standard 366 can be updated to automatic operation by returning the tool to the Pacific factory. Conversion kits to different gauges are available.

Ponsness-Warren Magn-O-Matic 10

Essentially a redesigned Du-O-Matic press, the Magn-O-Matic has all the same features, however, Magn-O-Matic is not convertible to other gauges. This press is exclusively for 10 gauge 3½″ shells. An extra-large shot drop tube allows up to #2 shot to be loaded easily while a special bushing access plug allows direct shot drop for even larger sizes. Shells are held in a sizing die throughout the five stations loading process. Ponsness-Warren's Magn-O-Matic 10 shotshell reloading press comes complete with 6-point crimp starter.

Ponsness M375 Du-O-Matic

A single stage tool requiring only 4 moves to produce a loaded shell. Change gauges in 5 minutes. No crimp starter needed for paper cases. Available in 12, 16, 20, 28 and .410. Conversion units to different gauges are available.

Ponsness 800-B Size-O-Matic Loader

A semi-automatic progressive loading tool; handles both paper and plastic shells, new or fired. Cases are resized full length and remain in the sizing die through all operations. Eight such dies are permanently assembled to the die cylinder which indexes automatically to position shells for each operation. A cam-operated carrier receives and positions wads for seating. Wad pressure is adjustable from 10 to 130 pounds. Powder and shot measures can be shut off or emptied at any time without disassembly. Handle can be positioned on either side.

With a helper available to keep components moving, up to 700 rounds per hour can be loaded. Available in 12, 20, 28 or .410.

Ponsness-Warren
New Mult-O-Matic 600B

Designed for the trap and Skeet shooters, this

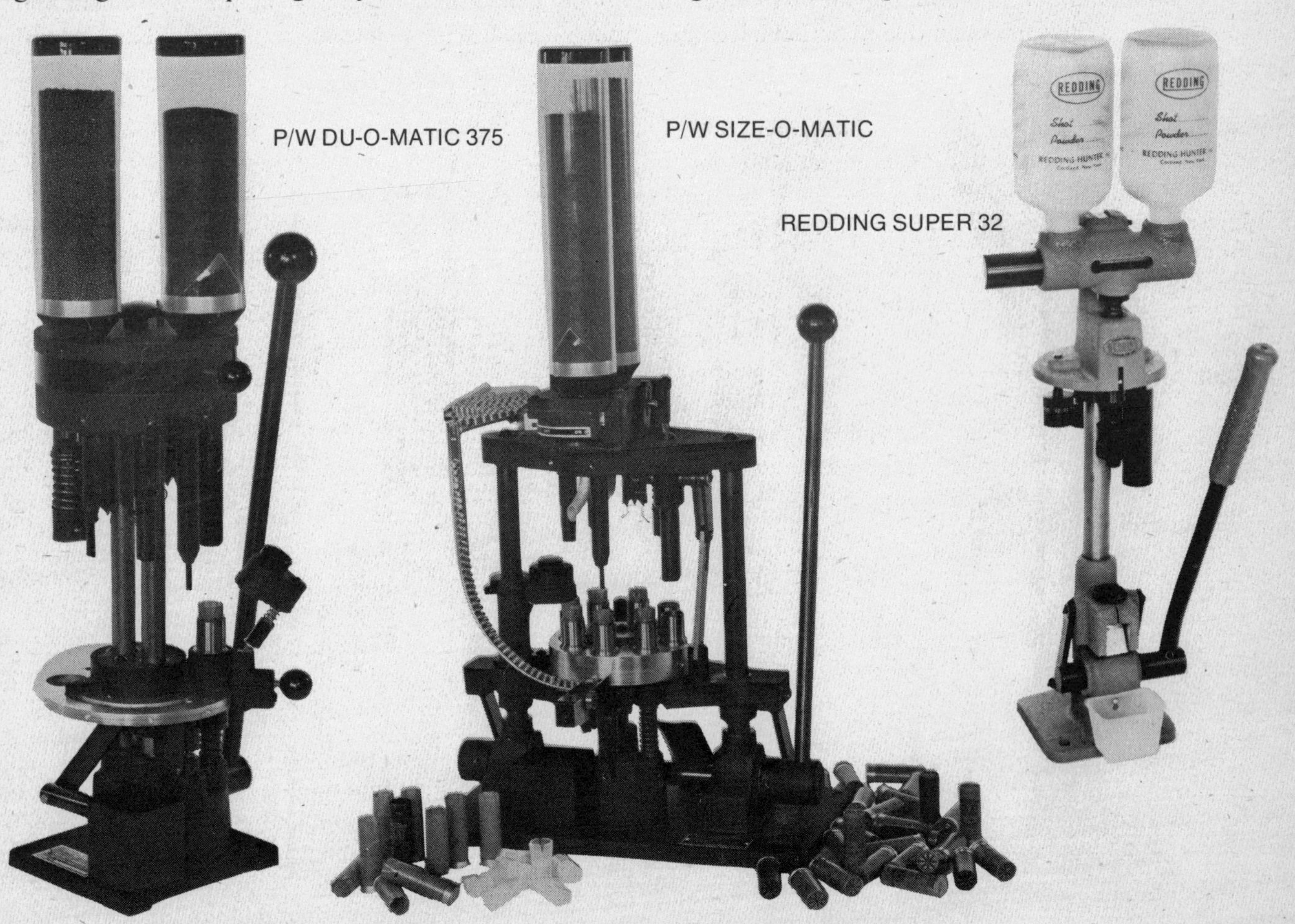

is an improved version of the original Mult-O-Matic. It gives high production rate and versatility. Each shell is contained in its own full length resizing die through the entire reloading operation. One operator can load up to 500 rounds per hour. Additional tooling sets available in all standard gauges and can be installed in 10 minutes. Complete in 12, 16 or 20, 28 or .410 gauge with 8 or 6 point crimp starter (specify).

Redding Super 32 Shotshell Loader

This is a turret-type shotshell press capable of producing 300 reloads per hour. All reloading operations are performed at one station to eliminate shell handling. Resizes high and low brass shells without adjustments. Fully adjustable wad pressure, fool-proof charge bar and a tilt-top for the easy change of powder and shot. The quick-release die head assembly allows a complete gauge change in seconds. Available in 12, 16, 20, 28 or .410.

Texan Model FW

Available in 12, 16, 20, 28 or .410, the FW resizes for high or low brass without adjustment.

Wad guide automatically lowers and raises for easy and fast insertion of wads. Crimp starter seeks out original fold for perfect crimps. Nylon wad guide fingers, double column design for rigidity and strength and accuracy. Quick changing of powder and shot without bar changes plus easy conversion to other gauges.

Texan Model MIV

A 10-station automatic turret tool, massive and heavy, that reloads 200 shells without refilling, delivers a loaded shell with every pull of the handle. Available in 12, 16, 20, 28 and .410.

Texan Model RT

A six-station progressive press. Adjustable wad pressure. Shot drops while wad pressure is being applied and the press has a self-aligning nylon crimp starter. Has powerful double-link leverage, swivel-top easy drain of powder or shot from reservoirs. Indexing turret, convenient primer catcher box on front of press. Has high speed production capabilities and is ideally suited to competition shooters. Available in 12 or 20 gauge.

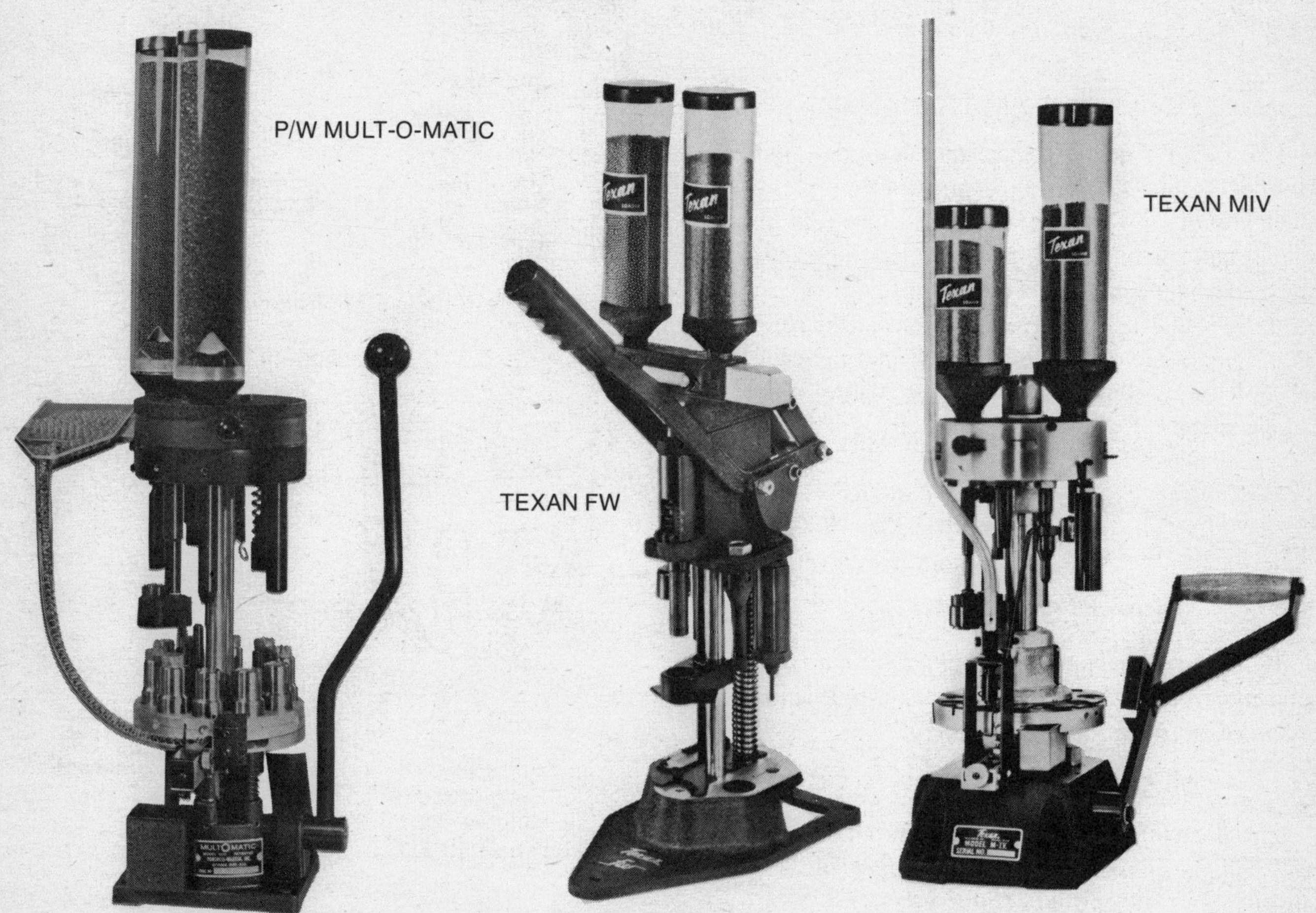

Notes on Shotshell Loading Dies . . .

Shotshell dies are designed to perform the following operations: decapping and recapping; seating wads under proper pressure; sizing and crimping. Provisions for inserting powder and shot charges must also be made, but this is not a function of the die set. Sequence of the operations may vary somewhat, depending upon the dies and press used. All shotshell presses as such in this volume perform the above operations with dies designed specifically for the individual presses. Their dies will not usually interchange. Other shotshell dies shown in this section are made for use in standard metallic reloading presses which can be converted to shotshell use if their die station(s) is threaded 1¼-18, the standard for this kind of shotshell die. This allows, perhaps, the conversion of one's existing press to shotshell use at a saving, compared with buying a separate press. Unless one plans on loading a great many shells in a short time, this is usually the most practical approach. Loading will be slow unless a turret type press is used, but the speed will be adequate for the average hunter. Loads produced in this manner can be fully equal in quality to those from a shotshell press, and of greater variety.

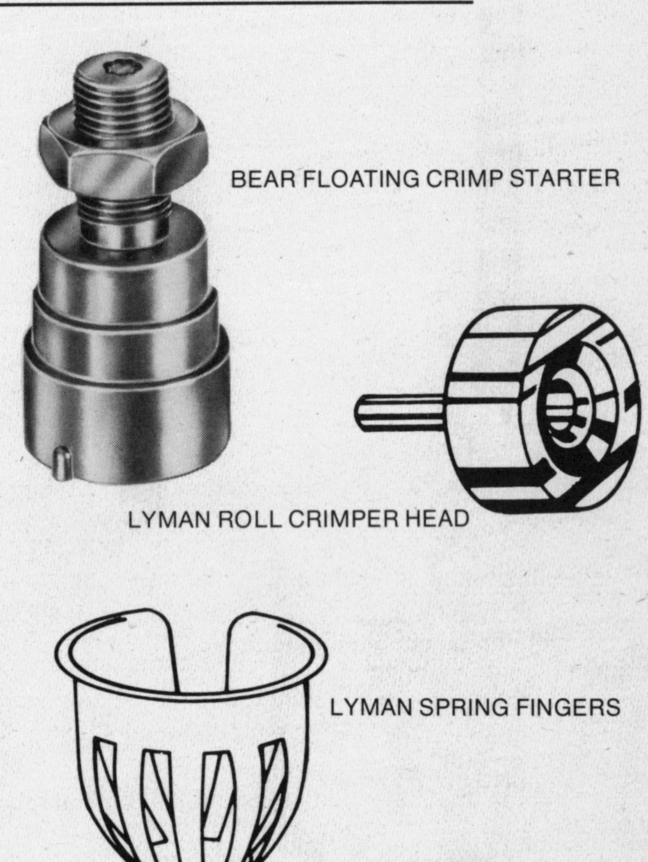

Bear Floating Crimp Starter

Free-floating crimp starter head aligns automatically with folds in shell mouth. Available for 6 or 8 segments in 12, 16 and 20 gauge; 6 segments only in 28 and .410. Specify gauge and segments when ordering.

Hollywood Shotshell Dies

Intended for use only in the various Hollywood presses; standard equipment in the big Hollywood automatic tool. A complete die is furnished for each operation so that no changing of parts is required. The complete set can be installed in the Hollywood Senior Turret tool. Well finished and polished, available in gauges .410 through 10 for paper, plastic or metal shells.

Lyman Roll Crimper Head

With drill press adapter. For roll crimping shotshells. Mounts in any drill press. Specify 10, 12, 16, 20, 28, .410 or 12 gauge for rifled slugs.

Lyman Spring Fingers

Replacement spring fingers to fit the wad chamber of the Lyman Easy Shotshell reloader. Available in all gauges (specify).

MEC Spindex Crimp Head

An 8-point crimp starter which rotates as it adjusts itself to the original creases in the case mouth. No indexing is required, yet a neat tight crimp is assured every time. Can be installed on all MEC presses (specify gauge).

Ponsness-Warren Crimp Starters

Six and eight point crimp starters are ball bearing lined and have an automatic pick-up to assure perfect crimp alignment.

Ponsness-Warren Paper Crimp Assembly

This conversion kit is intended for shooters who reload paper shells predominately. The standard crimp assembly on Ponsness-Warren tools is primarily for plastic shells. This assembly can be installed in a matter of minutes. Specify gauge.

Ponsness-Warren Wad Guide Fingers

Replacement wad guide fingers adaptable to most reloading tools and available in 10, 12, 16, 20, 28 and .410 gauge. These fingers accommodate all wads and assure exact wad seating. Specify gauge.

Redding Model 33 Shotshell Dies

Available in 12, 16, 20, 28 and .410 gauges, these dies consist of a decap rod, resize sleeve, rammer tube, wad guide assembly, crimp starter, crimp die assembly, and shell holder. For use with Model 32 and Super 32 reloaders.

Redding Model 23 Star Crimp Starter

This is a self-indexing, ball bearing crimp starter that fits all Redding shotshell loaders and many others ($5/16$-24 stem). Available in 6 or 8 point. When purchasing, be sure to specify gauge and points.

Redding Model 34 Conversion Kit

For use with the Redding Super 32 press only. Available in 12, 16, 20, 28 or .410 gauge. Consists of complete die head assembly, dies, crimp starter, shell holder, bushings and quick release pin. All that is necessary to convert the Super 32 from one gauge to another in seconds.

Texan Crimp Starters

These crimp starters are for crimping both paper and plastic shells and are available in both 6 or 8 point versions, for all Texan shotshell presses. Specify gauge and number of points.

Flambeau Twin-50 Loading Block

Bright yellow polyethylene block holds 50 shotshells on each side. One side is for 12 or 16 gauge, the other for 20 or 28 gauge.

Jasco Shell Caddy

A 50-shell, 1-piece, molded block that holds shotgun shell sizes from 10 to .410. Made of durable, oil-resistant, high-impact plastic, in natural white color.

Muti-Scale Model B201 Universal Charge Bar

A replacement charge bar fully adjustable for shot and powder charges. After finding scale settings on the chart (included), the knobs are adjusted accordingly. The same settings will yield the same load for any amount of shot from ½-oz. to 1¾-oz. and powder from 4.5 to 71 grains. The B201 is made to fit MEC 400, 600, 600 Jr., 700 Versamec, 250 and 250 Super models, and the Texan LT, GT and FW presses. From Multi-Scale Charge, Ltd.

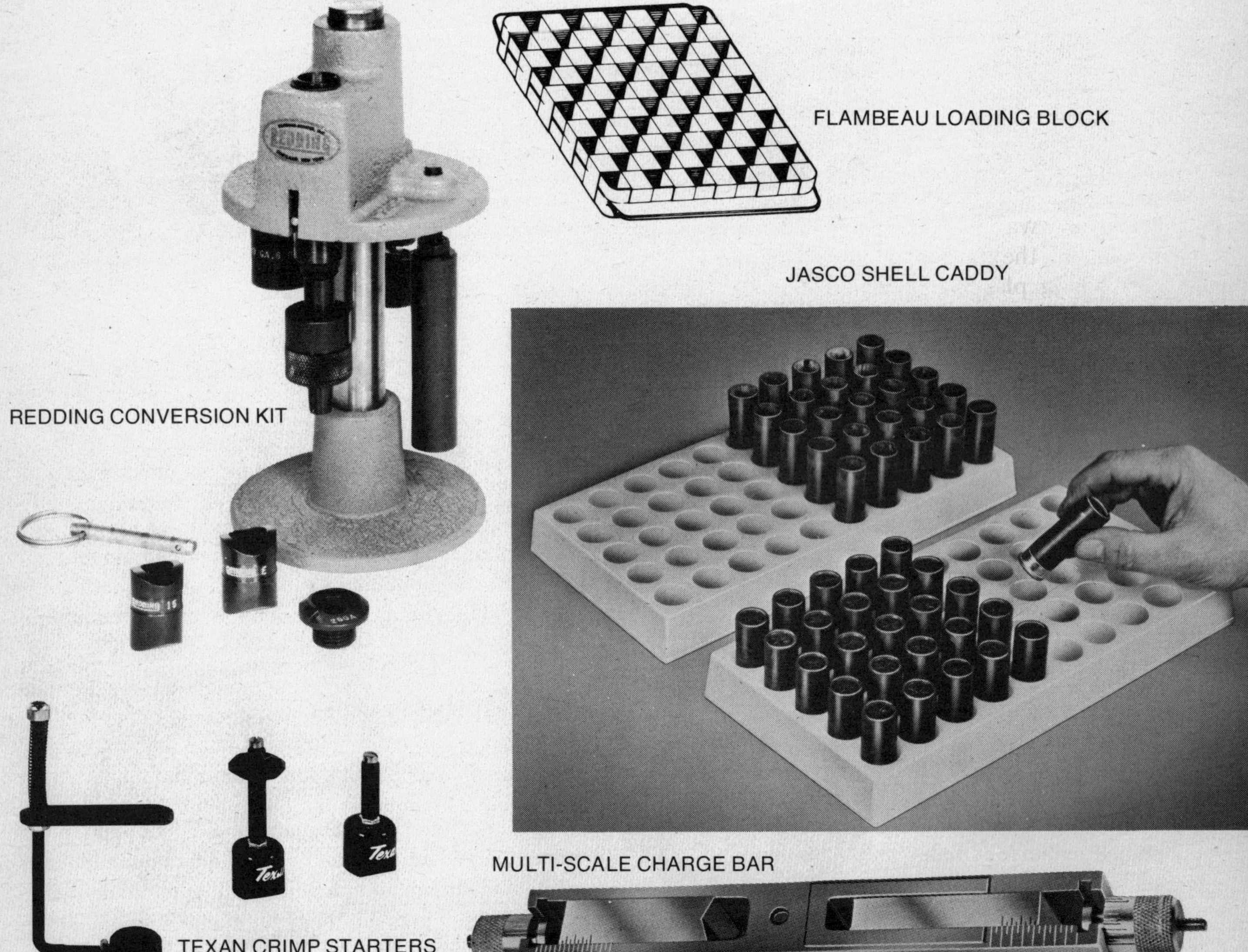

MEC E-Z Pak

The easy way to pack shotshells. As each shell is reloaded, they're placed in this device as if they were being placed in the box. After each 25 shells, the original box is slipped over E-Z Pak which is then turned upside down and removed. Available in all gauges.

MEC Super-Sizer

The new Super-Sizer accommodates 12-gauge shells only; however, the company advised that other gauges are to follow in the near future. One pull forces eight steel fingers against the brass. Sizing pressure is spread out evenly over the entire surface of base metal. MEC says that the metal is actually drawn back to factory specifications creating a resized shell that will work freely in any magazine tube and will chamber properly.

MEC E-Z Prime "5"

MEC's E-Z Prime "5" model auto primer feed is designed for the MEC Super 600, 650 and 700 Versamec series of shotshell reloaders. Primers transfer directly from carton to reloader eliminating tubes and tube fillers. Adapts to all domestic and most foreign primers with adjustment of the cover.

Pacific Primer Tube Filler

A fast and simple way to load primer tubes for shotshell presses—just turn the dial of this plastic device and the tube is filled. Will not drop primer with base inverted.

Ponsness-Warren Reservoir Tubes

These are two-foot long tubes for the active shooter who loads large quantities of shells. These tubes make it possible to load almost a full case of shells without refilling. Tube baffles assure consistent weight of shot and powder at all times.

Ponsness-Warren Canvas Dust Cover

This rugged and handsome cover provides a practical way to keep dust and dirt off the press when not in use. Specify your model of P-W press.

Ponsness-Warren Shot, Powder Bushings

For use with the Ponsness-Warren presses, these bushings are made with extreme care to assure accuracy. Shot and powder bushings are of different diameters to eliminate any possibility of their being reversed. Powder bushings are of aluminum.

Redding Model 28 Shotshell Bushing

For use with Redding Model 32, Super 32 and Model 16 shotshell reloaders. Bushings facilitate changing powder and/or shot charge from one load to another. Clearly marked, fool-proof design prevents shot bushing being used for powder and vice-versa.

Redding Model 35 Die Head Stand

Sturdy bench stand for holding the Redding No. 34 Conversion head assembly when not in use. Large diameter base protects dies from damage.

Texan Shotshell Conditioner

Plastic or paper shotshell cases can be completely reconditioned with this tool. One pull of the handle resizes both the body and brass head. Optional heating element. Complete for 12, 16, 20, 28 or .410 gauge.

Whit's Rotary Shotshell Ironer

Hardened tool steel device, carrying a ¼″ shaft for motor or drill press mounting, quickly restores shells to usefulness. Also for cleaning or re-paraffining case mouths. All gauges except .410.

Vitt Aerodynamic Shotgun Slug

Modified and improved from the old reliable Brenneke slug. The high, thin, helical ribs tightly fit the bore for accuracy, but because they are thin and soft they pass through the tightest choke with complete safety. Maker says the ribs induce rotation to improve accuracy. Available in 12 gauge only.

T & T Hollow Point Shotgun Slug
12, 16 & 20 Gauge

T&T's hollow point shotgun slugs come with three segmented grooves that are designed spe-cifically to ensure slug breakup once it gets inside the intended target. According to the manufacturer, the slug actually breaks up into three distinct projectiles; and, it isn't affected by shooting in, or through, normal brush cover. Slug made of pure virgin lead. Slugs come 25 to the box.

Hollywood Shot Measure

Identical to the Hollywood powder measure except for having a patented tapered lead on the drum cavity's cutting edge. The wedging action of this lead displaces pellets, does not cut or deform them. Throws accurate charges of all shot sizes up to BB; maximum is 2⅛ oz. #9 shot. Measure is furnished with flat bar and lock nut for attachment to bench or tool head, base is threaded ⅞-14 for use in most presses.

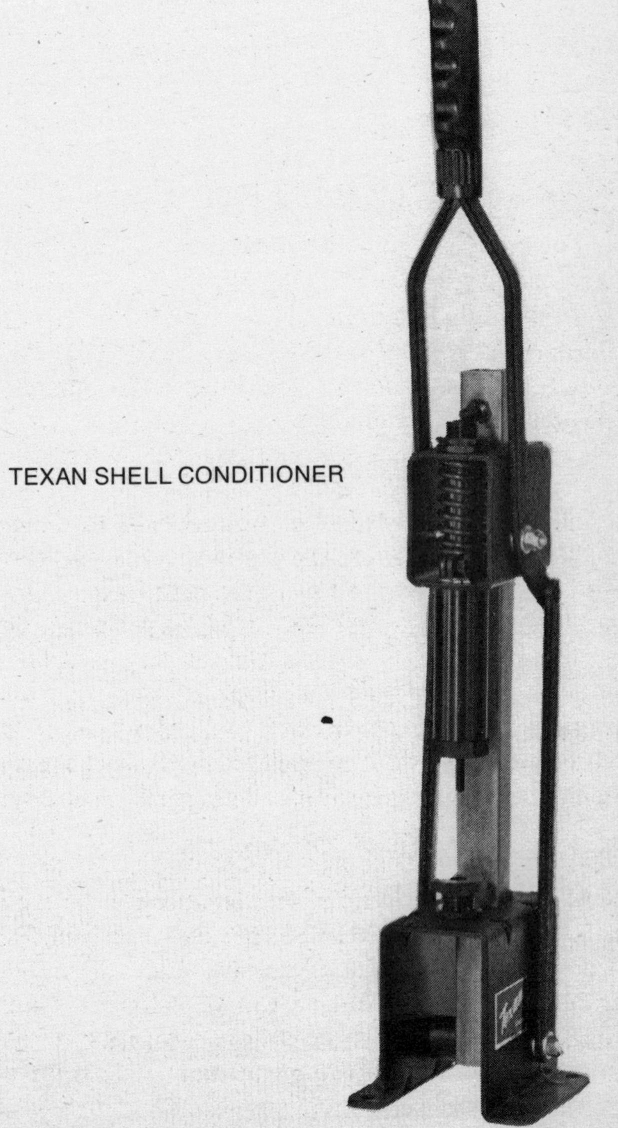

TEXAN SHELL CONDITIONER

Notes on Wads . . .

There are three basic wad types: overpowder, filler and overshot. The overpowder wads are available in card form (made of compressed paper), or as the newer plastic wads. The overpowder wad separates the powder from the softer filler wads and effects a gas seal ahead of the powder. Filler wads are resilient to cushion the initial shock, and are available in a variety of thicknesses to give the proper wad column height for perfect crimps and correct pressure. Since the majority of shotshells loaded today are star crimped, they need no over-shot wad. Only the older roll crimp shells require a wad which is held by the crimp to contain the shot.

Over-shot wads are made of compressed paper, similar to the over-powder type.

Lage Uniwad

This two-piece universal wad allows a change of powder charge for different cases and still stacks the proper height for a good crimp. Designed for 1⅛ oz. trap and Skeet loads, but it can be used for hunting loads too. Available in 12 and 20 gauge only. From Lage Uniwad Co.

Federal Wads

Federal makes a wide selection of wads for most popular gauges. The nearby chart provides complete information.

LAGE UNIWADS

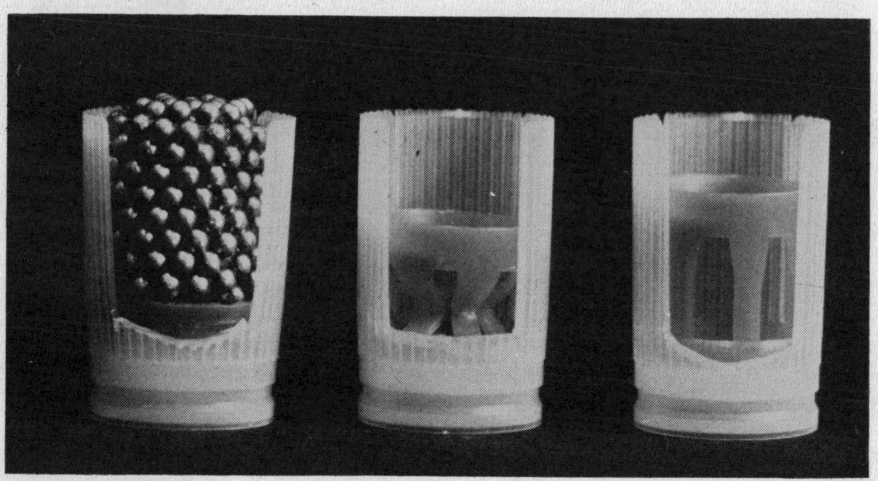

Federal Cartridge Corp.

Type	Gauge	Description
Champion		
Pellet Protector (plastic)	12	12 ga. ⅞" for 1⅛ oz. loads
Pushin'-Cushion Wad Column	12, 20, 28	12 ga. 1⅛, 1¼ oz. 20 ga. ⅞, 1 oz., 28 ga. ¾ oz.
Plastic Shot Cups	12 only	12 ga. 1½, 1¼ oz. or more
410 Wad Column (plastic)	410	Single-unit, ½ oz.
Card Wads	12 only	.045 inches .080 .135 .200
Fiber Cushion (waxed edges)	12 only	¼ inch ⅜

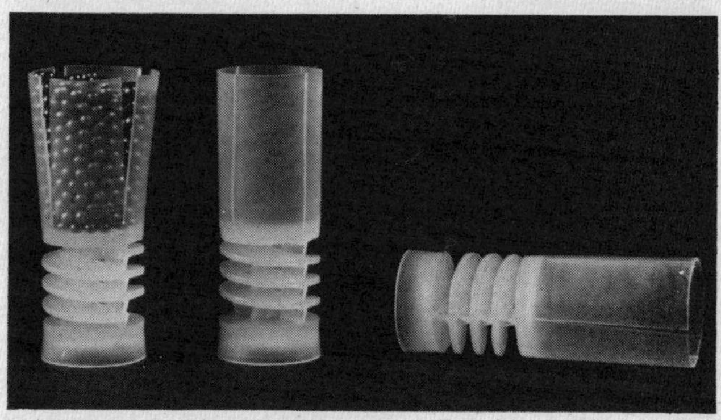
FEDERAL PUSHIN-CUSHIONS

Ljutic Plastic Mono Wad

Made in 12 gauge only, this wad features serrated runners the length of the wad to give less drag on the barrel. One piece design eliminates other wads and gives more consistent loads, greater speed with a reduction in powder charge. For use in Winchester AA plastic hulls and Federal plastic and paper shells.

Ljutic Mono Wad

A 1-piece wad for general use that eliminates the 2-piece, 2- or 3-stage wad column. Ljutic Mono-Wads give less recoil and make possible the use of less powder for the same muzzle velocity and pattern. Available in all standard gauges, including .410.

P & P Tool Co. American Wad

This wad is, so far, available only in 12 gauge. It has a thin-walled powder cup for better gas seal, a newly designed "X" mid-section for even pressure on the shot column. Wad material will not crack or brittle in cold weather. With 1⅛-oz.

of shot, wad will fit any standard shell such as Win. AA (red), Win. AA Handicap (black), Rem. (black), Rem. RXP, and Federal. Quantity discounts available.

Pacific Versalite Wads

A compressible center section in this wad will adjust to the correct wad column length. Available in 12, 20 and 10 gauge, the Versalite provides an excellent gas seal and shot protection. Shot

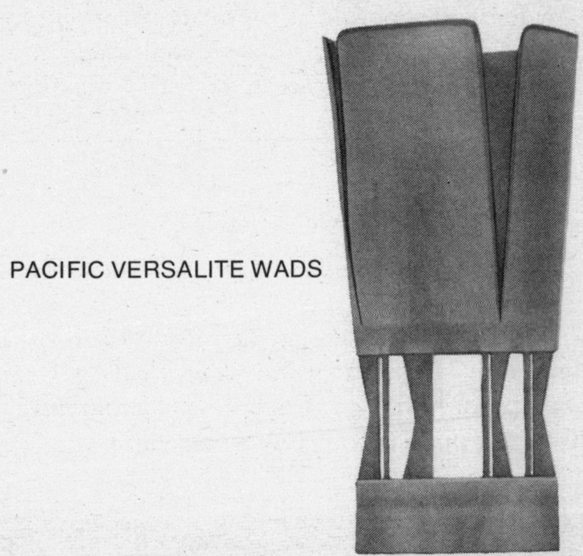

PACIFIC VERSALITE WADS

LJUTIC MONO WADS

cup is slightly flared to slip easily over the wad seating punch. From Pacific Tool Co.

Pacific Verelite Wads

The Verelite wad is made in two colors—green for 1⅛ oz. target loads in RP plastic target or WW paper target cases, and blue for 1¼ oz. loads in the WW AA or Federal paper hulls. 12 ga. only. From Pacific Tool Co.

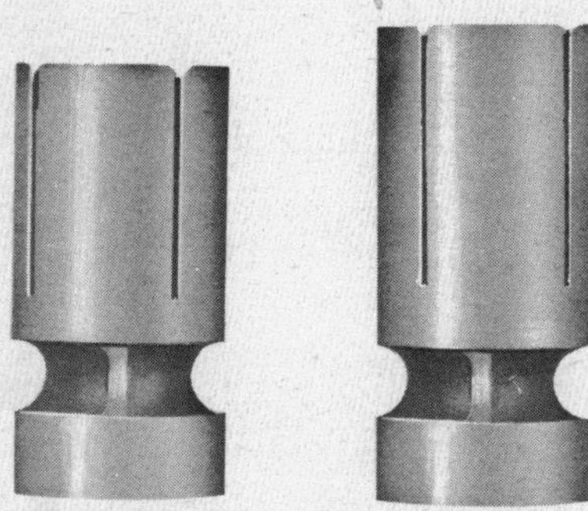

PACIFIC VERELITE WADS

Remington
Power Piston Wads
For Plastic Trap & Skeet Loads

Gauge	Wad No.
12	RXP12
20	RXP20
20	RP20
28	SP28
410	SP410
410	SP4103

RXP20 wad replaces R20 wad.

Power Piston Wads
For Plastic Field Loads

Gauge	Wad No.
10 (1⅝ or 2-oz)	SP10
12 (1 oz. load)	R12L
12 (1⅛-oz. load	R12H
12 (3¼x1¼-oz.)	RP12
12 (3¾x1¼-oz.)	SP12
16 (1-oz. load)	R16
16 (1⅛-oz. load)	SP16
20 (1-oz. load)	SP20

TRICO Precision Wads

These wads are available in 12, 20, 28 and .410 gauge. The 12 and 20 ga. are two-piece construction. They are designed with the MEC press in mind and the Precision 2 wads will fit all 20-ga. shells. Three different color-coded .410 wads are available, each for a different load.

Winchester Wads

Type	Gauge
WAA12	12
WAA12R	12
WAA12XW	12
WAA12F114	12
WAA20	20
WAA20F1	20
WAA28	28
WAA41	410

The Double A is designed to give straight line compression—no tipped wad. The vented skirt at the base allows trapped air to escape when seating the wad during reloading. When fired, hinged posts progressively collapse to absorb recoil. (Courtesy Winchester-Western)

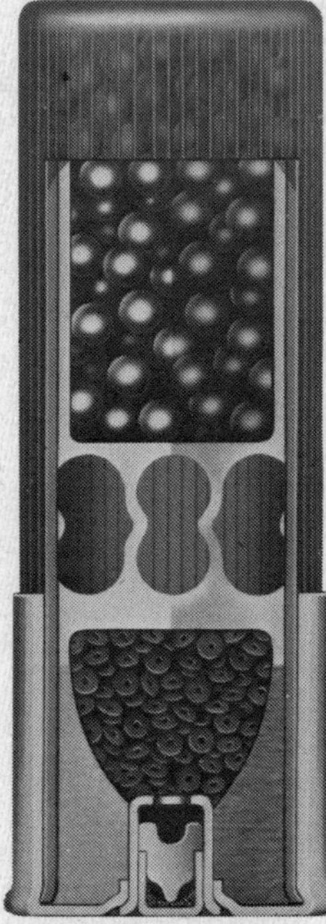

Plastic shotshell hulls are very reloadable — up to 10 times per shell in some instances.

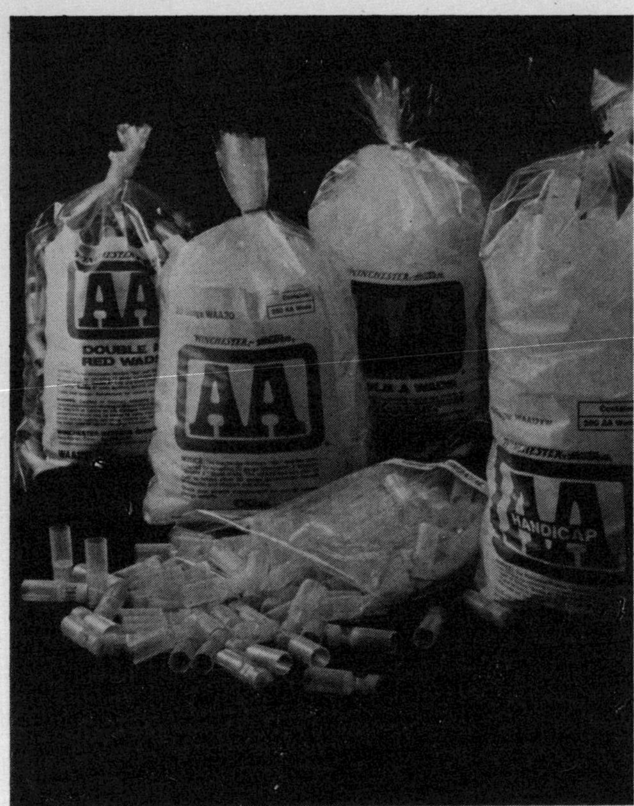

WINCHESTER WADS

Ballistic Products
Plastic Shotcup Wads

Available for 12 gauge 3-inch shells, these wads help improve patterns and extend the range of magnum loads. Holds 1⅝ ounces of shot.

Federal Plastic Shot Cups

These slit shot cups are made to combine with fiber and card wads for wad column. Come packed 250 per bag, 10 bags per case of 2500.

Federal 12 and 20 Gauge Card Wads

These card wads are available in .045, .080, .135 and .200. Packed 1000 per bag, 10 bags per case of 10,000.

Federal Shotshell Wads
in 12 and 20 Gauge

These fiber cushion wads have waxed edges and are available in ¼-, ⅜- and ½-inch heights. Come in 12 or 20 gauge. Packed 500 per bag, 10 bags per case of 5000 except for ½-inch 12 gauge, which comes 250 wads per bag, 2500 wads per 10-bag case.

Ballistic Products
10-Gauge Hunting Wad

Holding up to 2½ ounces of shot, these wads for 3-inch, 10-gauge shells provide top long range performance. Maker advises us they will hold killing patterns right up to the 80-yard mark.

Federal 1-Piece .410 Wads

This wad is of 1-piece construction and is segmented for easier loading. They come packed 250 per bag, 20 bags per 5000 case.

Miscellaneous Equipment & Supplies

Bonanza Powder/Bullet Scale

The Bonanza Model "M" scale has a 505-grain capacity, tempered stainless steel right hand poise plus a pan and beam made of Lexan. Guaranteed accurate to one-tenth of a grain.

C-H Powder/Bullet Scale

Comes with a chrome-plated brass beam, is graduated in 10-grain and 1/10-grain increments and has a leveling screw on the base. All metal construction, 360-grain capacity.

Pacific Bullet/Powder Scale

Pacific's Model-M has a 510-grain capacity, magnetic dampening and provides readout down to one-tenth of a grain.

RCBS Powder Scale

The RCBS 10-10 scale is a precision instrument that helps the reloader accurately determine the weight of a particular powder charge, case or bullet. The scale has a 500-grain capacity, magnetic dampener and other features.

Redding Reloading Scale

This Redding Model No. 2 scale has a 505-grain capacity, precision-milled V-groove beam, magnetic dampening and a 1/10-grain graduated over/under scale at the far left of the beam.

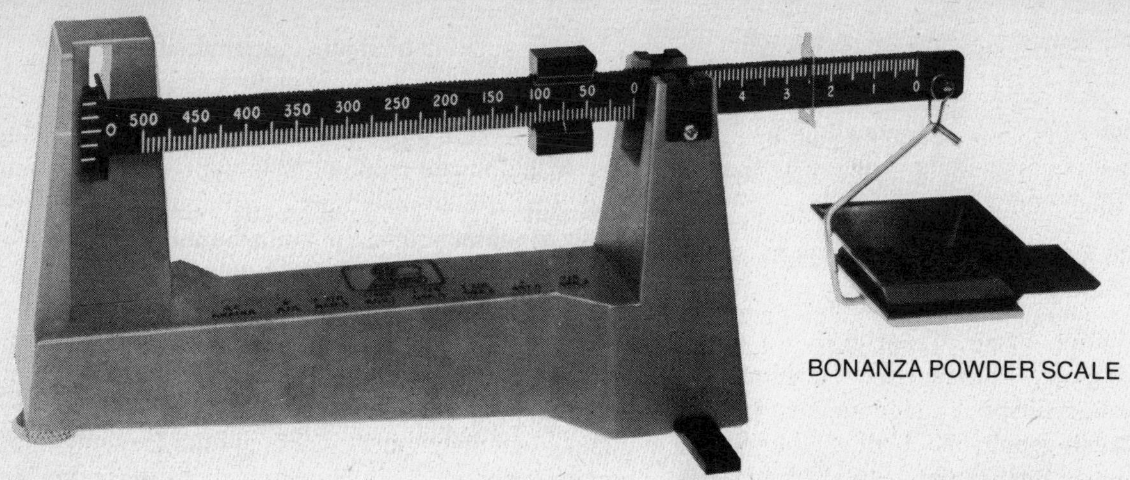

BONANZA POWDER SCALE

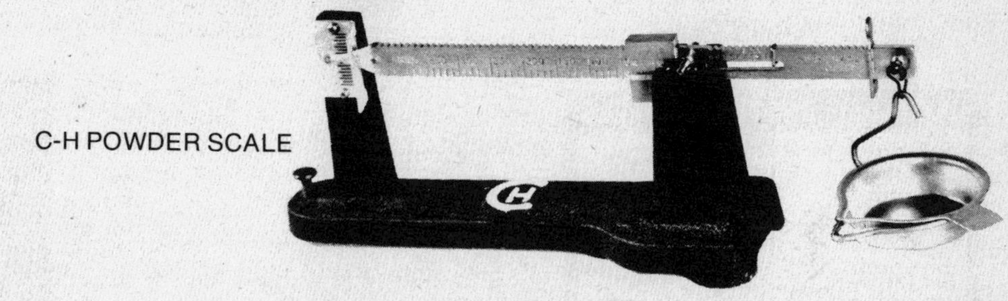

C-H POWDER SCALE

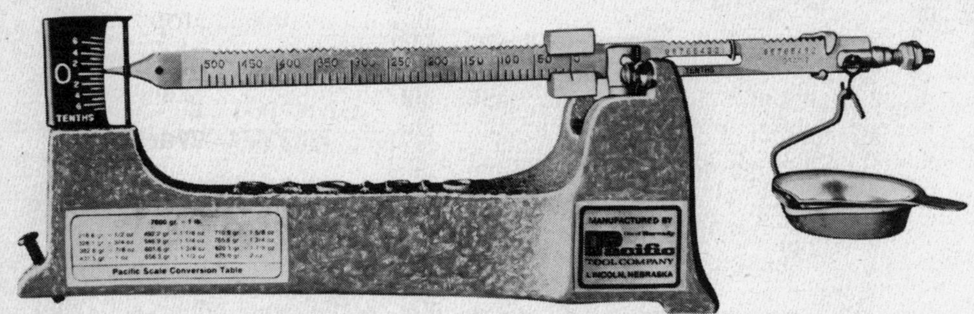

PACIFIC POWDER SCALE

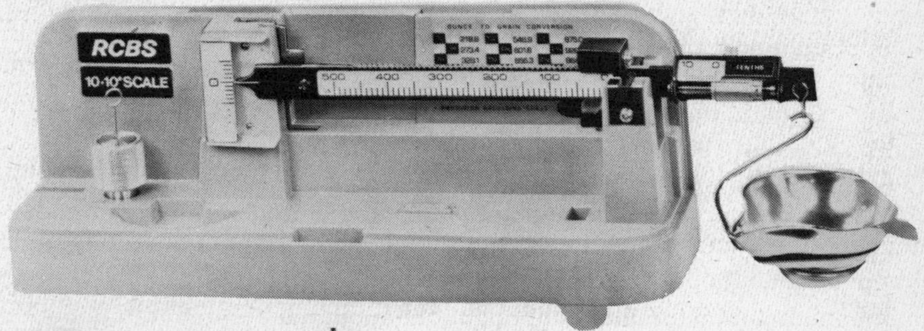

RCBS POWDER SCALE

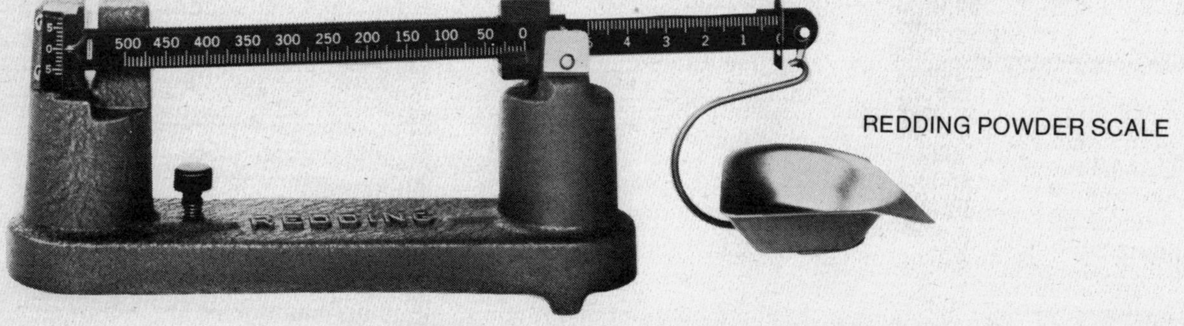

REDDING POWDER SCALE

Anderson Shotshell Case Trimmer

Quickly trims paper or plastic cases to desired length. Utilizes single-edge razor blade. Each trimmer comes with one dowel of proper gauge size; 10, 12, 16, 20 and .410 available.

Ballistics Engineering Company's Shotshell Scope

The Beco Shell-Scope from Ballistics Engineering Company allows the shooter/handloader to internally inspect a shotshell for proper powder/wad/shot position. Called the Shell-Scope, this handy unit might help stop an accident before it happens.

Jasco Shotshell Reloading Labels

Identifies the purpose for which a particular load is to be used, i.e., for Skeet, trap or hunting. Also helps the reloader record the components used in the re-making of shotshells. Identification of reloads, and the components used therein, is an additional safety factor for the reloader.

Dupont Smokeless Powders

Dupont shotgun propellants have been popular with shooters for years. Most of the powders in the nearby photos are available in 1-pound cannisters, 4- 5- or 8-pound caddies or 12- and 20-pound kegs.

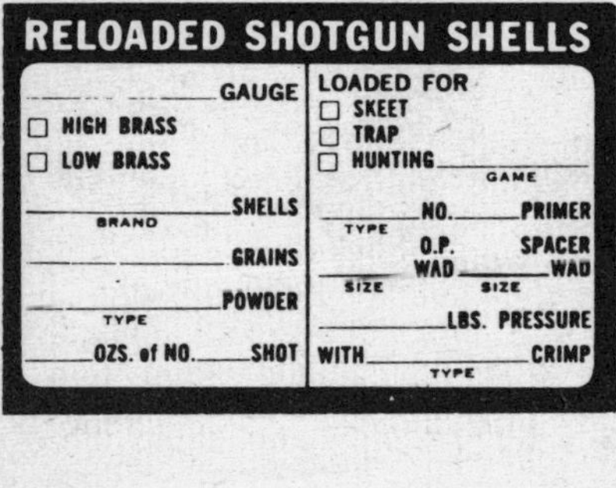

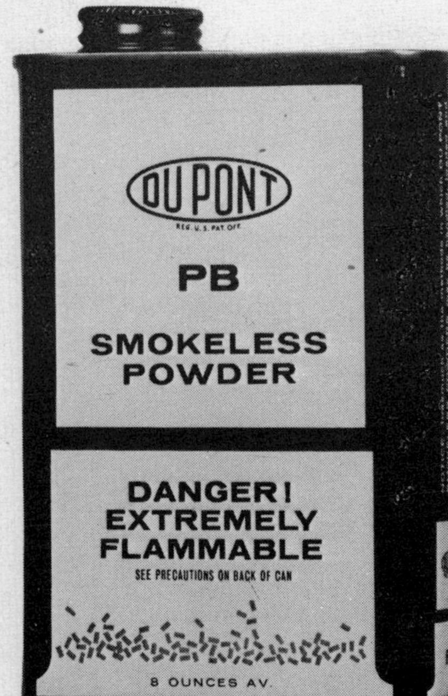

Winchester-Western Ball Powder

Winchester-Western's lineup of ball powders covers all of your rifle, pistol and shotgun needs. Ball powder has an excellent reputation for providing both low pressures and long barrel life.

Hercules Powder

Hercules powders have long been favorites with shotshell reloaders. Traditionally, Unique, Green Dot, Red Dot, Blue Dot and Herco are among the top propellant choices of shotgunners everywhere. Like all other reloading components, you get your best dollar buy if you do some shopping around and can afford to buy in quantity.

Shot

This is the one component that fluctuates greatly in price. Shot, in all sizes, is available from your local dealer or gun club. Prices—depending on where you live—can range from about $15 on up to around $19 for a 25-pound bag. Some gun clubs have even been selling cleaned, screened, salvaged shot at prices *well under* $10 a bag. Salvaged shot can represent tremendous savings. However, it is nothing like the "new" variety and may not suit your needs. The best cost savings advice we can give you is, "Shop around."

Ballistic Products' Plastic Shot Buffer

Ballistic Products offers the finely ground polyethylene plastic in half-pound bags. It's designed to be used in heavy waterfowl loads for shooting over 40 yards. Helps provide superb patterns.

Directory of Reloading Equipment & Components Manufacturers

(for shotshells and metallic cartridges)

AMMUNITION COMPONENTS—BULLETS, POWDER, PRIMERS

The Alberts Corp., P.O. Box 157, Franklin Lakes, NJ 07417/201-337-5848 (Taurus bull.)
Alcan, (see: Smith & Wesson Ammunition Co.
Ammo-O-Mart, P.O. Box 543, Renfrew, Ont., Canada K7V-4B1 (Curry bullets)
Austin Powder Co. (see Red Diamond Dist. Co.)
Ballistic Prods., Inc. 17510 19th Ave. No., Wayzata, MN 55391
Ballistic Research Inc., 935 E. Meadow Dr., Palo Alto, CA 94303 (BRI slug)
Barnes Bullets, P.O. Box 215, American Fork, UT 84003
B.E.L.L., Bell's Gun & Sport Shop, 3309-19 Mannheim Rd., Franklin Pk., IL 60131
Bitterroot Bullet Co., Box 412, Lewiston, ID 83501. 35¢ (coin or stamps) and #10 SASE for lit.
Brass Extrusion Laboratories, Ltd., 800 W. Maple Lane, Bensenville, IL 60106
Centrix, 2116 N. 10th AVe., Tuscon, Ariz
Kenneth E. Clark, 18738 Highway 99, Madera, CA 93637 (Bullets)
Division Lead, 7742 W. 61 Pl., Summit, Ill. 60502
DuPont, Explosives Dept., Wilmington, Del. 19898
Dynamit Nobel of America, Inc., 105 Stonehurst Court, Northvale, NJ 07647/201-767-1660 (RWS percussion caps)
Elk Mountain Shooters Supply Inc., 1719 Marie, Pasco, WA 99301 (Alaskan bullets)
Farmer Bros., 1102 Washington St., Eldora, IA 50627 (Lage wad)
Federal Cartridge Co., 2700 Foshay Tower, Minneapolis, MN 55402 (nickel cases)
Forth Five Ranch Enterprises, 119 S. Main, Miami, Okla. 74354
Godfrey Reloading Supply, Hi-Way 67-111, Brighton, IL 62012 (cast bullets)
Lynn Godfrey, see: Elk Mtn. Shooters Supply
Green Bay Bullets, 233 No. Ashland, Green Bay, Wis. 54303 (lead)
Gussert Bullet & Cartridge Co., Inc., P.O. Box 3945, Green Bay, WI 54303
Hardin Specialty Distr., P.O. Box 338, Radcliff, KY 40160 (empty, primed cases)
Hercules Powder Co., 910 Market St., Wilmington, Del. 19899
Herter's Inc., Waseca, Minn. 56093
Hodgdon Powder Co. Inc., 7710 W. 50th Hwy., Shawnee Mission KS 66202
Hornady Mfg. Co., Box 1848, Grand Island, Neb. 68801
N. E. House Co., 195 West High St., E. Hampton, CT 06424/203-267-2133 (zinc bases only)
J-4, Inc., 1700 Via Burton, Anaheim, CA 92806 (custom bullets)
Jaro Bullets, P.O. Box 6125, Pasadena, TX 77501
Keel Co., Bullet Metal Div., 327 East "B" St., Wilmington, CA 90744/213-834-2555 (bullet lead)
L. L. F. Die Shop, 1281 Highway 99 North, Eugene, Ore. 97402
Lage Uniwad Co., 1102 Washington St., Eldora, IA 50627
Ljutic Ind., Inc., Box 2117, Yakima, WA 98902 (Mono-wads)
Lomont Precision Bullets, 4421 S. Wayne Ave., Ft. Wayne, IN 46807/219-694-6792 (custom cast bullets)
Lyman Products Corp., Rte. 147, Middlefield, CT 06455
Michael's Antiques, Box 233, Copiague, L.I., NY 11726 (Balle Blondeau)
Miller Trading Co., 20 S. Front St., Wilmington, N.C. 28401
Norma-Precision, 798 Cascadilla St., Ithaca, NY 14850
Nosler Bullets, P.O. Box 688, Beaverton, OR 97005
Robert Pomeroy, Morison Ave., East Corinth, ME 04427
Red Diamond Distributing Co., 1304 Snowdon Dr., Knoxville, TN 37912 (black powder)
Remington-Peters, Bridgeport, Conn. 06602
Sanderson's, 724 W. Edgewater, Portage, Wis. 53901 (cork wad)
Sierra Bullets Inc., 10532 Painter AVe., Santa Fe Springs, CA 90670
Smith & Wesson Ammunition Co., 2399 Forman Rd., Rock Creek, OH 44084
Speer Products Inc., Box 896, Lewiston, Ida. 83501
C. H. Stocking, Rte. 3, Box 195, Hutchinson, Minn. 55350 (17 cal. bullet jackets)
Taurus Bullets, Alberts Corp., P.O. Box 157, Franklin Lakes, NJ 07417/201-337-5848
Taylor Bullets, P.O. Box 21254, San Antonio, TX 78221 (cast)
United Cartridge Co., P.O. Box 604, Valley industrial Park, Casa Grande, AR 85222/602-836-2510 (P.C. wads)
Vitt & Boos, c/o Mrs. Geo N. Vitt, P.O. Box 148, Wiscasset, ME 04578 (shotgun slugs)
Winchester-Western, 275 Winchester Ave., New Haven, CT 06504
Wood Die Shop, Box 386, Florence, OR 97439 (17 cal.)
Xelex Ltd., P.O. Box 543, Renfrow, Ont. K7V 4B1, Canada (powder, Curry bullets)
Zero Bullet Co., P.O. Box 1188, Cullman, Al 35055

LOAD TESTING and PRODUCT TESTING, CHRONOGRAPHING, BALLISTIC STUDIES

Hutton Rifle Ranch, 1802 S. Oak Park Dr., Rolling Hills, Tucson, AZ 85710
Kent Lomont, 4421 S. Wayne Ave., Ft. Wayne, IN 46807/219-694-6792 (handguns, handgun ammunition)
Plum City Ballistics Range, Rte. 1, Box 29A, Plum City, WI 54761
Russell's Rifle Shop, Rte. 5, Box 92, Georgetown, TX 78626/512-778-5338 (load testing and chronographing to 300 yds.)
John M. Tovey, 4710 - 104th Lane NE, Circle Pines, MN 55014
H. P. White Laboratory, Inc., 3114 Scarboro Rd., Street, MD 21154/301-838-6550

RELOADING TOOLS AND ACCESSORIES

Advance Car Mover Co., Inc., P.O. Box 1181, Appleton, WI 54911 (bottom pour lead casting ladles)
American Wad Co., 125 W. Market St., Morriston, IL 61270/815-772-7618 (12-ga. shot wad)
Anderson Mfg. Co., Royal, IA 51357 (Shotshell Trimmers)
Aurands, 229 E. 3rd St., Lewistown, Pa. 17044
B-Square Eng. Co., Box 11281, Ft. Worth, Tex. 76110
Bill Ballard, 830 Miles Ave., Billings, MT 59101 (ctlg. 50¢)
Ballistic Prods., Inc., 17610 19th Ave. No., Wayzata, MN 55391
Bear Reloading Equip., 2110 1st Natl. Tower, Akron, OH 44308
Belding & Mull, P.O. Box 428, Philipsburg, Pa. 16866
Berdon Co., P.O. Box 70131, Seattle, WA 98107 (metallic press)
Blackhawk SAA East, K2274 POB, Loves Park, Ill. 61131/812-633-7784
Blackhawk SAA Mtn., Richard Miller, 1337 Delmar Parkway, Aurora, CO 80010/303-366-3659
Blackhawk SAA West, Box 285, Hiawatha, KS 66434
Bonanza Sports, Inc., 412 Western Ave., Faribault, Miinn. 55021
Gene Bowlin, 3602 Hill Ave., Snyder, Tex. 79549 (arbor press)
Brown Precision Co., 5869 Indian Ave., San Jose, Calif. 95123 (Little Wiggler)
A. V. Bryant, 72 Whiting Rd., E. Hartford, CT 06118 (Nutmeg Universal Press)
C-H Tool & Die Corp., 106 N. Harding St., Owen, WI 54461/715-229-2146
CPM Industries Corp., 330 Elm St., Clyde, OH 43410
Central Products f. Shooters, 435 Route 18, East Brunswick, NJ 08816 (neck turning tool)
Camdex, Inc., 23880 Hoover Rd., Warren, MI 48089
Carbide Die & Mfg. Co., Box 226, Covina, CA 91724
Carter Gun Works, 2211 Jefferson Pk. Ave., Charlottesville, Va. 22903
Cascade Cartridge, Inc., (See Omark)
Catco-Ambush, Inc., P.O. Box 300, Corte Madera, CA 94926 (paper bullet patches)
Chevron Case Master, R.R. 1, Ottawa, IL 61350
Lester Coats, 416 Simpson St., No. Bend, Ore. 97459 (core cutter)
Container Development Corp., 424 Montgomery St., Watertown, WI 53094
Continental Kite & Key Co., Box 40, Broomall, PA 19008 (primer pocket cleaner)
Cooper-Woodward, Box 972, Riverside, Calif. 92502 (Perfect Lube)
D. R. Corbin Mfg. & Supply Inc., P.O. Box 758, Phoenix, OR 97535

Custom Products, 686 Baldwin St., Meadville, PA 16335/814-724-7045 (decapping tool, dies, etc.)
J. Dewey Mfg. Co., 125 Fenn Rd., Middlebury, CT 06762
Diverter Arms, Inc., P.O. Box 22084, Houston, TX 77027 (bullet powder)
Division Lead Co., 7742 W. 61st Pl., Summit, Ill. 60502
Eagle Products Co., 1520 Adelia Ave., So. El Monte, Cal. 91733
Edmisten Co. Inc., P.O. Box 1293, Hwy 105, Boone, NC 28607/704-264-1490
Efemes Enterprises, P.O. Box 122M, Bay Shore, NY 11706 (Berdan decapper)
W. H. English, 4411 S. W. 100th, Seattle, Wash. 98146 (Paktool)
Farmer Bros., 1102 Washington St., Eldora, IA 50627 (Lage)
Fitz, 653 N. Hagar St., San Fernando, CA 91340 (Fitz Flipper)
Flambeau Plastics, 801 Lynn, Baraboo, Wis. 53913
Forster Products Inc., 82 E. Lanark Ave., Lanark, Ill. 61046
Geo. M. Fullmer, 2499 Mavis St., Oakland, CA 94601 (sealing die)
Gene's Gun Shop, 3602 Hill Ave., Snyder, Tex. 79549 (arbor press)
Goerg Enterprises, P.O. Box 531, Renton, WA 98056/206-833-1529
Gopher Shooter's Supply, Box 278, Faribault, MN 55021
Griffin Mfg. Co., P.O. Box 935, Brownwood, TX 76801
The Gun Clinic, 81 Kale St., Mahtomedi, Minn. 55115
Hart Products, Rob. W. Hart & Son Inc., 401 Montgomery St., Nescopeck, PA 18635
Henriksen Tool Co., Inc., P.O. Box 668, Phoenix, OR 97535
Hensley & Gibbs, Box 10, Murphy, Ore. 97533
Herter's Inc., RR1, Waseca, Minn. 56093
Richard Hoch, The Gun Shop, 62778 Spring Creek Rd., Montrose, CO 81401/303-249-3625 (custom schuetzen bullet moulds)
B. E. Hodgdon, Inc., 7710 W. 50 Hiway, Shawnee Mission, Kans. 66202
Hoffman Prods., P.O. Box 853, Lake Forest, IL 60045 (spl. gallery load press)
Hollywood Reloading, (see: Whitney Sales, Inc.)
Hornady (see: Pacific)
Hulme Firearm Serv., Box 83, Millbrae, Calif. 94030 (Star case feeder)
Independent Mach. & Gun Shop, 1416 N. Hayes, Pocatello, Ida. 83201
Ivy Amament, P.O. Box 10, Greendale, WI 53129
JASCO, Box 49751, Los Angeles, Calif. 90049
J & G Rifle Ranch, Box S80, Turner, MT 59542 (case tumblers)
Javelina Products, Box 337, San Bernardino, Cal. 92402 (Alox beeswax)
Neil Jones, 686 Baldwin St., Meadville, PA 16335 (decapping tool, dies)
Kexplorc, 9450 Harwig #G, Houston, TX 77036
Kuharsky Bros. (see Modern Industries)
Lac-Cum Bullet Puller, Star Route, Box 240, Apollo, PA 15613/412-478-1794
Lage Uniwad Co., 1102 N. Washington St., Eldora, IA 50627 (Universal Shotshell Wad)
LanDav, 7213 Lee Highway, Falls Church, VA 22046 (X-15 bullet puller)
Lee Precision, Inc., 4275 Hwy. U, Hartford, WI 53027
Leon's Reloading Service, 3945 No. 11 St., Lincoln, Neb. 68521
Lewisystems, Menasha Corp., 426 Montgomery St., Watertown, WI 53094
L. L. F. Die Shop, 1281 Highway 99 N., Eugene, Ore. 97402
Dean Lincoln, P.O. Box 1886, Farmington, NM 87401 (mould)
Ljutic Industries, 918 N. 5th Ave., Yakima, Wash. 98902
Lock's Phila. Gun Exch., 6700 Rowland, Philadelphia, Pa. 19149
Lyman Products Corp., Rte. 147, Middlefield, CT 06455
McKillen & Heyer Inc., 37603 Arlington Dr., Box 627, Willoughby, OH 44094/216-942-2491 (case gauge)
Paul McLean, 2670 Lakeshore Blvd., W., Toronto 14, Ont., Canada (Universal Cartridge Holder)
MEC, Inc. (see: Mayville Eng. Co.)
MTM Molded Prod., 5680 Webster St., Dayton, OH 45414
Magma Eng. Co., P.O. Box 881, Chandler, AZ 85224
Judson E. Mariotti, Beauty Hill Rd., Barrington, NH 03825 (brass bullet mould)
Marmel Prods., P.O. Box 97, Utica, MI 48087 (Marvelube, Marvelux)
Marquart Precision Co., Box 1740, Prescott, AZ 86301 (precision case-neck turning tool)
Mayville Eng. Co., 715 South St., Mayville, Wis. 53050 (shotshell loader)
Merit Gun Sight Co., P.O. Box 995, Sequim, Wash. 98382
Modern Industries, Inc., 613 W-11, Erie, PA 16501 (primer pocket cleaner)
Multi-Scale Charge Ltd., 3269 Niagara Falls Blvd., North Tonawanda, NY 14120
NL Industries Inc., Metal Div., P.O. Box 3618, Hightstown, NJ 08520/609-443-2209 (Lawrence Brand shot)
Normington Co., Box 6, Rathdrum, ID 93959 (powder baffles)
Ohaus Scale, (see: RCBS)
Omark-CCI, Inc., Box 856, Lewiston, Ida. 83501
P & P Tool Co. (see American Wad Co.)
Pacific Tool Co., P.O. Box 2048, Ordnance Plant Rd., Grand Island, NE 68801/308-384-2308
Pak-Tool Co., 4411 S.W. 100th, Seattle, WA 98146
Personal Firearms Record Book, Box 201, Park Ridge, Ill. 60068
Ferris Pindell, R.R. 3, Box 205, Connersville, IN 47331 (bullet spinner)
Plum City Ballistics Range, Rte. 1, Box 29A, Plum City, WI 54761
Ponsness-Warren, inc., P.O. Box 8, Rathdrum, ID 83858
Marian Powley, Petra Lane, R.R.1, Eldridge, IA 52748
Precise Alloys Inc., 69 Kinkel St., Westbury, NY 11590 (chilled lead shot; bullet wire)
Quinetics Corp., 5731 Kenwick, San Antonio, TX 78238/516-684-8561 (kinetic bullet puller)
RCBS, Inc., Box 1919, Oroville, Calif. 95965
Redding Inc., 114 Starr Rd., Cortland, NY 13045
Reloaders Equipment Co., 4680 High St., Ecorse, MI 48229 (bullet powder)
Remco, 1404 Whitesboro St., Utica, N.Y. 13502 (shot caps)
Rifle Ranch, Rte. 5, Prescott, Ariz. 86301
Rochester Lead Works, Rochester, N.Y. 14608 (leadwire)
Rorschach Precision Prods., P.O. Box 1613, Irving, Tex. 75060
Rotex Mfg. Co. (see Texan)
Ruhr-American Corp., So. East Hwy. 55, Glenwood, Minn. 56334
SAECO Rel. Inc., P.O. Box 778, Carpinteria, Calif. 93013
SSK Industries, Rt. 1, Della Drive, Bloomingdale, OH 43910 (primer tool)
Sandia Die & Cartridge Co., Rte. 5, Box 5400, Albuquerque, NM 87123
Shassere, (Box 35865, Houston, TX 77096/713-780 7041 (cartridge case caddy/loading block)
Shiloh Products, 37 Potter St., Farmingdale, NY 11735 (4-cavity bullet mould)
Shooters Accessory Supply, see: D. R. Corbin
Sil's Gun Prod., 490 Sylvan Dr., Washington, Pa. 15301 (K-spinner)
Jerry Simmons, 715 Middlebury St., Goshen, Ind. 46526/219-533-8546 (Pope de- & recapper)
Smith & Wesson Ammunition Co., Inc., 2399 Forman Rd., Rock Creek, OH 44084
J. A. Somers Co., P.O. JBox 49751, Los Angeles, CA 90049 (Jasco)
Sport Flite Mfg., Inc., 2520 Industrial Row, Troy, MI 48084/313-280-0648 (swaging dies)
D. E. Stanley, P.O. Box 833, Ringold, OK 74754 (Kake-Kutter)
Star Machine, Inc., 418 10th Ave., San Diego, CA 92101
T.E.S., Inc., 2807 N. Prospect St., Colorado Springs, CO 80907 (Vibra-Tek)
T&T Products, Inc., 6330 Hwy. 14 East, Rochester, MN 55901 (Meyer shotgun slugs)
Texan Reloaders, Inc., 444 Cip St., Watseka, IL 60970/815-432-5065
Trico Plastics, 590 S. Vincent Ave., Azusa, CA 91702
WAMADET, Silver Springs, Goodleigh, Barnstaple, Devon, England
Walker Mfg. Inc., 8296 So. Channel, Harsen's Island, MI 48028 (Berdan decapper)
Wammes Guns Inc., 236 N. Hayes St., Bellefontaine, OH 43311 (Jim's powder baffles)
Weatherby, Inc., 2781 Firestone Blvd., South Gate, Calif. 90280
Webster Scale Mfg. Co., Box 188, Sebring, Fla. 33870
Whits Shooting Stuff, P.O. Box 1340, Cody, WY 82414
Whitney Sales, Inc., P.O. 875, Reseda, CA 91335 (Hollywood)
L. E. Wilson, Inc., P.O. Box 324, 404 Pioneer Ave., Cashmere, WA 98815
Xelex, Ltd., P.O. box 543, Renfrow K7V 4B1, Canada (powder)
Zenith Enterprises, 361 Flagler Rd., Nordland, WA 98358

Shotshell Reloader's Guide to Press Operation

MEC 700   P/W Du-O-Matic   Pacific 366 Auto

Step-By-Step Press Operation Using the MEC 700

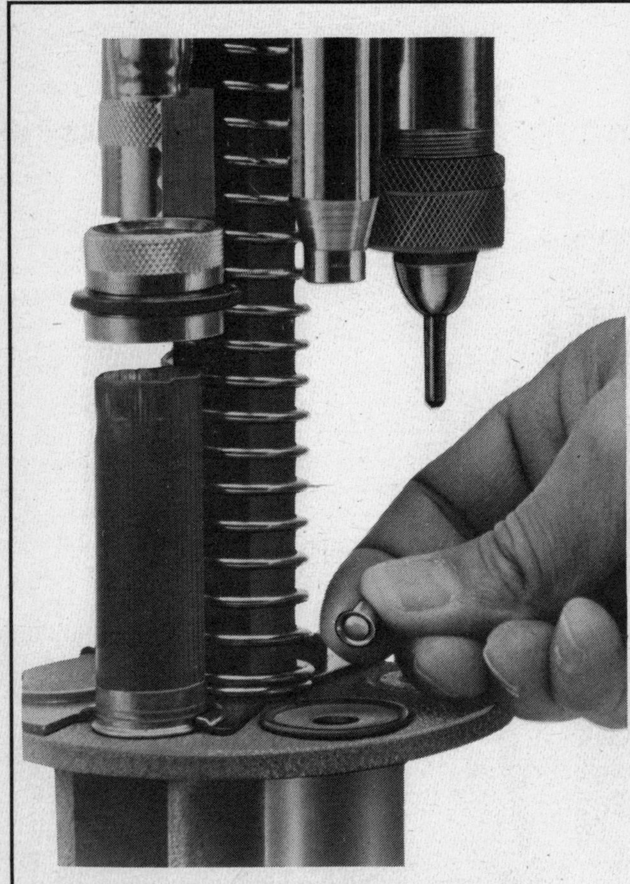

1. POSITION PRIMER

Place primer in Primer Seating Assembly, base down.

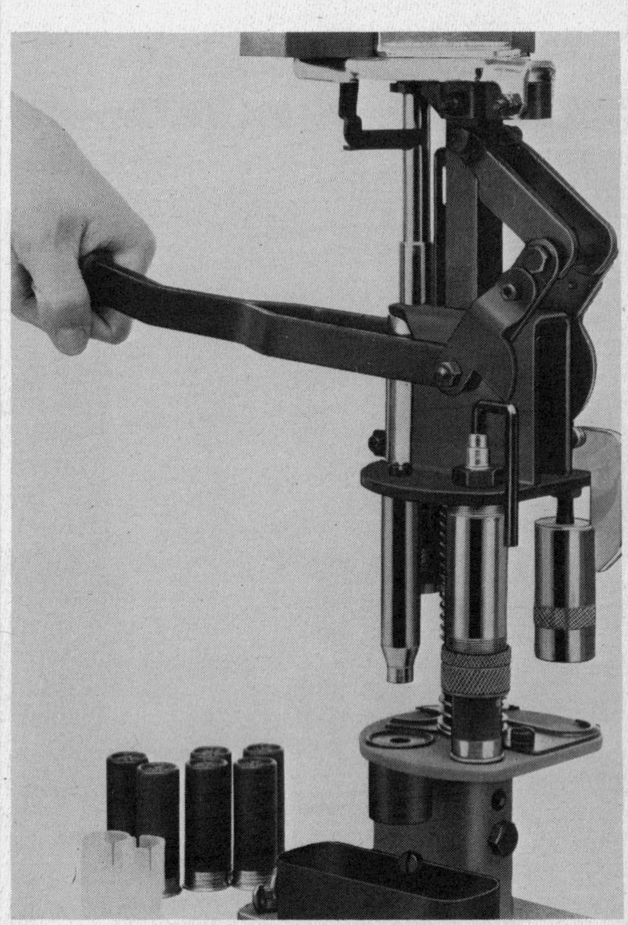

2. DEPRIME & SIZE

Start shell into Reconditioning Die and depress handle. The spent primer will drop in the Primer Catcher below and the die will resize the metal base of the shell for diameter and head space and recondition mouth. *Avoid excessive flexing of the rim.* Expanded rims could cause failure to feed from the magazine tube or chamber properly. Reconditioned shell is ejected from die by exclusive cam-actuated ejecting mechanism on upstroke of handle. (Note: Do *not* snap handle up.)

3. REPRIME

Slip shell on Repriming Punch and depress handle until new primer is seated properly in base of shell. Use only the pressure required to seat the primer to avoid distortion of the base wad or expansion of the head.

4. PREPARE FOR POWDER CHARGING

Place shell under Rammer Tube with shell rim under the shell holder.

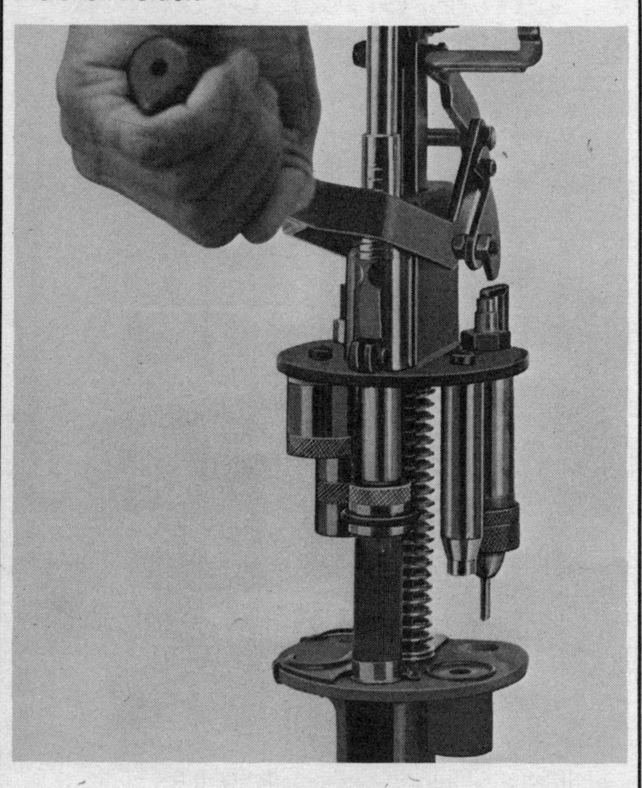

5. POWDER CHARGING

Depress handle, lowering Rammer Tube into shell. Charge powder by moving Charging Bar to left.

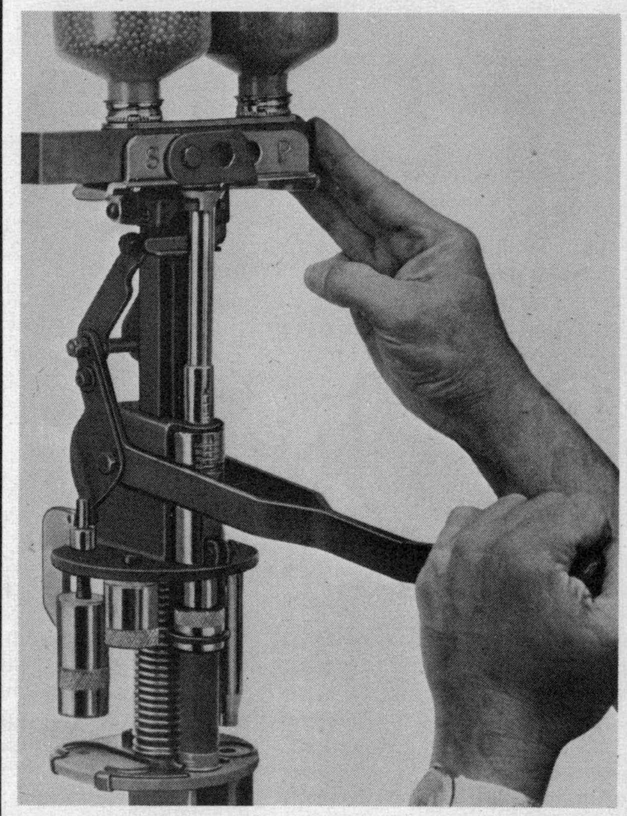

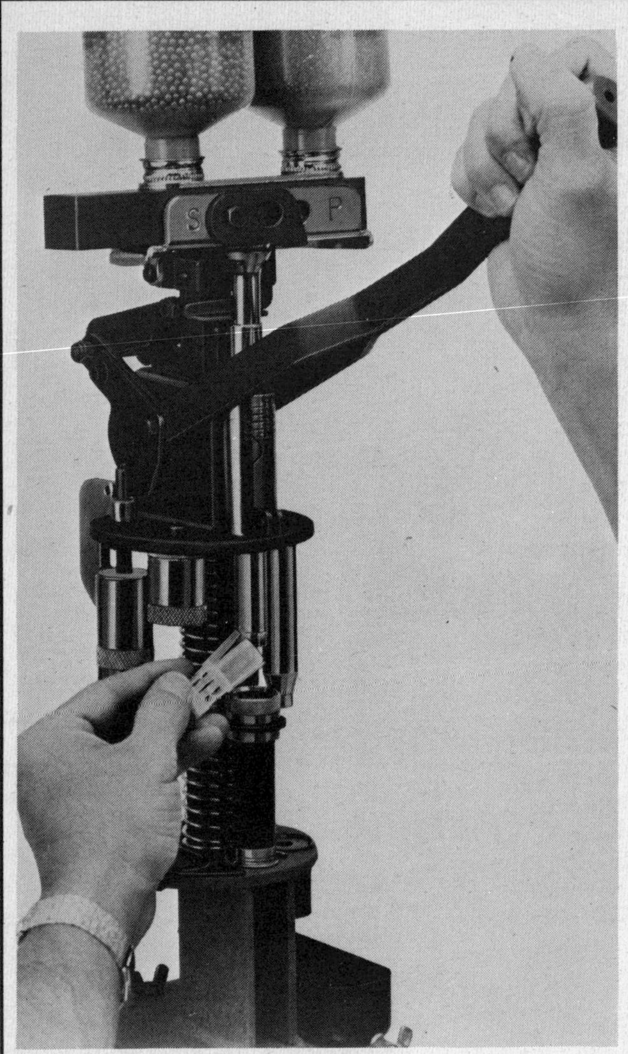

6. PLACE WAD

Raise handle to clear Rammer Tube from shell. With the left hand, pick up and place a wad column in the Adjusta-Guide wad starter. With the right hand, depress handle to positive stop. Pro-Check will automatically position wad guide to provide maximum clearance for easy wad entry.

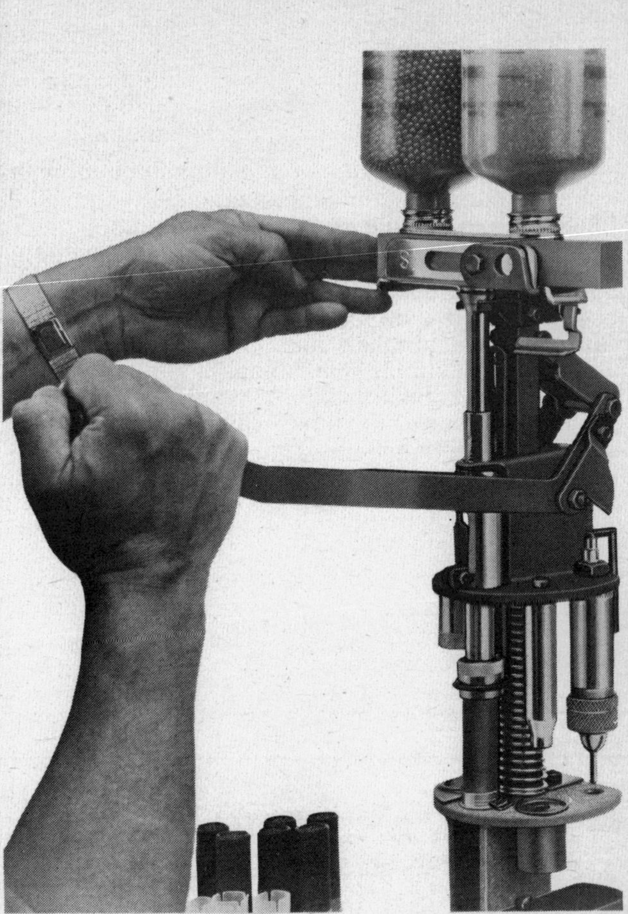

7. DROP SHOT CHARGE

With handle depressed, charge shot by pushing Charging Bar to right. Pro-Check will release wad guide and upon raising the handle, shell will be free to be positioned at pre-crimp station.

8. CRIMP START

Place shell under Crimp Starter with shell rim under the holder. Depress handle. The self-aligning Crimp Starter will follow the original folds of the plastic shell. Close the shell to approximately one half its original diameter, partially depressing the handle may be adequate, depending upon the condition of the case mouth. Choice of 6 point or cone insert included to start the folds on new cases or fired paper shells.

9. FINAL CRIMP

Place shell under cam-operated crimping die with shell rim in shell holder. Depress handle all the way (above). This performs complete crimping operation in one stroke of the handle (below).

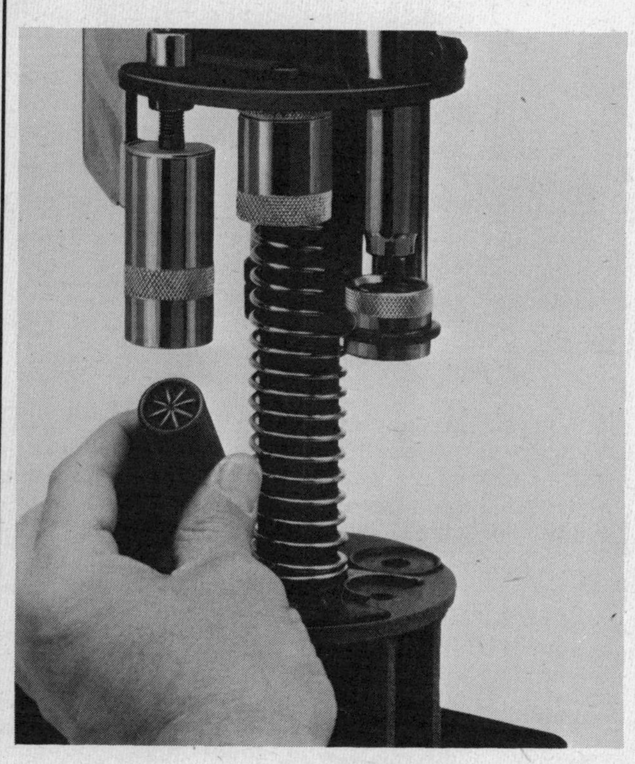

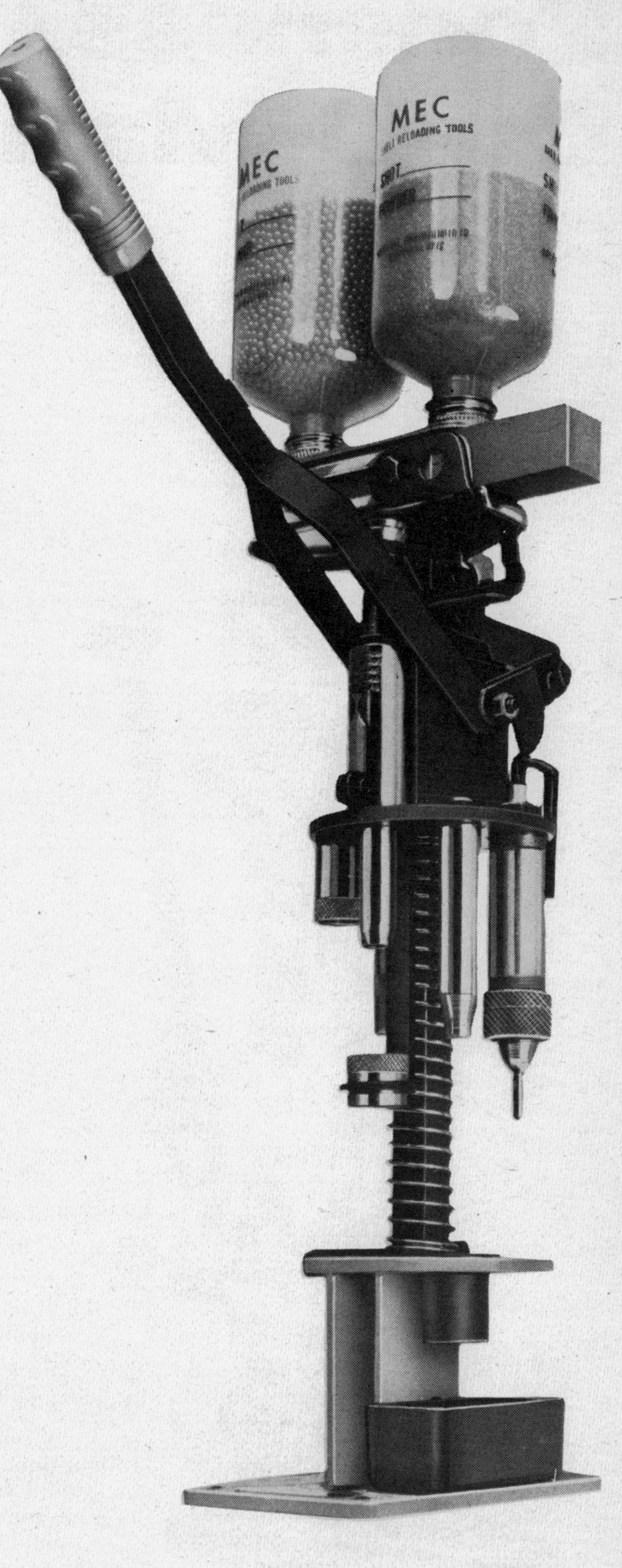

Step-By-Step with the Ponsness/Warren Du-O-Matic 375

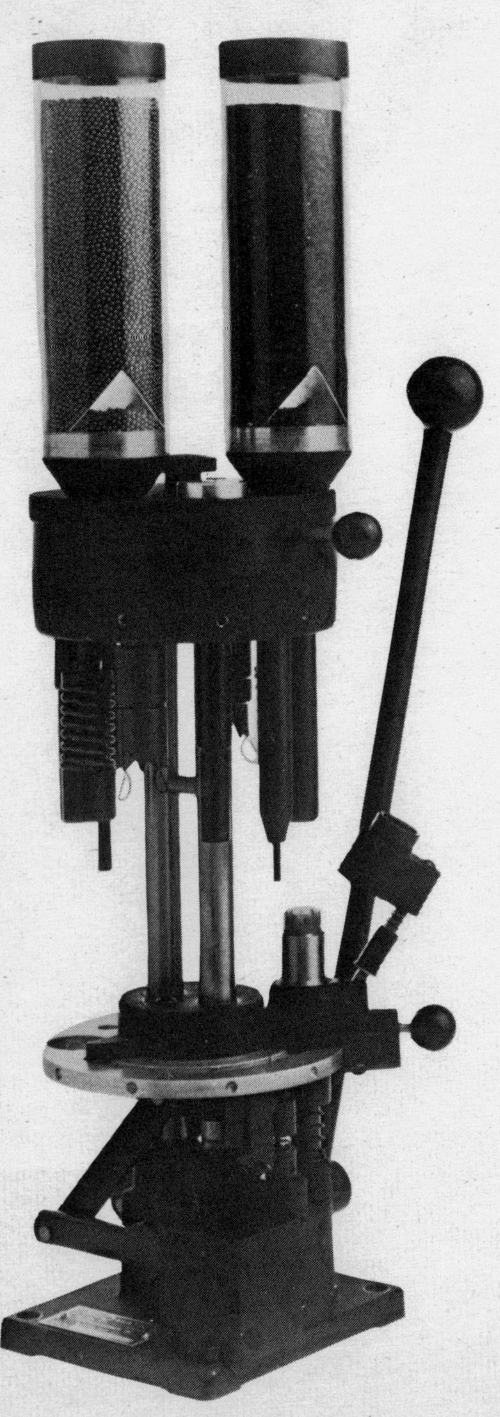

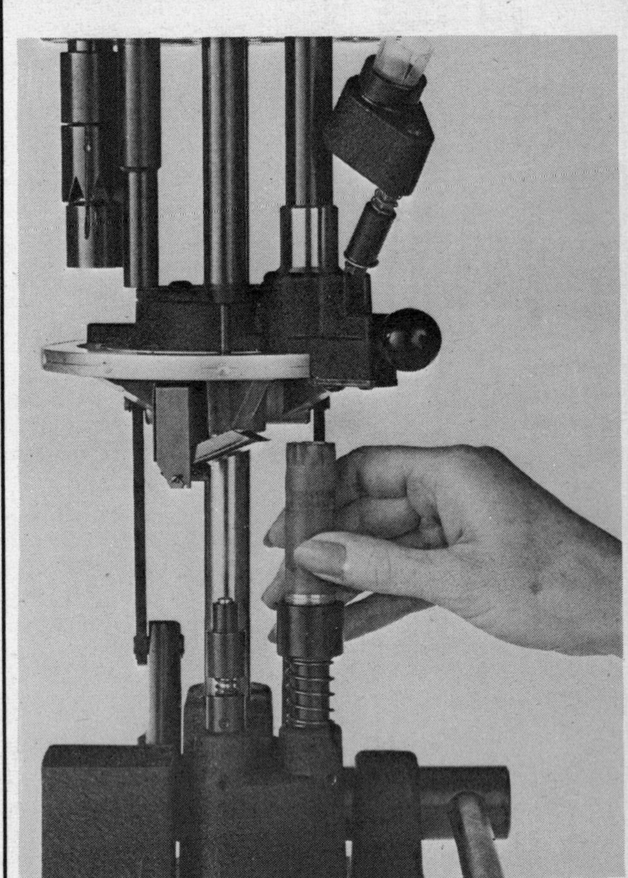

1. SEAT SHELL

With the sizing die at station 1, pull the operating handle all the way down. Place an empty shell on the shell seating post, a primer on the primer seating post, and a wad into the wad cup. Push the operating handle all the way up, seating the shell in the full-length die.

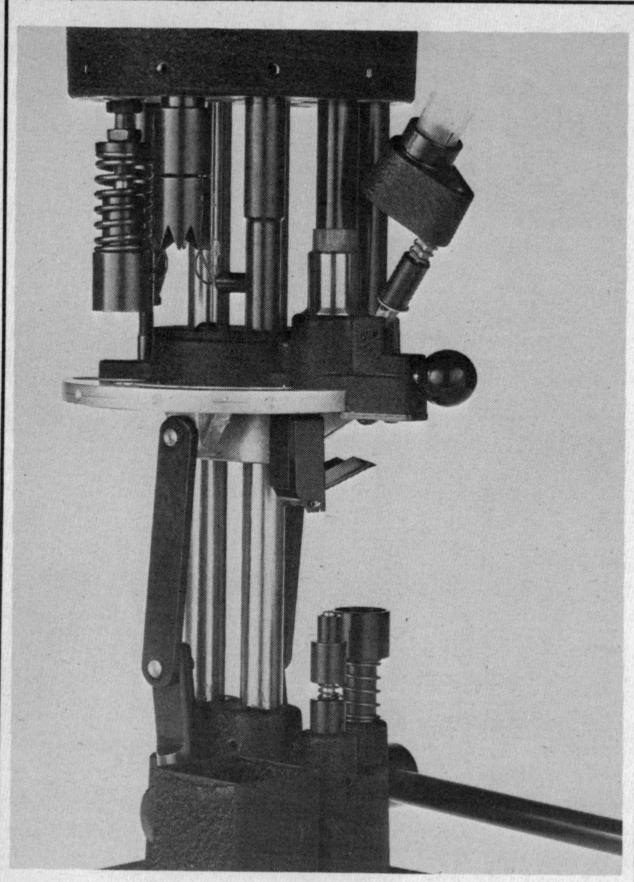

2. DEPRIME, PRIME

Move the sizing die one notch to the left to station 2. At the same time, pull downward slightly on the operating handle to allow for clearance over the primer post. With the sizing die set at station 2, pull the operating handle on down. The spent primer will be punched out, dropping down on the primer deflector and into the spent primer box below. Now bring the operating handle to the full up position to seat the new primer.

3. DROP POWDER

Move the sizing die to the left to station 3. Pull the operating handle on down. Move the charging ring handle to the left. This drops your powder charge into the shell.

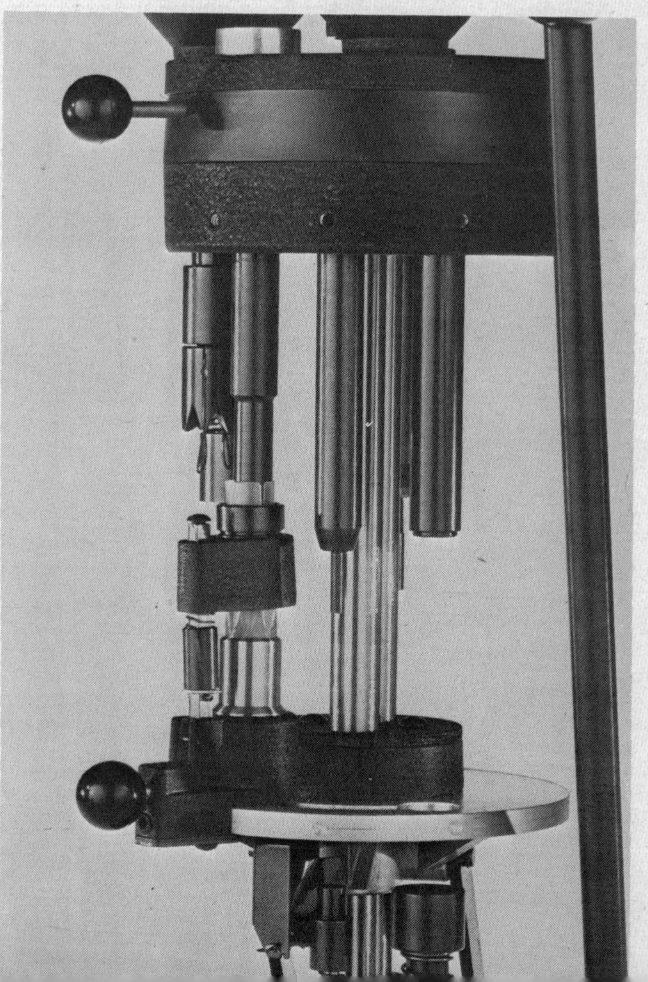

4. SEAT WAD, DROP SHOT

Now move the operating handle to the up position. Push the spring-loaded wad cup containing the wad over and down on the shell, then bring the operating handle down, automatically inserting the wad into the shell. While the operating handle is still down, move the charging ring handle to the right, dropping your shot charge into the shell. Now move the operating handle back to the up position.

5. PRE-CRIMP

Move the sizing die to the left to station 4 for the pre-crimping operation. Bring the operating handle down to engage the shell with the crimp starter.

6. FINAL CRIMP

Bring the operating handle to the up position and move the sizing die to station 5. Bring the operating handle down firmly to finish the crimping operation.

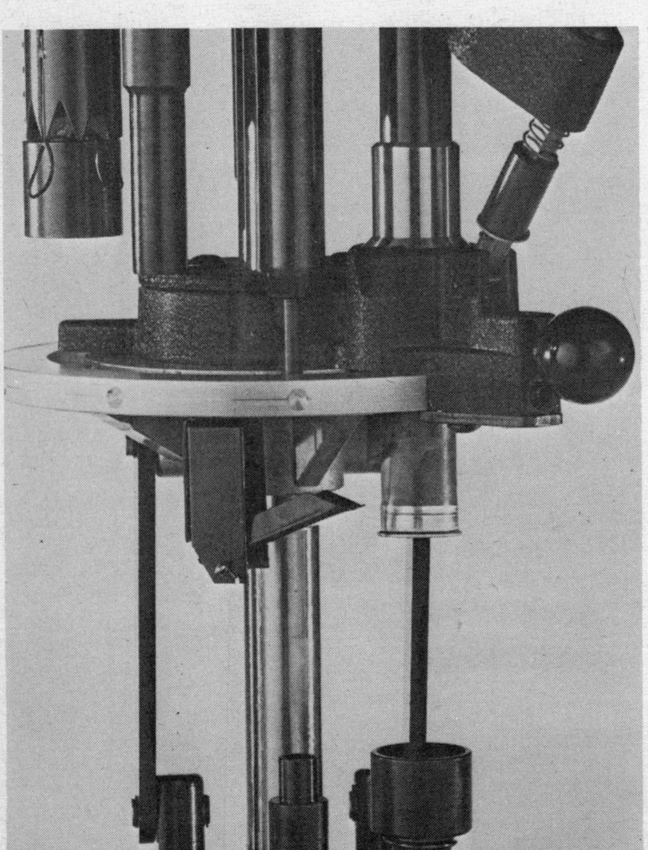

7. SHELL KNOCKOUT

Bring the sizing die all the way back to the right to station 1. Bring the operating handle down and your perfectly resized, finished reload is ejected down and out through the full-length sizing die.

Step-By-Step with the Pacific 366 Auto Reloader

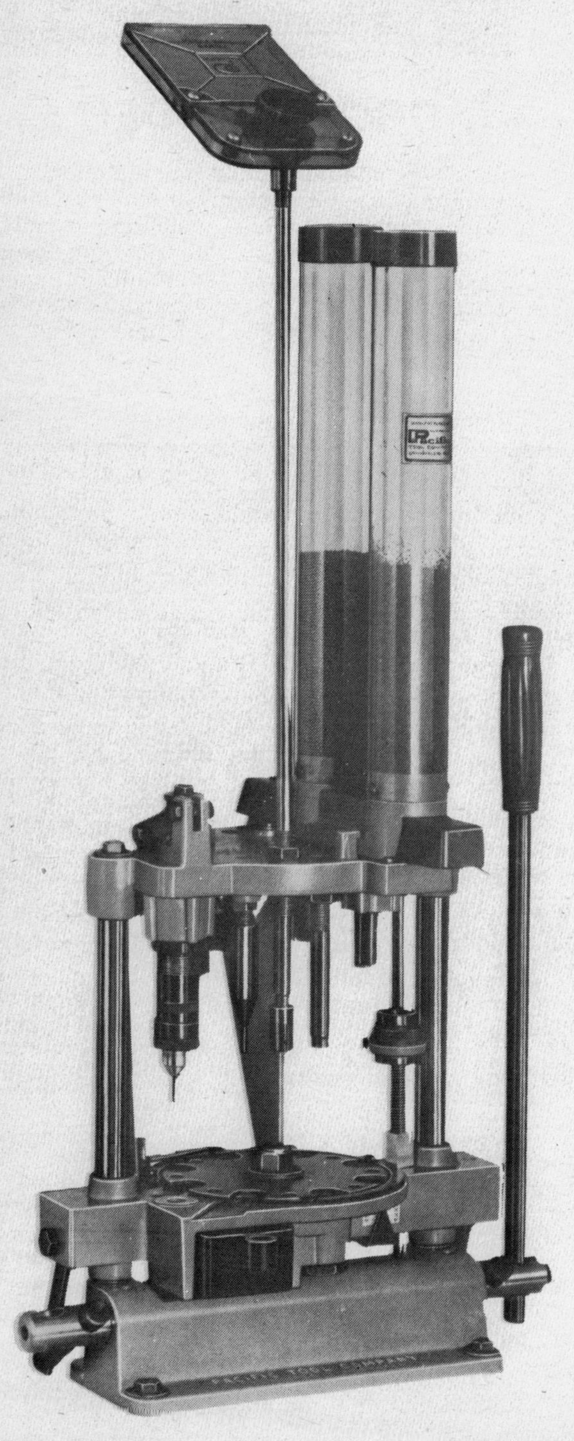

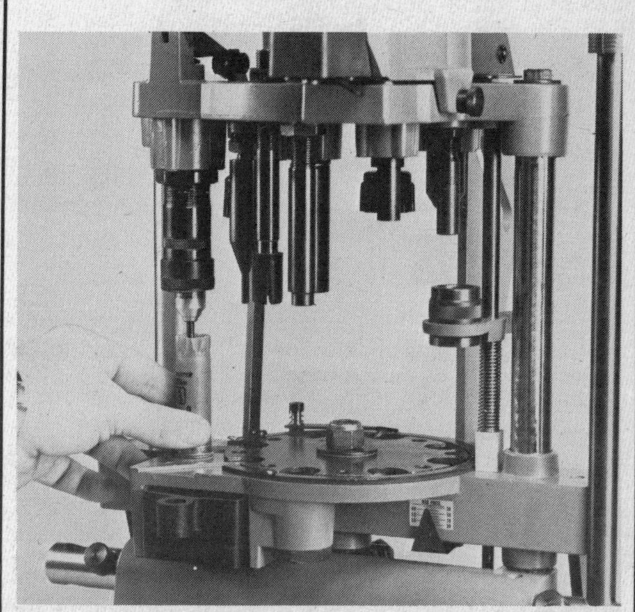

1. RESIZE AND DEPRIME

Place an empty shell in station 1A (the position shown) making sure the deprime punch enters the case mouth and the shell is reasonably centered under the size die. Pull the operating handle to the bottom of the stroke. Make sure nothing interferes with the handle reaching bottom. When the platen is at the top of the stroke make sure the shell has completely entered the die and there is no gap between the die and the casting. Return the handle to the top completing the stroke and the shell will be ejected from the die. Place case in station 1.

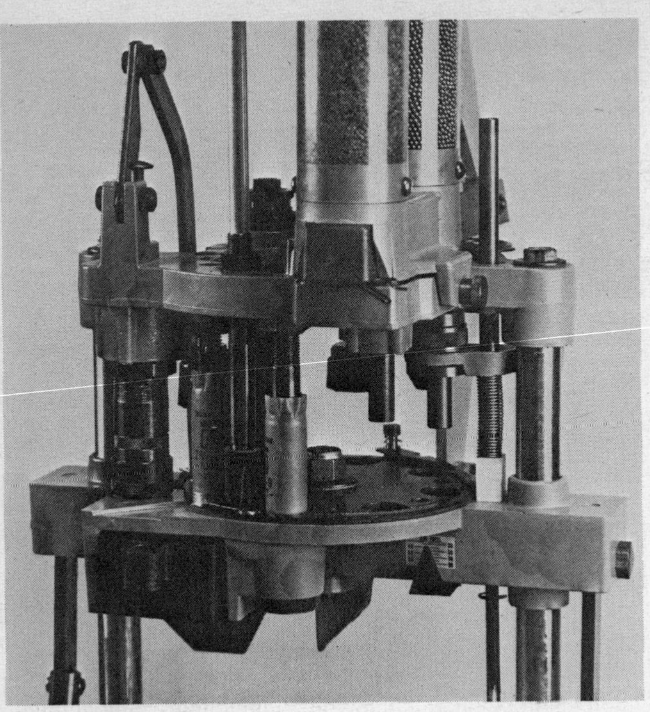

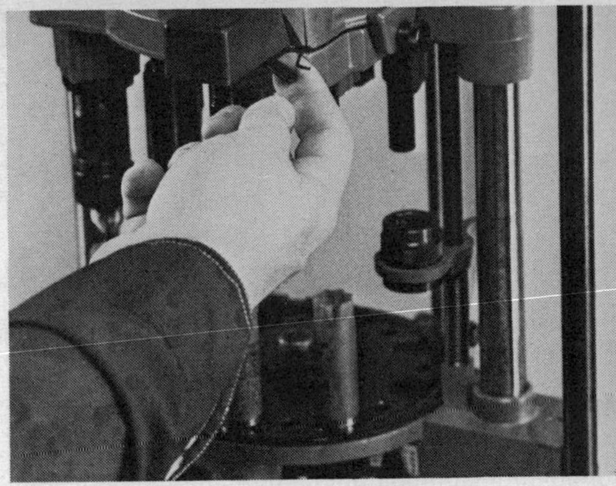

3. DROP POWDER

Before pulling the handle, pull the powder slide toward you. The spring will lock the slide in place. Place another shell in station 1 and pull the operating handle. During the stroke the powder drop tube will enter the case mouth and a powder charge will drop. Upon completion of the stroke the shells will advance to the next station.

2. PRIME

Before pulling the handle remember to insert another shell in station 1. Pull the handle through a complete stroke. The seating punch will enter the case and push the case down, over the primer in the seating pad. On the return stroke the primer seating pad will push the case back up into position and the shell plate will advance to the next position while a fresh primer drops into station 2 and the next shell is moved into position above the primer.

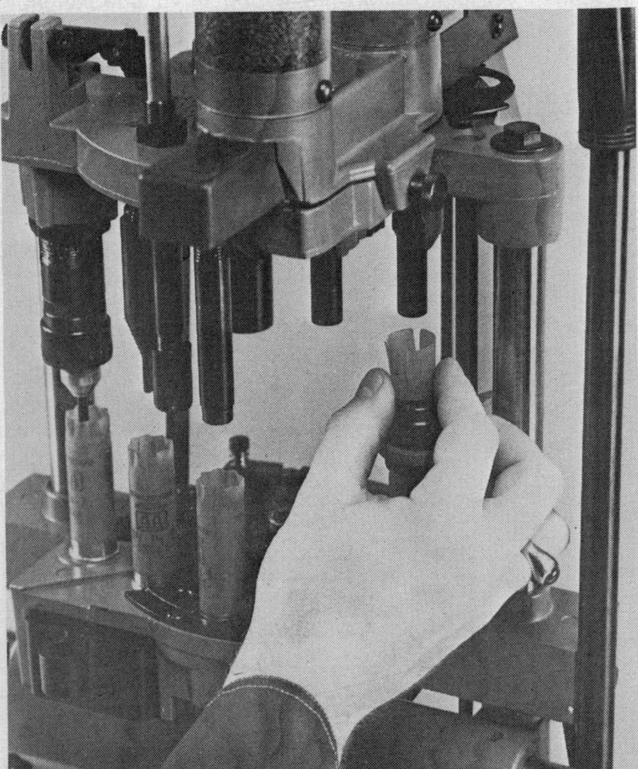

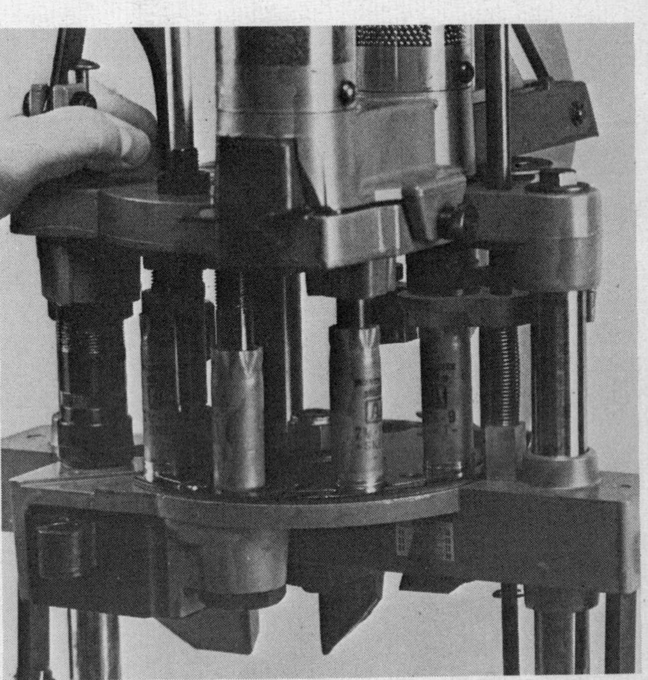

4. SEAT WAD

Insert a new shell in station 1 and insert a wad (left) in the wad guide. Pull the operating handle through a complete stroke (above). As the handle comes down the wad guide will swing into position over the shell, the wad ram will enter the wad, push it into the shell and, as the handle completes the stroke the wad guide will swing toward you for the next wad and the shell will advance to the next station.

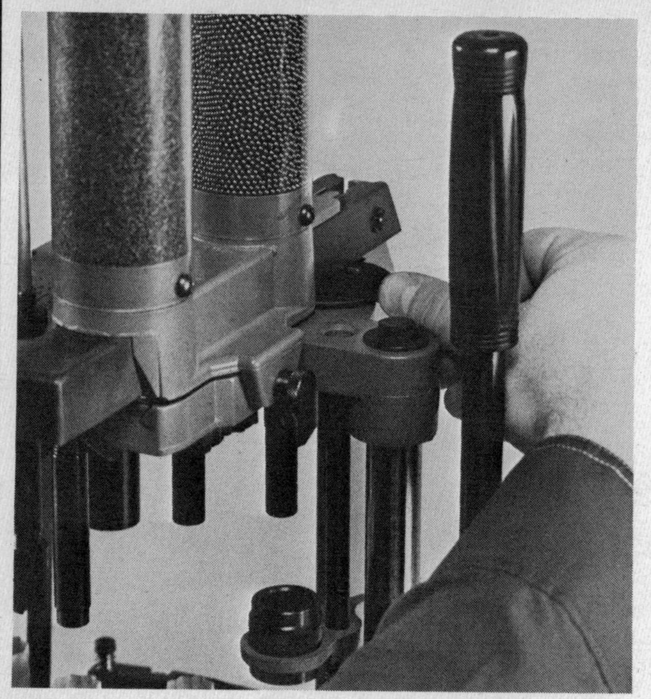 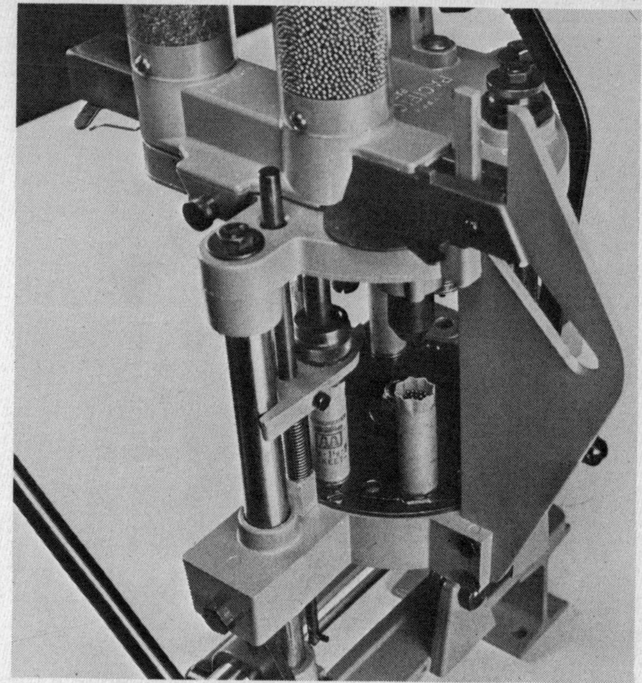

5. DROP SHOT

Before pulling the handle, rotate the shot shut-off backward (left), place another shell in station 1 and a wad in the wad guide. During the down stroke the shot drop tube will enter the case mouth before the shot has dropped. Near the bottom of the stroke the shot drops ensuring the complete charge (right) is in the case. Upon completion of the stroke the shells will advance to the next station.

6. *START CRIMP*

Insert another shell in station 1 and a wad in the wad guide and pull the operating handle. The shell at station 6 enters the plastic unit and the mouth of the case is partially closed. The plastic crimp starter unit is ridged on the inside to conform to the partially crimped shell. Upon completion of the stroke the shell will advance to the next station.

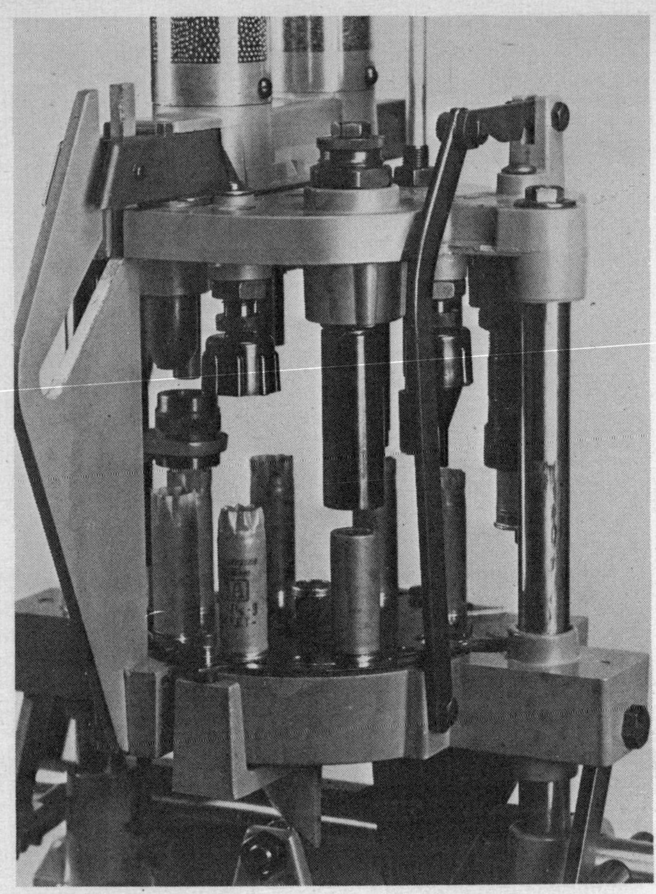

7. CRIMP

Place another shell in station 1 and a wad in the wad guide and pull the operating handle. The shell at station 7 will enter the crimp die which will also start to rise when it comes in contact with the platen casting. As the spring in the double action die is compressed the shell will be pushed over the crimp plunger and the crimp formed. On the return stroke the shell will be pulled from the crimp plunger but the crimp die will keep pressure on the case to retain the proper shape.

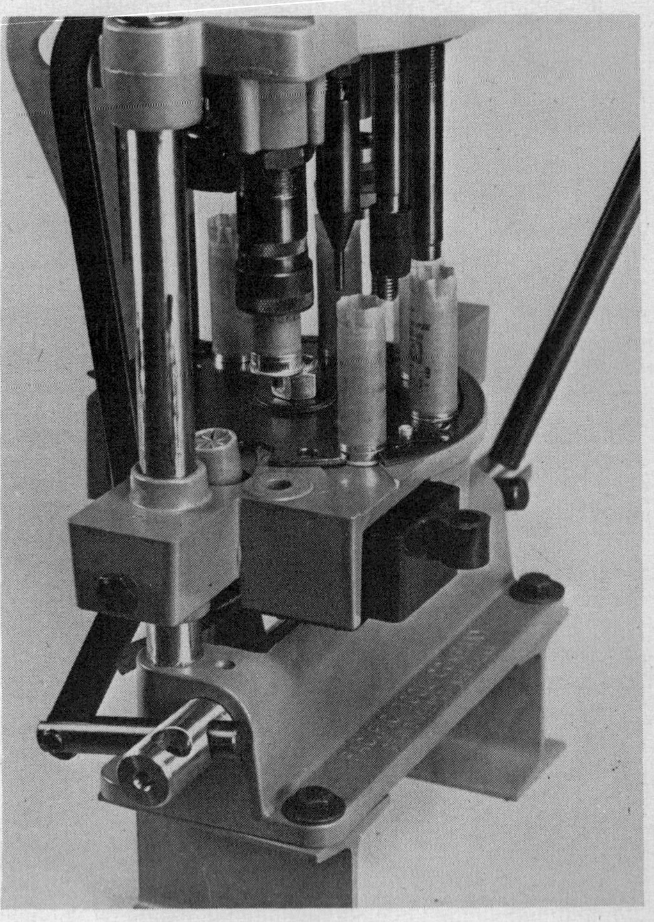

8. TAPER CRIMP

Insert another shell in station 1, a wad in the wad guide, and pull the operating handle. The taper crimp is a smooth crimp starter and will taper the finished case exactly like the factory loads. As the shell at station 8 enters the taper crimp die the plastic mouth of the crimped shell will be "rolled." On the return stroke, the shells advance to the next position but, the shell in station 8 contacts a cam in the platen casting, moves to the left, and drops through a hole in the casting down the chute to the back.

Your loader should now have a shell at each station ready for the next stroke. You should have a shell in station 1, and 1A if you resize, and a wad in the wad guide. You can continue the sequence until all your empty shells have been reloaded but, always remember to check the powder and shot hoppers and make sure a primer drops on each stroke. If you will refill the primers, shot, and powder after each 100 rounds you will never load shells without components.